The
Sensitives

THE NOTEBOOKS OF PAUL BRUNTON
(VOLUME 11)

THE SENSITIVES
(DYNAMICS AND DANGERS OF MYSTICISM)

PAUL BRUNTON
(1898–1981)

An in-depth study of
category number sixteen
from the notebooks

Published for the
PAUL BRUNTON PHILOSOPHIC FOUNDATION
by Larson Publications

International Standard Book Number (cloth) 0-943914-35-3
International Standard Book Number (paper) 0-943914-34-5
International Standard Book Number (series, cloth) 0-943914-17-5
International Standard Book Number (series, paper) 0-943914-23-X
Library of Congress Catalog Card Number: 87-82655

Manufactured in the United States of America

Published for the
Paul Brunton Philosophic Foundation
by
Larson Publications
4936 Route 414
Burdett, New York 14818

Distributed to the trade by
Kampmann and Company
9 East 40 Street
New York, New York 10016

88 90 91 89 87
2 4 6 8 10 9 7 5 3 1

The works of Dr. Brunton

A Search in Secret India
The Secret Path
A Search in Secret Egypt
A Message from Arunachala
A Hermit in the Himalayas
The Quest of the Overself
The Inner Reality
(*also titled* Discover Yourself)
Indian Philosophy and Modern Culture
The Hidden Teaching Beyond Yoga
The Wisdom of the Overself
The Spiritual Crisis of Man

Published posthumously

Essays on the Quest

CONTENTS

EDITORS' INTRODUCTION

The Sensitives is a timely, informed evaluation of mysticism, paranormal experience, sects and cults. Grounded in a clear distinction between productive spiritual practice and dangerous fascination with the occult, it will be extraordinarily useful to a variety of readers: to individuals involved in or about to undertake any sort of spiritual practice, to psychologists and psychiatrists, and to people unable to understand or assess the interests and practices of friends or relatives associated with a sect or cult.

The Sensitives is a necessarily complex volume, covering one of the three largest sections in the notebooks series; the others are the *Human Experience* section of volume 9 and the *What Is Philosophy?* section of volume 13. During our visits with P.B., he often stressed the urgent need to differentiate spiritual and psychic practices—in oneself, in others, and in various groups and teachings. This concern carries over into his writings, from the early works on India and Egypt, through the several notebooks of interviews with mystics around the world, and into the 4000 paras of this volume.

There comes a time when a little success in meditation, study, or self-discipline begins to show itself: a time when some parts of the ego thin out sufficiently to let a little light in. This light shines through the cracks in the ego, but also powerfully lights up the ego itself. These refracted colors are so bold and beautiful, the pure light is so hard to look into, that most questers begin to wander from their intended goal. This volume addresses the nature and end result of following these lesser lights—the revelatory, intuitive, visionary, psychic, mediumistic, and magical. It examines the groups of eager followers which spring up around leaders who have sought and gained some mastery of these lights, but who themselves are, in one form or another, powerfully misled. As the light of the soul shines into the recesses of the ego, it activates the latent desires for fame, power, wealth, physical immortality, seership, and wisdom. It is only this last desire, the desire for wisdom, that leads on through what P.B. has termed the intermediate zone, on into the region of true spiritual practices, which he calls philosophy.

Why does this volume fall between arts and religion? It follows the arts because all visions, voices, messages, and psychic phenomena are processes involving the imagination, which is also the primary tool of artists. The difference is that many artists intentionally use the imagination as a lens through which to peer at the spiritual world, which is at once their limitation and their protection. Mystics and occultists, on the other hand, often believe that there is no significant difference between their images and the reality behind them, and this contributes to the contradictory nature of their doctrines. This volume precedes religion because, after all, all religions are based on someone's revelation; all formal and informal religion works with some image—visual, verbal, or mental—of Divinity. Before we dare yield up our faith to such icons, it behooves us to know what is authentic in them and what is man-made, what is original and what is a potpourri of our background, past lives, presuppositions, biology, and education.

So who should read this book? Every quester, for it is written to all of us. The beginner will find guidance for understanding the weaknesses, innocence, and naïveté that influence the choice of who and what to follow. The practicing quester when encountering these dream-world phenomena is often lured strongly into the maze through blind beliefs and unbalanced strengths. For such a person, this volume provides explanations for what is happening, suggestions for evaluating the outcome, and directions for further progress. For the advanced mystic faced with the prospect of leadership, P.B. points out exactly how obstacles to truth, rationality, and involvement in the world will be raised by their enthusiastic followers or their own short-sighted follies.

This volume lies at a crossroads between the earlier topics dealing with the preparatory phases of the quest and the later volumes, written for those old souls ready to enter into the life of higher philosophy. Many topics are covered in each part of the series—searching out relationships to groups and teachers, the practices of meditation, emotional and moral development, intellectual work, and the mysterious forces of light and darkness present in nature. Here, P.B. presents these subjects as they are seen through the vitalized powers of the inward-directed mind, while in the earlier volumes they were treated in the light of our ordinary consciousness. In the categories that follow, P.B. writes from the unique perspective of philosophic insight—on reverential and devotional life, the balanced character of the philosopher, the inquiry of mentalism, intuition from the Overself, advanced meditations, and the encounter with those authentic teachers who have attained enlightenment. To read this volume alone without reference to these other works is to read a dream, with no knowledge of the waking personality, and no conclusive insight into the reality it seeks to symbolize, so we earnestly hope that you will reference these other works when reflecting on the issues presented here.

In his own terse outline of this category, P.B. made no indication as to the order, or hierarchy, of the development of feeling, will, and intellect; since he does treat them separately, we had to put them in some order, based on the continuity we perceived among the paras; their sequence (in chapter 2) is our own, not his, and should be taken only as a working model. Similarly, there are many paras of blunt criticism of practices, beliefs, and activities intrinsic to this region of imagination; some readers who have traveled far in this realm and have gained something for their efforts may object to the potency of these lines. P.B. traveled here extensively as well, and in his decades of inner and outer travel around the globe he observed the long-range consequences of following the colored lights, rather than the pure. He has approached these wanderings with philosophic insight, and so helps us to adjust our compasses, that we too may end our days in the light of the Overself, not in the shadows of the mind.

This eleventh volume of *The Notebooks of Paul Brunton* contains paras drawn only from category sixteen of the original twenty-eight topics arranged in the "Ideas" notebooks reserved for posthumous publication. As in the earlier volumes, (P) at the end of a para indicates that the para has been previously published in *Perspectives*, volume 1 of this series. We have continued the conventions outlined in preceding introductions regarding the quantity of material chosen, spelling, capitalization, and other copy-editing practices. We would like to thank the many people at Wisdom's Goldenrod and the Paul Brunton Philosophic Foundation who provided tremendous help in meeting the many challenges this volume presented us with. Further information about publication schedules and related activities may be obtained from the

Paul Brunton Philosophic Foundation
P.O. Box 89
Hector, New York 14841

THE
SENSITIVES

We should distinguish the theories and doctrines woven round the mystic's experience from the significant features of the experience itself. And those features are: the awareness of another and deeper life, a sacred presence within the heart, the certitude of having found the Real, the gladness and freshness which follow the sense of this discovery.

The real is more miraculous than the illusory psychic, more occult than the so-called occult world, more fascinating than the fantastic.

1

MYSTICAL LIFE
IN THE MODERN WORLD

Mysticism is simply an attempt to provide a system for those whom ordinary religion has ceased to help. It says, in effect, here is a practical means and a demonstrable method whereby you may verify for yourself the essential basic truth that there is a soul in man.

2

The devotional life consists of prayer and worship; the mystical life consists of intuition and meditation.

3

Mysticism is not a new creed which one slips on with the ease with which we slip on a new dressing gown; it is a LIFE.

4

Few are able to have genuine mystical experiences and yet be able to reflect on them impartially and knowledgeably. One who is able to do this successfully should go far on the Spiritual Quest.

5

Mysticism is a mode of feeling which elevates consciousness to its highest self.

6

There are certain conditions of the mystical life which remain indispensable, quite irrespective of the century or the milieu in which aspirants live. There are certain laws of mystical progress which remain immutable under any or every kind of human situation.

7

Despite the large variations of belief, doctrine, method, and experience, it would be fair to say there still remains a considerable number of important principles which have been held in common by mystics everywhere.

8

The dangers of a misguided mysticism are real, but with the proper safeguards and protective disciplines they vanish. The shaping of a sound, worthy, and strong character as prerequisite and accompaniment to all intuitive or mystical experiences is the very first of these safeguards.

9

Mystical life is not merely a matter of set times only, but is, for other types and temperaments, a matter of constant remembrance and continual thinking which leads in the end to precisely the same result as got by those who practise formal exercises at set periods. I know of mystics who have attained the goal of self-realization without having passed through the formal practice of meditation in the orthodox sense.

10

If the differences of view and teaching in mystical circles are wide and striking, they ought not be allowed to obstruct the more significant fact that the resemblances far outweigh them. Here on their foundation there exists ready-made the material for a synthesis of Truths that would be incontestable and universal.

11

Mysticism is not a thing we learn from clever textbooks. It is life!

12

It must be clearly understood that mysticism is distinct from religion; yet nonetheless, it is deeply religious.

13

The definitions of mysticism vary as widely as the standpoints of the definers themselves vary. Thus we arrive at a curious situation. A Theosophist like Annie Besant could applaudingly call it "esoteric religion," whereas a theologian like Karl Barth could only disgustedly call it "esoteric atheism."

14

It is a hard fact that few people possess the mystical faculty and an even harder one that most people cannot acquire it by conscious effort.

15

The list of things which are classified as *mystical* has come to include such contradictory matters as the diabolical and the divine. Could there be greater confusion in any field of thought?

16

My Webster defines a mystic as "one who relies chiefly upon meditation in acquiring truth." This is a good dictionary definition, but it is not good enough because it does not go far enough. For every true mystic relies also on prayer, on purificatory self-denial, and on a master.(P)

17

So many persons make the mistake of confusing not only religion with mysticism but also occultism with mysticism. The true mystic possesses in himself all that is best in religious feeling but does not necessarily show any outward signs of being religious.

18

Mysticism extends both in thought and practice to points far beyond the limits of religion.

Development

19

There is no justification in this century, as there was in an earlier one, for any mystic to make a statement of truth so obscure and ambiguous that it needs another mystic to interpret it.

20

Culture has been continuously developed and enriched, revised and enlarged, improved and perfected as human mentality and experience have themselves expanded. Mysticism as a branch of culture cannot exempt itself from this growth.

21

Such will be the shape of mysticism to come. It will not seek to keep the old traditions alive but rather to create new ones in conformity with twentieth-century needs.

22

After all, the prime business of such teaching is to illumine the mind. Yet these exponents do their utmost through heavy veilings, cryptic symbolism and overmuch mystery-mongering to darken it!

23

Life is too short, our days too hard-pressed to spare the time to dig out the shadowy meanings of these unnecessarily obscure writers of occultism and alchemy when the plain statements of those writers who do not belong to such cults will yield clear meanings with only one-twentieth of the study. It is an insult to modern intelligence to ask it to get itself involved with all the tortuous draperies which have been wrapped, fold upon fold, around truth.

24

Certain schools of medieval writers on mystical subjects leave most readers the impression that the subject is too unintelligible and too mysterious to be worth troubling about. They were overly fond of writing in riddles, leaving their unfortunate readers to decipher toilsomely much that could have been stated plainly. The tortuous expressions and mystery-mongering phrases for which the alchemists, especially, acquired a reputation irritate rather than inspire the modern mentality when it takes up their belauded work—weighty with a dark jargon and mazed by a plethora of cryptic metaphors. This applies to the interpretative side, while on the material side one looks in vain for authentic evidence of successful results. How many of the whole crew of medieval alchemists who wrote elaborate treatises on the art of turning lead into gold, themselves died as paupers! The consequence is that those moderns who do not investigate more deeply form the natural but hasty conclusion that to adopt mystical practices is to turn back the clock and to revert to worn-out superstition. But this conclusion is unfair and mistaken. First, because amid all the ponderous gibberish and inflated imaginations of the medieval stews of pure mysticism and adulterating magic, there was an important residue of genuine irrefragable truth. Second, because the price of religious heresy in those times was often persecution, imprisonment, or even death and consequently mystical writers had to express themselves guardedly, brokenly, symbolically, and vaguely. Today they are under no such necessity. Today, on the contrary, it is their duty to try to leave no opposite impression in their writings. The highest meanings can now be expressed in the plainest possible manner. All mystical teachers are now free to put their thought into direct and understandable language. And if they do not do so, it is because they fail to remember that this is the twentieth and not the fifteenth century, because they are mesmerized by the past, and because their enlightenment is a borrowed and not a directly personal one. The wise student will waste no time with them but rather will study the work of those whose thoughts leave their pens not in dark symbol but in direct clear-cut statement. For only those who know what they are thinking about are likely to know what they are writing about. And only those readers who know what they are reading about are likely to derive any profit from it.

25

The time has come for the more intelligent among those who have followed these paths to re-examine their techniques and re-define their goals. The others would deem such a procedure damnable heresy. But history is curiously eloquent about the heresy of today being the orthodoxy of tomorrow.

26

Mysticism must try to extend itself today to bring the everyday life of ordinary people within its sphere. But can this be done? It seems so hard, nay impossible. Yet how else are those who feel attracted towards it to benefit by it? Merely to spend the years reading about its achievements in other and earlier times under other and different skies may be interesting but does not solve the present problems.

27

The time has come when the ancient religions—however many and fine the truths which they contain—must take note of the changed circumstances in which we live today, must ruthlessly prune their teachings and dogmas by the light of enlightened science without deserting the religious intuition. If this is not done then new, vigorous, and modern sects will keep on coming to birth, because they have more and better appeal to the young minds.

28

It is dangerous to use terminologies and vocabularies which the past and the present have associated with particular cults, movements, groups, and organizations. It is better to find new ways of presenting spiritual truths, new words with which to name them.

29

The seekers of the modern era still gaze backward into the past, mesmerized by its revelations and fascinated by its records. In doing this they are still antique or medieval and as out-of-date as a bullock-cart on a transcontinental journey. The wisest among them, however, will refuse to sell their birthright as twentieth-century individuals. They cannot regard the ancient methods of devotional or introspectional patterns as ones to be undeviatingly followed. It is true that all the forms and techniques which they have at their disposal are not necessarily superior to those which the ancients had. But the task of bringing both up-to-date has become historically necessary. Therefore, contemporary living needs must dictate the pattern under which to absorb them. Of course, the reference here is not to the essential truths of the mystical life; its needs of sinking intellect in intuition, ego in soul, and desire in serenity are unshakeable by time. They will never change by one iota.

30

The time has come in this twentieth century to bring into the daylight of scientific understanding all those occult matters which have hitherto been playthings of esoteric societies, and the hour is ripe to skim all useless verbiage from those explanations which have been handed down to us by Oriental tradition. We may then find something useful where before we could formerly find only difficult symbolism or incomprehensible mystification; we may then be able to express in clear terms such ideas and facts as are infinitely important for the life and well-being of modern man.

31

The modern mind does not favour the ancient wrappings of mystery and magic around these deeper layers of human consciousness. It believes that knowledge today ought to be shared and spread.

32

How can the Western mentality, brought up on logical thinking and the scientific method as it is, become naturalized in the incoherencies of Zen enigmas, puzzles, and riddles any more than it can do so in the modern attempts to resuscitate the obscurities of medieval alchemy and medieval occultism?

33

To try to live in blind imitation of the ways of medieval men is sentimentality, not by itself spirituality.

34

Mystical human experience does not alter and cannot alter from age to age. At its highest and best, it is always and ever the same. But because human intelligence is itself evolving, then our thought about such experience must evolve too. If the voice of contemporary inspiration is to speak faithfully, it must speak in its own way and utter its own ideas.

Continuing the tradition

35

The mystic who offers his special experience of living to others may be ridiculed or ignored by a materialistic epoch, but the fact is that he belongs to a continuing tradition that extends backward to the beginnings of human culture. And because this experience is rooted in what is basic and best in the human entity, the tradition will extend forward so long as any culture remains at all.

36

Until a few years ago, very few had done more than play with these ideas and not many had even heard of them. Here and there some solitary individuals or occasional groups took them up and made queer and freakish cults out of them. But today there are several signs of rapid change.

37

The occult groups and religious sects have multiplied in our time—and not only among the uneducated or even the half-educated.

38

It is good that world catastrophe, religious decay, and scientific advance are turning more and more people towards mysticism. But it will be bad if they turn towards an uncritical mysticism.

39

The failure of the historical element in orthodox religion to withstand modern scientific examination is also one of the reasons why educated minds have turned towards mysticism. For here they become quite independent of the truth of the records or falsity of the myths of certain past events.

40

Today the mystic is no longer a voice crying in the wilderness, even though mysticism is still far from having a multitude of voices.

41

Mysticism cannot continue to remain forever an esoteric system cultivated only by an exclusive coterie and unknown to the rest of humanity. It could easily remain aloof and apart only under the old forms of civilization, but not so easily under the new forms which are emerging today, with the immense widening of culture, communications, and privilege involved in them. We are indeed coming closer and closer to the time when more people shall be able to understand its teachings and many more people follow its techniques. The reasons which kept this knowledge hidden in the past, or in extremely limited circulation, are to a large extent less valid today. The spread of popular education helps to support this view, but there are other grounds. The fact is that esotericism has largely accomplished its function. So many conditions and circumstances which formerly justified its continuation have been so altered by time that they now justify not its cessation but, rather, its modification. The truth in its dazzling fullness could not be dispensed to the multitude while there was still no inward preparedness for its reception. If today the ban has been partially withdrawn, that is because there has been sufficient development to justify it. The old obscurantist attitude which would forbid public instruction in mysticism and prevent promiscuous circulation of mystical books cannot be fully justified today. The power which has been manifesting itself will sweep aside the resistance of such selfish exclusionists with the force of stunning shocks. If the esoteric path cannot entirely be made into a common highway, it can at least be made into a useful one for the increasing number of war-awakened minds who are fit to understand and follow it. Although the promiscuous communication of these teachings is still a rash and ill-advised undertaking, its judicious communication is now so no longer. If this integral philosophy can be interpreted to those few whose right knowledge and timely inspiration will thereby be used for the mental and physical betterment of the masses, it will surely be helping, however indirectly, the masses themselves. Taken as a whole, the masses are still not ready for the higher philosophy. But there are individuals as well as large groups among them who are quite ready for mysticism. It is a duty therefore to make it available to such individuals, to see that their inner needs are not neglected, and to leave all others to be taken care of by religion. The patriarchal age cannot last forever. Humanity is on the move. It is beginning to develop intellect, to read, learn, think, and observe for itself. This is to some degree apparent everywhere, although its result will be apparent to the fullest degree only in a few. And these are the few who will accept and appreciate the philosophic mysticism here expounded. The others can be greatly helped by religious mysticism.

Purpose

42

What the mystic seeks is a direct experience of the soul. This is an uncommon goal and calls for an inner boldness, a spiritual venturesomeness which orthodox religion usually prohibits.

43

The rites and forms of religion arise logically from the point of view that God is separate from, and external to, the creatures in the universe. Hence the worship of, and communion with, God must be an external affair too. The theories and exercises of mysticism, however, arise from the point of view that God is internally linked to all creatures.

44

If the mystics' world is a world of imagination therefore, from a practical standpoint, some imagination is worth having for we have to live personally as well as enquire analytically. Art and its creations are not rejected even if imaginary but on the contrary they are most valuable in everyday life. Similarly the peace and absorption of the mystical experience may even be imaginary but they provide a useful if temporary refuge from the pressure of troubles and burdens. Even the illusiveness of his fantasy experience is not entirely worthless when it reveals little-known powers of the mind in giving back to man what he has once thought, thus proving their subconscious existence. And like dreams, his mysterious visions and occult experiences illustrate the wonderfully creative powers of the same mind. If the forms taken by these phenomena are the working of imagination, the activating power behind them is not necessarily so. We must never forget that the initial movement of these experiences (in those cases where they are authentic and inspired) starts in the Overself and is a manifestation of its Grace. If, therefore, we want to understand the mystic's highest experience aright we have got to get away from its concrete details and the intellectual paralysis that often accompanies them and pay attention primarily to the state of being in which it arises. He often tells us that its atmosphere is so sublime, so peace-fraught, as to be beyond all human verbal description. It is indeed a temporary expansion of consciousness because through it he has been led into the presence of the Overself.

45

Yoga methods, meditation practices, and religious mysticism have all been given to the world for a twofold purpose: (a) as temporary disciplines, to sharpen the mind and enable it to concentrate on abstract themes, and to purify the character so that strong worldly desires should not interfere with one's power to think without prejudices such as, for instance, the preconception that the material world is ultimate reality, and (b) because at the end of enquiry, when all ideas are seen never to reach the Thinker, the Yogi enters the Silence.

46

The right kind of mysticism is definitely useful. At the least it helps those who are out of tune with life and brings a serene temperament, a poised mind, equable emotions; it brings awareness of spiritual truths about oneself which flood life with illumination.

47

It is wise and proper to recognize the limitations and admit the mistakes of mysticism. But to ignore or abandon it on that account is foolish and wrong.

48

The intellectual metaphysical and rational path is secondary to the mystical feeling path, which is primary. For the Overself has much more to be felt as a presence than merely thought as idea.

49

If there were nothing other than our ideas of things, and if it were impossible to cross their boundaries, all that we could discover would never be anything more than an exploration from our own imaginings and conceptions. Then, everything holy and divine would be robbed of its value and meaning. But mystical experience intrudes here to show us a world beyond thoughts, a reality beyond ideas.(P)

50

When we tire of groping our way through the misty profundities of metaphysics without ever arriving at any worthwhile goal, we return to mysticism.

51

The true mystic does not look to other men for enlightenment, does not fix his gaze outward but inward. He cultivates over a long period, and at last fixes, the habit of sitting in quiet introspection, in perfect repose, and in mental stillness.

52

Reject the one-sided narrowness of V.S. Iyer and John Levy, successor to Atmananda, which makes them reject mystic experience and mystic feeling. For then the intellect alone is made to serve the quest so that the result is hardly a balanced one. Fanaticism is too limited a way to trace down truth. Mysticism has its valuable service to render on its own level in feeling and devotion.

53

Mysticism makes communion and worship wholly an interior process.

54

Those who consider the mystical experience as being a private hallucination or a piece of wishful thinking, are themselves in error.

55

The mystic quietly declares that he has experimental knowledge of a higher self, a diviner self than the everyday one.

56

Even if these mystical doctrines are doing nothing more, they are at least bringing peace and solace and comfort to troubled souls who can find help nowhere else.

57

The illusions and aberrations of historical mysticism or religion need not make anyone reject its values, beauties, intuitions, facts, and experiences. They remain unassailable and are entitled to exercise their influence.

58

In religion the Divine is regarded as utterly beyond, something outside, transcending the familiar or the ordinary, and quite unreachable. But when this inaccessibility of the Supreme lessens and finally disappears, a tremendous mystical experience arises.

59

What is often criticizable in persons who pursue mystical studies is unfortunately quite true of most and partly true of many others, since they turn to mysticism in search of escapism or consolation and, more often than not, it remains little more than a branch of religion for them. However, such criticism is thoroughly unjust to the few who are earnest seekers of Truth. To those pioneers, mysticism, with or without its pleasurable experiences—more often without—represents a necessary step forward on their path of spiritual progress, one which will help to bring them closer to their Goal.

60

If the metaphysician rejects the fallacies of religion, if he abandons the exaggerations of mysticism, and if he expunges the deceptions of occultism, let it not be forgotten that he also retains whatever is valuable in them.

61

These explanations of mystic experience are not intended to explain it away altogether. We must not discount either its reality or its value merely because it may not be quite what the mystic himself sincerely believes it to be. We must not dismiss it as worthless phantasy. We must comprehend that it is the way in which a genuinely transcendental existence necessarily expresses itself to the human mind at a certain stage of the latter's development.

62

Here in mysticism is a world of thought, doctrine, practice, and achievement which seems strange, remote and mysterious, for which most people simply do not have the time but to which a few people are tremendously attracted.

63

The masses are entitled to their surface satisfactions of which several kinds exist. But a smaller group exists which seeks better and higher ones. It is not the sensational and dramatic occult experience they want, nor the self-flattering psychical one, but rather entry into the inner stillness. They are the connoisseurs.

64

Though it moves in a quiet and unobtrusive manner, the work of mysticism is no less vital and important.

65

The rhapsodic experience which culminates devotional mysticism gives an intensity of bliss which amply pays for whatever renunciations the mystic himself has made.

66

It is an error to say that mysticism and metaphysics are on equal levels. The first is more important than the second. There is no way to realize the Self which does not include going inside consciousness. Thinking, however metaphysical, cannot do it. Action, however self-denying, cannot do it. It must be found inside in the heart. The other things are needful but secondary. Without the inner consciousness, action becomes at best humanitarianism and thinking a photographic copy of the Real.

The scientific and the superstitious

67

The point was reached where the possession of strong interest in mysticism was regarded as an archaic and singular superstition, suitable only for the neurotic among the educated and for the credulous among the uneducated. But this picture is now changing before our eyes. There is more respect, more attention, and more study of this subject than there has been for two hundred years.

68

If we have the satisfaction of knowing that we do not live in those miserable medieval times when the mystically minded were persecuted with fire and steel, we nevertheless have the less lovely fact that today we may be regarded as dupes and fools, as hallucinated at the least.

69

Where the factual and the fictional are so mixed together that one can hardly be separated from the other, it is not surprising that so many people sceptically dismiss the whole subject as unworthy of investigation.

70

In the minds of several scientists the very term mysticism is a synonym for credulity. This is as deceptive for them as it should be disturbing for us.

71

The materialistic opponents and critics of meditation fasten triumphantly on its unhealthy phenomena as constituting sufficient grounds for condemning the practice outright. Nevertheless we reply that those so-called scientific psychologists who analyse and expose only the fantastic aberrations of mysticism, in the belief that they are analysing and exposing mysticism itself, are themselves self-deluded. For unless they can approach mysticism from the inside, from their own personal experience, as well as from the outside, from what the observing world sees, they will blunder badly into undue scepticism, unnecessarily materialistic explanations, and even wholly false interpretations. But because few scientists possess such equipment, few can offer an accurate, fair, sympathetic yet critical estimate of mystical claims, or comprehend that all mystical experiences are not on the same level, or that even those which are differ in kind and degree.

72

People with genuine mystical experiences are rare enough—so rare that they are looked upon either as abnormal by sceptics or supernormal by believers.

73

Religious people denounce a mystic as a heretic. Worldly people denounce him as a fanatic. All this because he has the moral courage to withdraw from religious tradition and to deviate from worldly custom.

74

That the mystic can possess dignity and display intelligence is what has to be shown. That he is not necessarily a charlatan but may well be a man of virtue is what also has to be shown.

75

Despite the swiftly begotten yet swiftly forgotten enthusiasms and amid all this shallow omniscience which skims the surface of a multitude of subjects and penetrates to the core of few, there is undoubtedly a genuine public interest in mystical experience.

76

Because some kinds of mystical experience are clothed in forms which are really projections of ordinary all-too-human feelings, the materialist rejects the whole experience as being a fantasy. He tears it to pieces by his criticism and imagines he has satisfactorily disposed of the subject. But he fails to account for that part of it which is the deepest and least human, the holiest and least ordinary, the truest and least imaginary. He fails to account for the message which every genuine mystic receives when standing on this sacred ground: that here is the ultimate significance of *all* experience, including everyday experience.

77

The difference between a practising mystic and a talking one is hard for the ordinary observer to detect.

78

For a long time—a hundred years at least—the world did not want us mystics, had no use for our mysticism. And now it is beginning to want us again. The wheel has turned full circle.

79

It is a poor logic which asserts, because some "mystical" experiences are admittedly pathological and others illusory, that all mystical experience is pathological and illusory. The fairest criticism such detractors could make would be silence, so that they would then cease to profane what they cannot understand.

80

The perils which beset the mystic's path have been eagerly pointed out by critics and used by them as being sufficient reason for forswearing that path altogether. We may admit the perils without admitting the absurd counsel based upon their existence.

81

Mystics who have dared to carry a brightly flaming torch into the dark places lit only by dim candles of avaricious priests, have been reviled and slandered by the many, but received with love by the intuitive few. Their accomplishments are not to be measured by the narrow and decaying walls of societies and cults which are built by later followers. The mystic's work is infinitely wider than that, and lives on apart.

82

Most critiques of mysticism stem from a character and an experience which have certain limitations. Most are satisfied with current scientific psychologic knowledge because they know almost nothing of Oriental mysticism, which has thousands of years of experience and tradition behind it.

83

To say that mystical experience has no validity because it is subjective, is to say little.

2

PHASES OF MYSTICAL DEVELOPMENT

The transience of mystical emotions

If wisdom is dependent on a transient ecstatic or yogic state, we must presume that it disappears with the passing away of that state. What then is the use of seeking a wisdom which cannot be permanently understood and must leave us in ignorance for most of life?

2

The mystic is given a beatific foretaste, as it were, in the ecstatic experiences which are intermittently his. But this is only a halfway house and he must not be satisfied with it. To make the thing permanently his own, to come into lasting peace, he must first pass through the metaphysical region and then that of disinterested deeds.

3

Those of you who are trying to find a closer contact with your spiritual selves through the practice of meditation, through inspiration, and through prayer ought to understand the limitations of what you are doing. Realize that you may get exalted experience, but do not deceive yourselves about them. Experiences which come and go are not experiences of the Real: they are experiences of the thoughts.

4

It is certainly satisfying: pains and sorrows are no more for the time, cares and anxieties make a temporary exit. But to stop here and not advance farther is to accept oblivion under the mistaken belief that it is salvation.

5

The ecstasies of the meditation-chamber can no more constitute the final goal of mystical life than the ecstasies of the nuptial-chamber can constitute the final goal of married life.

6

Mystics who seek quivering ecstasies alone take the risk of becoming victims of their own emotional workings. For then the aberrations of mystical experience may be numerous and peculiar, the exaltation of imaginative emotionalism to the status of divine experience is often inevitable, and the possibilities of psychological camouflage may be many. Moreover, if their emotional overturning is carried too far and if it is mingled with concentration on pictorial visions of a saviour or saint who belongs to the opposite sex, it may easily develop into something quite unspiritual. A mystical eroticism which is rooted in repressed sex complexes may then be the undesirable consequence. The history of religious mysticism and devotional yoga has several cases on record of those whose excited ecstasies showed all the symptoms of strong erotomania. These cases have been offered as instances of "union with God." The truth must be told and it is that they are only emotional extravaganzas.

7

To fly off on the wings of ecstatic union at one time and to fall down into an agonizing sense of forsaken separation another time is an experience common enough at the mystical stage when emotion and not knowledge rules the aspirant.

8

An ethical content is lacking in the ideal of this kind of mysticism. It seeks only to enter into raptures that are satisfying to the emotions but not necessarily edifying to the character.

9

They reach the divine centre with their imagination or with their feeling, but not with their mind nor with their will.

10

One fact about most mystical phenomena is that they are transient. Strains of heavenly music may be heard by the inner ear and intoxicate the heart with their unearthly beauty—but they will pass away. Clairvoyant visions of Christ-like beings or of other worlds may present themselves to the inner sight—but they will not remain. A mysterious force may enter the body and travel transformingly and enthrallingly through it from the soles of the feet to the crown of the head—but it will soon vanish. Only through the ultramystic fourfold path can an enduring result be achieved.(P)

11

It is a common practice for aspirants to mistake their emotional extravaganzas and mental projections—however noble they appear to be—for glimpses of the infinite reality. It is a common error for them to take the creations of their own thought and the suggestions of other minds for genuine mystic revelations. For the path of meditation is beset with hosts of long-nurtured notions which reappear in mystic visions and oracular messages as though they were independent and separate visitants from outside. It is also beset with influences drawn from past reading or authoritarian dogmas which mislead the mind or play queer tricks upon it. The average mystic is easily deluded by the masks which vanity, desire, or egoism assumes. Too quickly does he believe that he is God-guided; too readily does he imagine that great angels or noted Masters are hovering around to display supernatural visions; too willingly does he go astray in the mist of illusion which always hangs dangerously near the credulous, the inexperienced, and the unphilosophical.

12

Emotion there must be in every experience that is to mean anything to one's life, be it aesthetic or painful, amatory or mystical. But if in a mystical experience the emotion becomes violent and excessive then the new consciousness of the Overself, which is on a higher level than emotion, can only be confused and not clearly attained.

13

When there is intense pleasure without any outer object or other person to account for it physically, then there is mystical experience in some form, high or low, sane or mad.

14

The meditation upon bliss may give him bliss, but it will not remove his ignorance of reality, his misapprehension of truth, his defects of character.

15

Ecstasies come and go outside the mystic's own will, but philosophic enlightenment is something which we win and keep because we work for and earn it.

16

The unfinished mystic who makes too much of his raptures or his darknesses alike, does so because he still identifies himself with his personal feelings—that is, with his ego.

17

The mystic who resolutely refuses to fall into this trap, who does not hallucinate himself with the belief, and claim, that he is the only man in the Western hemisphere to achieve such a realization, will be free to make further progress.

18

Wallowing in heavy, syrupy emotionalism is not the same as experiencing Reality—and consequently does not produce the same results.

19

It is natural and pardonable for a mystic to regard his most vivid experience as his most important one. But it need not be so.

20

These short spells of meditation, if it is successfully practised, will give peace and understanding; but when they are ended, you return to ordinary consciousness and lose both.

21

"The desire to enjoy ecstatic union with God is one of the things which most effectively separate us from God," said Abu Hasan Al Shadhili.

22

Those Indians who still assert that realization is the ecstasy of the mystic should study the life of Swami Rama Tirtha of North India. His books breathe the spirit of mystic joy and spiritual bliss. Yet during the last year or two of his life he became a victim of melancholia, and although it is not published to the world I have been assured by a *sannyasi* who knew him that he left a note saying that he was going to commit suicide. Anyway he was found drowned. The moral is that yogic ecstasy is a temporary thing.

23

The sentimentalities of the emotional devotee are absent from the philosophical devotee. Indeed, they are regarded by the latter as signs that a man is still filled with the thought of himself, still attached to his own ego.

24

That the greater length and higher intensity of a sitting meditation have a purificatory effect is true; that if such profound and prolonged meditations are repeated often enough the trend of thought and feeling, the shape of character, and the quality of consciousness may be reshaped is also true. But the change may not be of a lasting nature if philosophy is absent.

25

Emotional excitement is not necessarily baptism by the Overself. It may or may not accompany such baptism. Those who look for it as an authentic token of the divine visitation open themselves to a likely self-deception. It is safer to look for a different and better sign, such as lasting intellectual conviction or improvement of outward conduct.

26

The peace which they possess is an excellent thing but it is not, and cannot be, a lasting one. Even though the circumstance which could upset it may not arise for many years, the hidden weakness will always be there.

27

It is easier to gain mystical experiences than to gain a clear and right understanding of them.

28

If his goal is only to induce a mystical experience in himself, he ought to be warned that this will pass away as it came, that it is no less transient than the physical experiences of life.

29

How can a mental state be the final realization? It is temporary. Mystic experience is such a state. It is something one enters and leaves. Beyond and higher is realization of unchanging truth.

From personal vision to impersonal being

30

Students must guard against faulty technique. They misuse meditation when they force it to serve their fantasies and errors, ascetic phobias and religious fanaticisms. Then they become bogged in their own conceptions or in idealized projections of their own selves. It is easy to mistake the voice of the ego for the voice of the Overself. And it is not hard for the meditators to see things in their imagination which have no reality corresponding to them or to cook up a deceptive mixture of fact and imagination.

The sceptic's doubts—whether in this condition one acquires spiritual affinity with the Divine or merely creates a hallucination—are not infrequently justified. Much that passes for mystical experience is mere hallucination. Even where there is genuine mystical experience it is often mixed with hallucinatory experience at the same time. The subconscious mind easily formulates prepossessions, preconceived notions, externally received suggestions, and so on, into visual or auditory experiences which emphatically confirm the ideas or beliefs with which the meditator originally started. Instead of liberating him from errors and delusions, mysticism thus practised may only cause him to sink deeper and more firmly into them. For he will convert what formerly he held on mere faith to what he now holds as assured mystical realization. In the course of an extensive experience, we have found that meditation, unchecked by reason and unbalanced by activity, has not infrequently produced monomaniacs. A "pure" experience is rare and belongs to a highly advanced stage. Only where there has been the proper preparation, self-purification, and mental discipline can a genuinely pure experience arise.

If these twisted truths and disguised emotions are such common fruit of mystical orchards, may it not be because they are inescapable corollaries of mystical attitudes? With a higher criterion, could they even come into existence?(P)

31

These experiences, because of their delightfulness and strangeness, may deceive and detain him as they have deceived and detained a multitude of yogis and mystics through the ages. They cannot be avoided—indeed, they are extremely valuable stages—but they must not be regarded as the end of man's spiritual quest. The purely emotional interpretation of experience endangers the attaining of the knowledge of higher truth, if indeed pleasant.

32

It is a mistake to believe that because some saints and mystics saw pictorial visions of a striking kind, he also must see them. On the contrary, he may not. They not only are not to be sought after but, if they should come, are to be treated as of secondary or even no importance.

33

Just as pseudo-intuitions deceive many an unwary novice, so pseudo-realizations deceive some unwary intermediates. We should be suspicious of sudden realizations. Such overnight changes belong only to the sphere of the emotions.

34

Visions are a far less plentiful phenomenon of meditation than are intuitions, inspirations, directions, predictions, and messages. Almost every mystic has them. Many may be remarkably true but others are a fruitful source of delusions; where the mystic's imaginative faculty is stronger than his critical judgement, and where it then gets to work upon metaphysical, religious, and psychological matters it cannot help falling victim to strange fantasies and deceptive chimeras. Unfortunately the mystical temperament is too inclined to indulge in undisciplined thought and to let its imagination run riot. The wishful thinker and uncritical self-deceiver quickly finds several excellent arguments to fortify his beliefs in his own mental creations.

35

The clairvoyant phenomena do not make truer the mystical utterance; that still has its own worth, which is neither increased nor reduced by the visible figure or audible voice which accompanied it.

36

Psychic phenomena are often an accompaniment of certain stages of meditation. When they are sensory in form, it is only necessary to note if they hold any useful meaning, if they are authentic and not illusory, and to pass on.

37

It is a failing of many an intense devotee that he loses his sense of proportion. In frequent flushes of egoistic emotionalism he may, for instance, often ascribe most events—however petty—in his personal life to divine interference or magical manipulation or supernatural intervention.

38

Krishnamurti scornfully calls these experiences "a form of hypnosis . . . visions, sensations, all that silly business and other forms of entertainment . . . and immaturity."

39

The question of how authentic his experience really is does not usually arise in him. For it is debatable whether a mind mostly preoccupied with the subject of its weaknesses, faults, failures, deficiencies, and sins—that is, mostly with its personal ego again—could penetrate the Overself's sphere.

40

Neurotic persons who are eager for the mystical experience more out of self-regard than out of reverence for the Other, may gain one form of it through developing the psychological capacity for concentration and withdrawal of thoughts in meditation, often having already a favourable temperament for it. In that case, they will congratulate themselves on this success, admire themselves all the more, possibly tell others freely about it, and thus offset their gain by strengthening their egoism. This is ambition in disguise. Although it has some features resembling the authentic mystical experience, it is not that but an adulterated deceptive form.

41

The uninstructed, the simple, the pious, the mystical are apt to be satisfied with their personal reactions to gurus, temples, rituals, mantras, and meditations. But the reactions may be pleasant illusions, giving birth to comforting fallacies or false consolations. That is, the seekers get beyond their ordinary selves and believe that they are experiencing the Transcendental, the Absolute. They do not know that counterfeits exist, or that there are inferior states which may be joyful or peaceful or exciting or sensational but are still not the real, the authentic goal.

42

In this field it is prudent for the seeker and beginner to beware of alleged illuminations in himself and, even more, in others.

43

Where the emotional nature is very powerful there is some danger during mystical experience of giving to its thrills the seat of authority, which ought to be given to the calmer but more reliable voice of intuitive conviction. For intuition will bring him closer to that egoless life toward which he ought to be ever striving, whereas emotion, if unpurified and unbalanced, may bring him farther from it.

44

The workings of imagination and the movements of emotion are used by the ego to deceive the mystically minded.

45

The genuine experience possesses certain marks and may be recognized. Then why is it so many are deceived by the false one?

46

The manic psychosis of Western psychology has some startling points of similarity to the highly emotional states of certain religious mystics.

47

Until their ideas are freed from illusions and their psyches from unbalance, meditation may be as harmful to them as it can be beneficial to others.

48

They are meditating, it is true, but with their thoughts centered on the ego more subtly if less strongly than when they are back in the world.

49

The novice who begins his mystical experience with personal visions to be seen in mental pictures will end, if he progresses far enough, with a pictureless impersonal state of being.

50

Quite a number of mystics have never even had the trance experience although they have had ecstasies, intuitions, messages, visions, and other exalted phenomena. It is not at any stage a necessity of the mystical path.

51

The seeker who has no psychical experiences, no pictorial visions appealing to the senses, no clairaudient voices delivering a supreme message, should have no regrets. His progress is not belittled in any way.

52

There are mystics to whom no vision has come, no voice has sounded, no phenomenon has appeared. Yet they are farther on the quest than so many to whom these things have happened.

53

Visions which one may experience, though interesting, are at best only symbolic and temporary. One should not trouble about interpreting them. Their real meaning becomes clear in the course of time in a way that affects character and consciousness.

54

The experience of knowing one's own being is a natural one which will come to all in time. The thrills, visions, revelations, and ecstasies which may accompany it are not essential parts and, if allowed, will pass away.

55

It is better not to try to get inner experiences but to let them unfold as and when they will.

56

Calm, quiet, and deep meditation is a more manifest sign of divine presence in the heart than thrilling psychic experience or enrapturing excited emotion.

From inner peace to inner reality

57

The ordinary mystical experience cannot automatically sustain itself and cannot naturally continue itself. It evaporates, to the intense disappointment of the mystic, who imagines each time that he has undergone the supreme changeover of his whole life, but imagines in vain. He may catch a glimpse of the higher state of being but alas! he cannot keep it long. He may climb to the mountaintop but he cannot stay there. He may enjoy the rarefied atmosphere of its heights but he cannot live in it. He is forced by the ebb of inspiration to come down again to walk the common pedestrian roads. This is partly because his experience does not rise above the level of emotion and partly because it does not emerge from the self-centered attitude.

In the first case, a mysticism that is only emotional and nothing more, that lacks a reasoned metaphysical supporting structure, lacks also unity and continuity, inner principle and binding significance. In the second case, an aspirant who is seeking religious or mystical satisfactions is usually preoccupied with his own wants, his own emotions, his own reactions, and his own experiences. He is still egotistic, however higher his egoism may be than that of the common level. If he wishes to obtain a durable enlightenment, he will have to develop it out of something which, while necessarily including emotion, gathers in the whole of his being at the same time. That is, he will have to seek through the fourfold path for the philosophic experience. Even his first initiation into philosophy will teach him that reality and truth are not to be found here and will point to an order of being beyond it. From that moment he begins to look on life from the Overself's side, which although it does not exclude the personality's side, at the same time transcends it. He begins to shift the object of thought and feeling from his ego to his diviner self.

58

The object of the average yogi is to attain inner peace whereas the object of the philosopher is to attain inner reality. The two paths coincide up to a point but the second then proceeds farther than the other one. For example, asceticism which is a finishing point for the mystic is only a starting point for the philosopher.

59

The excessive joy and throbbing ecstasy of which the annals of mysticism so often speak belong mostly to the novice and intermediate. The truly advanced man experiences quite the contrary, which is a deep sadness, although it never shakes his unalterable serenity. This is because the first two are primarily preoccupied with their personal feelings whereas the third has also brought compassion for all mankind within the orbit of his outlook.

60

Mysticism is not a couch to sleep on but a step to tread on.

61

However exalted the feelings may be by the experience, however immaterial the perceptions may be, however deep the trancelike absorption may be, it is not the Infinite Reality with which he is in contact but still only his idea of it, plus the vivification and intensification which come from his closer approach to that Reality.

62

Buddha certainly glorified the worth of compassion, but he also glorified the worth of insight. He never said that universal compassion could alone bring one to Nirvana. Buddha recommended the first as a disciplinary practice for the attainment of the other. Why? Because personal feeling either blinds us to truth or distorts our mentality. Often we cannot see things as they really are because we are warped by our egoistic prejudices and passions. If we can get away from the personal, we can get rid of these obstacles. Compassion thins the ego's strength and assists us to become properly equipped to achieve insight into Truth. Similarly, Jesus gave the masses the golden rule of doing unto one's neighbour as one would be done by. They needed to be dislodged from their strong selfishness. Hence, he taught them that "Whatsoever you sow that shall you also reap" but he did not suggest that this was sufficient guidance to the Kingdom of Heaven. Love is not enough.

63

The initiation into mystical experience may come dramatically and convulsively through ecstasy in the case of one aspirant but unobtrusively and gently through quietude in the case of another. Because individuals differ so widely in the personality and the history with which they meet the experience, no general rule may be affirmed in the matter, no dogma laid down. When aspirants and their half-grown teachers constantly confuse these ecstasies with the highest and fullest enlightenment, it is necessary to protest and point out the error. That this is an error is shown by the fact that the ecstasy passes away, the emotions subside, and the man quickly recedes from these high levels and begins to revert back to his prosaic everyday condition once again. He soon discovers that these holy experiences, alas! cannot be kept up for long. They are as ephemeral as the colours of sunrise. Saint Bernard complained that the clear vision of the Divine is only for a moment. Jacob Boehme compared his mystic ecstasy to lightning which flashed and vanished. Such emotional ecstasies are always transient; they come and go simply because it is the nature of emotion to do so. Nature never intended mystical raptures to be anything more than weekend guests, as it were. She has not made the man who can enjoy them forever at the same pitch of passionate intensity which they possess at the start. In his ignorance the mystic desires to cling to his ecstasy but always fails. Consequently the experience is always succeeded by a mood either of depression or of frustration. He does not perceive that this very desire to hold on to it is something which must be conquered, as much as any other possessive desire, if he is ever to attain a lasting inner peace. The foregoing may prompt the question, "Why then is inward joy one of the accompaniments of mystic experience?" In the early stages it comes to make easier his revaluation and overcoming of outward and earthly joys. Hence it is then highly emotional and tempestuous. In the advanced stages it is to tell him what the divine Overself is like. Hence it is then profoundly mental and tranquil.

The bliss which accompanies a mystical experience is not only accounted for by these causes but also by a further one, or by all in combination. And this is that every such experience is a renewed discovery of the glorious fact that he is not engaged on an impossible quest. That the latter can be successfully completed by conscious union with the Overself is joyously evidenced anew by each such temporary union. It is through such momentary glimpses or vivid intuitions of the transcendental reality that he is encouraged to continue with this long-drawn quest. The heavens have opened for him and closed again. Whoever has once had this vivid experience cannot go on again as though it had never been. He will be uneasy, restless, alternately fascinated and haunted by its memory, tantalized into seeking how he may recapture it again. And it is well that such gleams of encouragement do come to him. For there are times when he realizes the Himalayan altitude of the road he has undertaken to climb. With this realization there arrives despair, even the desire to withdraw from it altogether.

The conclusion from all these considerations is that if blissful psychic experiences or rapt ecstasies come to him, he ought not let his attitudes and utterances be too jubilant; if they fail to come, he need not be too sad. It is interesting to hear about them and pleasant to have them but they are not essential to the higher life.

64

"Where thou findest not emotion, thou wilt find a door whereby thou mayest enter into thine own Nothingness."—Miguel de Molinos: *A Guide to True Peace*

65

The rush of agitated emotions which the experience brings to beginners and the enormous excitement it stirs in them, are absent from the psychological state of proficients.

66

Wonderful, exalted, joyous feelings accompany this state. The unphilosophical mystic is carried away and regards them as being the state itself, but the philosophic mystic understands that it is rather a different kind of consciousness.

67

The devotional mystic enjoys being lifted up to rapturous heights. But insofar as he luxuriates in his mystical experience as he would luxuriate in a beautifully furnished bedroom, it is nothing more than a personal possession, a component of his private property. It is good that he has it, of course, but it is not enough. For how different is this from the philosophic experience, which opens egotistic ears to the call of mankind's needs! He will enjoy the thrills of being emotionally swept off his feet by mystical ecstasies; but when eventually he comes to understand, whether by his own intuition or by someone else's instruction, that such excitement prevents him from reaching the fullest consciousness of the Overself, he will come to respect the preachments of philosophy in this matter. Here an analogy may be useful to clarify our meaning. The mystic is like a man who carries away the flower, knowing that the perfume will come with it also. The mystic is so enraptured by the exalted ecstasy of peace of his experience that he tries to seize hold of it, only to find that it soon eludes his grasp. The philosopher does not dally his attention with the ecstasy of peace but directs it straight toward the source whence the peace emanates—to the Mind itself—and tries through comprehension to seize hold of its very nature. In the result he gets both reality and its emanated peace at the same time. He absorbs the ecstasy instead of being absorbed by it.

68

The more advanced a man is, the less he looks, or should look, for inner experiences. Despite popular belief, they are more frequent among beginners.

69

We do not need to seek our vindication in the witness of contemporary conditions and inside ashrams; it exists in the writings of mystics themselves and as far back as the Middle Ages. Suso, Tauler, Guyon, Saint Teresa, Saint John of the Cross, Ramakrishna, and others have all had occasion to observe the same sad consequences which we also have observed, and they have passed caustic comments upon their fellow aspirants in their own writings. One of the most illustrious and advanced of medieval mystics, John Ruysbroeck, vigorously criticized his fellow mystics for defects he had observed among them. He denounced those who mistake mere laziness for meditative sanctity, as well as those who take every impulse to be a divine one. (See E. Underhill's *Mysticism* for a quote from Mme. Guyon criticizing visionary experiences of mysticism.) The Spanish Saint John of the Cross wrote: "It is very foolish, when spiritual sweetness and delight fail, to imagine that God has failed us also; *and to imagine that because we have such sweetness we have God also.*"

Four centuries ago another Spanish mystic perceived the subtle selfishness which underlay this attitude. He was Saint Pedro de Alcantara, who wrote that such devotees of spiritual joy "are much rather loving themselves than God." Even many a genuine mystic of high achievement is not altogether exempt from this charge of spiritual selfishness. His ineffable ecstasies deceive him by their very sweetness into barring himself from concern with the woes of the outside world. This often arises quite innocently because the sense of joy which follows success in meditation is easily misinterpreted to mean the end of the quest. It may indeed be the end of most mystical quests, but it is only the beginning of the ultimate one! Only a few of the wisest and most advanced mystics have placed it where it rightly belongs. The danger was so clearly seen by Buddha that he specifically warned his disciples not to stop at any of the four degrees of rapt meditation, where, he said, they might easily be deceived into thinking that the goal had been attained. It was seen too by Sri Ramakrishna, the renowned Bengali yogi. He once disclosed to a disciple: "Mystic ecstasy is not final." He severely chided his famous pupil, the monk Swami Vivekananda, when the latter replied to a question about his ideal in life with the words: "To remain absorbed in meditative trance." His master exclaimed, "Can you be so small-minded as that? Go beyond trance; it is a trifling thing for you."(P)

70

An important query now arises, although hardly a mystic ever conceives the challenge of its existence and consequently ever seeks its answer. We have to enquire about what really happens during the highest effort of the meditator, when thought is so overcome that it appears as if about to lapse. Will he enter a higher dimension of existence as he believes? Will the self-revelation of the hidden reality really occur? Is this thrilling ecstasy or this stilled peace, which has begun to supervene, the peculiar sign of a revolutionary shifting of spiritual gravity from mortal concerns to eternal life, from mere appearance to basic reality? Many mystics think that the mere elimination of thoughts during self-absorption is a sufficient achievement. The world is then forgotten and with it all the personal cares. This state really arises from the extreme diminution of the working and tempo of thought, with the consequent diminution of attention to the man's own personality, to its varied cares and affairs, as well as to the external world with its insistent claims and constant demands. Thus it is simply one of exquisite relief from human burdens (whether of pain or pleasure, for here there is no distinction between both), from attention to the external world, and from the strain of supporting a continuous series of thoughts. The result is a delightful lightness and soothing peace. But the feeling of peace is alone no guarantee of the attainment of true realization. Peace is admittedly one of its signs. But there are different grades of peace, ranging from the negative stillness of the tomb to the positive mind-mastery of the sage. The arrestation of thoughts touches the fringe of the transcendental state, but not more than the fringe. When I wrote in *The Hidden Teaching Beyond Yoga* (page 309, British edition) that the mystic only penetrates to the illusion of reality, I referred to visions of forms and ecstasies of emotion. If however the mystic does achieve a visionless serene unexcited beness, then it is the Overself, for he touches the Void wherein is no form and no thoughts; then he does touch reality. I admit this. But his task is still incomplete, because this experience which occurs in trance is transient; hence the need of gaining metaphysical insight also for permanency.(P)

71

There are three major and progressive goals open to the mystic. The first is to become conscious of the fringe or aura of his divine soul, the Overself. Most mystics, elated by the emotional thrill of its discovery, stop here. The second is to penetrate to its serene centre and pass during trance into the undifferentiated void of its non-sensed, non-thinged essence. The more intelligent and superior mystics, who are naturally much fewer in number than the first kind, are not satisfied until they reach this attainment. It is upon this world-vanishing experience that most Indian yogic metaphysicians base their theory that the universe is an illusion. To the ordinary yogi, this is the summit of achievement and represents for him the goal of human existence. But the trance itself is only temporary. How can a mental self-abstraction, however prolonged, a merely temporary condition, be a final goal for mankind? This is the problem which indeed was stated in *The Hidden Teaching Beyond Yoga*. All such theories merely show that such mystics have their limitations, however admirable may be their capacity to enter into and sustain the trance state. The third goal is to bring the true self, the essential emptiness and the universal manifestation, into a harmonious, unified experience during full normal wakefulness. This last is philosophical mysticism. Being a complex and complete attainment, it naturally calls for a complex and complete effort. Careful analytical and historical study of mystical practices and mystical biographies will show that it is these three different goals which have always been pursued or achieved, no matter to what external religion, country, or race individual mystics may themselves have belonged. Thus the ordinary mystic's account of the Overself is true but incomplete, his experience of it authentic but insufficient. He has yet to undergo the whole, the complete experience which mysticism can yield. But then, if he does so, if he refuses to remain satisfied with an incomplete and imperfect attainment, he will no longer remain a mystic. He will become a philosopher.(P)

72

Questionable excitements have often been mistaken for the true mystical experience. But the serene and clear-sighted tone of authentic realization is lacking in them. The excited ecstasies of lower mysticism should not be confused with the dignified exaltations of ultramysticism. In extreme cases the former sometimes bear a resemblance to the merry elations felt in moments of Bacchic enthusiasm, whereas even here the rapturous feeling passes away eventually as a sense of supernatural calm, of noble quietude which is rated as being far superior, takes its place. Passionate joy is something which comes and vanishes, a mood which can [not—ed.] be kept permanently, here today and still here tomorrow. Joy belongs to the person. Peace belongs to the higher individuality. The absence of passion, however exalted it be, is a noteworthy feature of the genuine supreme realization. Emotional intoxication is not the final stage. Steady illumination—as steady as a flickerless lamp—is philosophically higher and transcends it. He who attains the heights will always evidence it in permanent dignified serenity, not in fitful egoistic excitement. Emotions are quiescent thereon.

73

Saint John of the Cross wrote, in *The Ascent of Mount Carmel*: "Would that I could persuade spiritual persons that the way of God consisteth not in the multiplicity of meditations, ways of devotion or sweetness, though these may be necessary for beginners, but in one necessary thing only, in knowing how to deny themselves in earnest, inwardly and outwardly, giving themselves up to suffer for Christ's sake, and annihilating themselves utterly. He who shall exercise himself herein, will find all this and much more. And if he be deficient at all in this exercise, which is the sum and root of all virtue, all he may do will be but beating the air—utterly profitless, notwithstanding great meditations and communications."

74

The beginning mystic is very much aware that he is having an unusual experience. This makes him feel that he is being favoured, that he is being lifted high above his fellows. The personal ego is being mixed into the very centre of an impersonal power. The reaction of an advanced mystic—that is, a philosopher—is free from these egoistic blemishes.

75

Let them not confuse a merely psychological state, however strange it may be, with a truly mystical state. For the first is within the ego, the second with the Overself.

76

Just as there are three degrees of the spiritual journey—religion, mysticism, and philosophy—so there are three degrees of spiritual illumination—the child, the adolescent, and the adult.

77

A man who himself passed through various kinds of mystical experience, Ibrahim al Jili, who lived in the fourteenth century at Yemen, Arabia, pointed out in his book, *The Perfect Man*, that although meditation was the noblest activity of man, he should beware of resting continuously in it to enjoy its bliss. He added that the philosophical mystic will leave it even before it has yielded all its secrets to him, lest it become a barrier to his further advance towards the highest goal.

78

Yoga takes a man to a certain level, philosophy to another, whilst the ultimate *sahaja* path takes him to a more complete experience and the highest vantage point of all.

79

Far safer than endeavouring to reach the trance state, he had better devote his efforts to control of thought and a search for inner tranquillity.

80

Those alone will ever understand the mystery of the Overself who are willing to penetrate beyond the fitful beatific consciousness of the mystical ecstasy to the continuous equanimity of the Sage.

81

Whereas ordinary mysticism seeks only to discipline the personality, philosophical mysticism seeks both to discipline and develop it.

82

The medieval monk emotionally enjoying a rapturous union with God in his cell was not necessarily farther on the way than the advanced Quaker sitting rapt in the still, silent meeting-house three centuries later.

83

From the philosophical standpoint, it is not enough to say that a man is illumined and leave it at that. The depth and permanence of his illumination need also to be considered.

Moral re-education

84

At this stage of our brief study of the mind and its mystical powers, personal observation and experience involving thousands of contemporary cases among Asiatics, Africans, Europeans, and Americans no less than wide reading in and deep reflection over the past annals of mysticism in the West as well as yoga in the East dictate the stern duty of a warning utterance. In this matter at least we have the privilege of practice as well as the theories of yoga at our fingertips and hence may be presumed to know what we are talking about. If our statements are strongly worded, that is because the importance of the matter justifies it. Many have deplored the innumerable aberrations and the countless delusions, the intellectual vagaries and the pathological states, the hysterical emotionalisms and the half-concealed eroticisms to which mysticism too easily leads its votaries. Why does this happen? Part of the answer is that meditation exercises are often practised incorrectly. This is still true even when they are done under a teacher's guidance, for scientifically imparted instruction is usually difficult to obtain, whereas superstitious or superficial instruction is more easily found. The consequences of wrong practice make themselves marked in time upon both character and capacity. They may appear in the following forms: fancy being mistaken for reality; the decay of reasoning power and the growth of credulity; the surrender to emotional impulse, miscalled intuition, in the belief that this is a higher guide to behaviour than right thinking; and the adoption of a holier-than-thou attitude towards others. Moreover, meditation of a merely self-hypnotic character unaccompanied by philosophical or practical discipline may lead to pathological neuroses, or to dissociations of personality, or to deep self-deceptive hallucinations of personal attainment. Just as the right kind of meditation will expand and develop spiritual life, so the wrong kind will cripple and dwarf it. Those who do not estimate the creative powers of meditation at their real worth may ridicule such a statement. But the fact remains—and is indeed a commonplace matter of mere observation to any competent investigator—

that the whole character, mentality, temperament, motives, and reactions of the student who continues for a sufficient period with such practices will undergo a marked change for the better or for the worse. They will indeed either benefit or harm him.

Nevertheless, if erroneous meditation has led some to fantasies and illusions, this is not a warning to give up its practice but to meditate rightly and to gain metaphysical clear-sightedness to see through phantasms and mistakes. Indeed, it is quite possible to erect a shield against these errors by undergoing the philosophical training, which puts its students on their own guard and enables them to protect themselves. Meditation is supremely necessary but the pitfalls that surround it are so grievous as to make it most desirable to practise it as part of the fourfold balanced path, and not merely alone. Moreover, in this world crisis, the service enjoined by this path and usually neglected by unphilosophical meditators is at least as urgent as self-development.

85

If a man gives up several hours every day to religious devotions, mystical exercises, and metaphysical study, but has not given up his feelings of envy, spite, and malice, then his spiritual development is a superficial affair. True spirituality always penetrates into a man's heart, changes his attitudes toward other people, and purifies his relations with them. If he has no results to show in the moral sphere, do not be deceived by his mystical tall talk or pious mouthings.

86

Whoever disregards this requirement of a balanced total effort may advance too rapidly for a time and become jubilant over his advance. But sooner or later he will experience a setback and settle in a cul-de-sac. For nobody can outwit the integral evolutionary purpose of Nature.

87

When the search for inner peace is conducted through meditation alone, ignoring moral re-education, intellectual strengthening, and altruistic service, the result will be deplorably lopsided.

88

If he is well-grounded in the metaphysics of truth and well-balanced in character, neither the plausible voices of false doctrines nor the pretentious claims of false prophets can deceive him.

89

The errors into which so many mystics have fallen, could not have lain in their path if their emotions had been submitted to the philosophic discipline and if their thoughts had been conformed to philosophic knowledge.

90

The more I travel the world of living men and study the recorded experiences of dead ones, the more I am convinced that mystical powers, religious devotion, intellectual capacity, and ascetic hardihood do not possess anything like the value of noble character. I no longer admire a man because he has spent twenty years in the practice of yoga or the study of metaphysics; I admire him because he has brought compassion, tolerance, rectitude, and dependability into his conduct.(P)

91

We personally believe that Gandhi is as self-realized a mystic as his contemporaries like Ramana Maharshi, Aurobindo, and Ramdas. His whole life and thought, his writing and speech, his deeds and service proclaim it. He himself has declared that he feels "the indefinable mysterious power that pervades everything" and that he is "surer of His existence than of the fact that you and I are sitting in this room." Then why is it that Gandhi's view of the world war was so widely different from Sri Aurobindo's, if both are divinely inspired men? The answer is that in Gandhi we find a perfect illustration of the defects of ordinary mysticism, of the insufficiency of its spiritual self-realization, and of the need for philosophical mysticism. There is no need to doubt, as so many doubt, that he is a genuine saint turned to the genuine service of humanity. But he has carried into that service the unbalance, the fanaticism, and the impracticality which mark so many saints throughout history. This conclusion may be unpalatable to some, but it is unavoidable. Perfect mystics are not the same as perfect beings. They are liable to error.(P)

92

If a man spends a total of six hours a day in meditation practices, as some I have known have done, but is unable to perceive the truth about the character of other men with whom he is brought into contact, then it is absurd to believe that he is able to perceive the truth about the immeasurably more remote, more intangible and ineffable Transcendental Reality.(P)

93

Where is the definite evidence in moral excellence, or even moral improvement, that a diviner life has been found? If this is lacking, then the would-be mystic is merely deceiving himself, merely stagnating in an illusory attainment which still remains outside the true soul.

94

Look for the results of spiritual attainment in character and conduct. If a man has lived his whole life in a yogic ashram but is still mean, petty, treacherous, spiteful, unjust, and unreliable, be sure that all his religious devotions and meditation exercises have only affected his surfaces, not his depths.

95

I have been asked to explain the phrase "that God whom meditating mystics and trance-wrapped yogis prematurely grope for within their hearts" which occurs on page 313 of the British edition of *The Hidden Teaching Beyond Yoga* and page 365 of the American edition. Some seem to think that the criticism implied therein is directed against the heart as a place wherein to search for God. They have misread my meaning and put the emphasis in the wrong place. The emphasis should be laid on the word "prematurely." The time factor is not seldom as important as any of the others. Its importance should not be underestimated. The right act done at the wrong time itself becomes a wrong act. Mystics who prematurely try to seize the fruits of philosophy without taking the trouble to undergo the philosophic training commit an error. For the fruits thus gained are inevitably transient. And when they advise suffering worldlings to resign themselves to God's will and cease bewailing their lot, they often commit another error in timing. For it may be that the discontented worldling is moved through his very discontent to exert his latent capacities and better his lot, and if he does this rightly he will thus improve both his character and intelligence. Each individual case will necessarily differ, for there are times when it is right to resist karma and times when it is wiser not to do so. To lay down a universal rule of absolute nonresistance, as these mystics do, is to ask many men to invite needless suffering.

96

The philosophical student must keep clear of the quicksands into which others may fall. He must show how he can keep reasonable and balanced when others become fanatical and hysterical, and how he can continue to be faithful and persevering in this quest while fickle emotionalists try and discard one cult after another.

97

There are a thousand candidates for adeptship in occult powers. There is scarcely one candidate for adeptship in goodness, self-control, and piety.

98

The wiser teachers among the ancients advocated asceticism only as a temporary practice, as a means of getting some self-discipline, whereas the more fanatical teachers insisted that all their followers should become ascetics. Life is not limited to disciplinary mysticism alone. It has many other things to offer man's many-sided nature.

99

This personal wholeness is not so much a means of attaining reality as a guarantee that no personal complexes will intervene in the attainment itself.

100

Even the man who does not fall into such a deep and dark unethical abyss because his inherent decency is too strong to allow it, is still likely to fall into a lesser danger and involve others in his fall, if he has not undergone the philosophic discipline or if he has not the restraining hand of a personal guide to protect him.

101

Reason is rightly offended by these notions that a mere physiological trick like changing the manner of breathing or even a psychological trick like stopping the thinking process can confer everlasting inner peace upon a man and give him entry into the kingdom of heaven. This is the error of the rigid hatha yogi. No man can cheat God and find his way into the kingdom without changing his sense of values, his moral character, his desires, and his conduct. Only if he has really done this may such tricks help him to achieve his high purpose.

102

Only after his first fervour is shaken by doubts is he at all likely to understand that discrimination balance and critical judgement are not less needed in the spiritual realm as in the physical.

103

He is not set free from the evolutionary task of developing his personality because he has developed the capacity to enter mystical states. He must fulfil this task and thus bring all his capabilities into equilibrium; until he has done this, his enjoyment of the divine bliss will be only a sporadic and broken one. But this task fulfilled, it will become a natural and continuous one.

104

It is good and important that people practise meditation and thus seek within themselves what can never be found outside themselves. But it is not enough. There are serious obstructions which blur, distort, or prevent our seeing what is within. Unless they are also tackled and removed, the seekers may spend half a lifetime either looking in vain or seeing wrongly.

105

There are many who are earnest in thought and steadfast in aspiration but who, despite this, have never had any mystical experience, never known any psychical phenomena, and never felt any ecstatic uprush. They may be consoled to learn that, philosophically, these happenings are not at all the most significant indicators of spiritual advancement. The ennoblement of character, the development of intuition, and the cultivation of inner equilibrium are more important.

106

A sane mysticism is needed if aspirants are to keep their balance in such rarefied atmosphere, as also a metaphysics which does not get lost on its way to philosophy.

At home in two worlds

107

The eccentrics and fanatics have had a long inning in the mystical field. It is now the turn of the sane and normal.

108

Why should the mystic not like the two worlds, the practical as well as the mystical, the world of self-indulgence as well as the world of self-discipline, and be at home in both? Why should so many people find it impossible to imagine the mystic being an efficient professional or business man, or being able to enjoy an evening at the musical comedy theatre?

109

So long as they are withdrawn into and united with the Overself their consciousness is richer than all others. So soon as they leave it, mingle with and apply themselves to human affairs, their consciousness is shaped again by what they habitually are, and largely limited by it. From the Perfect they have returned to the Imperfect. From this moment error may creep into their minds, unwisdom into their actions.

110

There is an escapism which ignores all events other than personal ones. A form which, in our own experience, it commonly takes is shown by the announcement that "I never read newspapers!" It is pleasant to put out of consciousness the muddle and misery of our times, but in the end it is futile and self-deceptive. The escapist is justified in seeking a defense-mechanism against the constant reports of world tragedy and wickedness, but he should find a better one.

111

The helplessness of so many mystics in the face of social danger is an instructive symptom. It arises from the fact that mysticism possesses no social trend. Its ideal is specifically inner peace, which—however desirable for all—is, when pursued as the highest aim, an individualistic and non-social one.

112

He may get inner experiences but however much others may praise or envy him for them, they make him unfit to carry on a career in the world: in short, he is now quite unpractical. For there is a deficiency here, a lack of preparedness, an omission in the instruction.

113

The student who is busily engaged searching inwards through meditation is justified in resorting to social isolation. But he will be very unwise
and also very egoistic if he makes it a total and permanent isolation.

114

Under the pressure of this revision of values and hunger for spirituality
he may feel the futility of going down to the office every morning, but can
he afford to stop doing so? Can he renounce the world merely by staying
at home or by going off to the woods instead?

115

"Such a man remains seated within himself, useless and inert. This
repose is simply laziness, and this tranquillity is forgetfulness of God, one's
self and one's neighbour. It is the exact opposite of the peace of divine, the
opposite of the peace of abyss; of that marvellous peace which is full of
activity, full of affection, full of desire, full of seeking, that burning and
insatiable peace which we pursue more and more after we have found
it . . . men seek it themselves, and no longer seek God even by their
desires. Yet it is not He whom they possess in their deceitful repose. The
possession of God demands and supposes perpetual activity. He who
thinks otherwise deceives himself and others. All our life as it is in God is
immersed in blessedness: all our life as it is in ourselves is immersed in
activity. And these two lives form one." These words of John Ruysbroeck
(1293–1381), a European mystic who had refused to be content with a
merely self-loving mysticism, were uttered in a denunciation of those
mystics, whom he called "Quietists," whose goal is simply to enjoy the
repose which comes when, as he said, "they abstain from every interior
and exterior act."

116

One kind of mystic who regards time as an illusion, history as a dream,
and progress as a myth inevitably comes to take less and less interest in
men and events, more and more in himself and his thoughts. In the end,
he becomes entirely preoccupied with his own life, entirely indifferent to
the lives of others. He makes no practical contribution towards the welfare
of society because he does not think it worth making. Life in the world has
become, for him, bereft of meaning. For it is God's *Lila*—sport, dance, or
play. Intervention would be senseless, beneficent intervention would be
self-deceit.

117

One wonders how those mystics would behave who have little knowledge of business offices or industrial factories, if they were forced by
destiny to earn their living by working in such a world after illumination.

118

In their metaphysical talk and doctrine they may rant and rave against the world but in their daily life they have to admit its existence. It is then no longer illusion, no longer falsely real. Confronted with its harsh or rosy spectacle they discover it to be quite substantial; it refuses to dissolve and vanish.

119

There is no direct gearing between the two. A man may be capable of drawing into a rapt absorbed condition but incapable of properly handling practical affairs or correctly judging a course of action.

120

Mysticism, when psychologically comprehended and correctly practised, can certainly give man—weak-willed, passion-driven, and earthward-bent, as he often is—definite disciplinary, emotional, and ethical benefits. But so far as it shuts him up to lounge in his inner recesses and enjoy their peace alone, or so far as it persuades him to cast society permanently aside and withdraw like a tortoise into his own shell, it does not directly advantage others. The mystic wants to be left alone to meditate without external distractions. His peace is precious to him and he is unwilling to disturb it by sacrificing any part of his personal life for the benefit of others. The serious yogi-in-training usually spends most of a lifetime in segregation from his fellows, untrammeled by family burdens and unperturbed by social responsibility, because he is seeking something whose attainment the presence of others hinders and disturbs. He is naturally wrapped up by his discipline in a cloak of self-centeredness. Every manual of yoga which recommends the novice to turn hermit and forsake cities in moderation at the proper time in the proper place and for a limited duration, is a perfectly justifiable rule. He needs solitude and silence for the practice of his meditations. It is difficult to get these things in society so he quite properly avoids society. The very essence of all genuinely mystical exercises is the process of introversion. But carried to the point of excess, as it usually is when the practitioner is ignorant of the fact that mystic discipline is a means and not an end, it is likely to finish in callous self-centeredness. When he does not realize that asceticism is but a temporary discipline, a jumping-off ground, whence to arrive at the higher and permanent condition of *internal* disentanglement, he is likely to fall into the trap of making such external disentanglement the goal of life and even become callously indifferent to the well-being of others—not deliberately, of course, but as a consequence of his unbalanced introversion.

Philosophy and mysticism

121

Whereas an incomplete mysticism arrests progress and leads to lethargy, because it regards worldly indifference as the necessary result of worldly detachment, the riper philosophic mysticism stimulates progress and inspires action. This is because it regards first, inner value rather than outer appearance, and second, altruistic duty as well as personal satisfaction.

122

If he cannot enter the spiritual state without shutting himself up in an undisturbed room and meditating, then it is assuredly not the final state. If he has to pass into a trance or close his eyes, he has still to travel to reach the goal. If he cannot keep the higher awareness when he returns to social existence, it is not the eternal one. All these have to be transcended if the philosophic experience is to be attained.

123

Its refusal to separate the inner life from the worldly one is perhaps one of the features which distinguish philosophical mysticism from the ordinary kind.

124

When the whole world lies stretched out before them, how dare they go on ignoring it, or else dismissing it as a device of Satan to entrap and ensnare them! We must enquire into the world which the senses contact no less than into the self which is viewing that world. How can the ascetic obtain the knowledge of the All when he gives up such a huge portion of it? Giving up the world does not lead to Reality, but it leads to peace of mind. Men who lack intelligence, who possess little brains, must take to mysticism and yoga, but only the mature and developed mind can enter the quest of enquiry into Truth. This means therefore that pupils are generally not initiated into this enquiry by gurus prematurely. They must first have developed their egos and their minds to a high degree, and only after that should they be taught to renounce what has been fostered with so much pain. This is evolution: although Truth is ideally attainable here and now, technically it is attainable only at the end of the pageant of evolution, when the whole being of man has been highly developed and is ripe to receive the greatest of all gifts.(P)

125

Not all mystics have settled down to make the enjoyment of a self-centered peace their loftiest aim in life. Some, like the Quakers, have been generous enough to include the relief of human suffering in such an aim.

126

To seek no meaning in the universal life but only in one's own life, to limit enquiry solely to the self without caring to extend it to the world in which that self finds itself, is to shut one's eyes to the divine purpose in endowing man with intelligence and all the possibilities of developing it.

127

This indifferentism has been tersely put on record by Thomas Traherne, the seventeenth-century English mystical clergyman and poet. The result of his inner experiences was that he understood, "All things were well in their proper places. Whereupon you will not believe, how I was withdrawn from all endeavours of altering and mending outward things. They lay so well, methought, they could not be mended; but I must be mended to enjoy them." Traherne merely expressed what every mystic must feel when the beauty of the Inner Reality is revealed to him and the task of withdrawing himself from earthly enchantments and disturbances to its unhindered enjoyment is confronting him. Such a mood is inevitable, necessary, and natural. It is quite right at this stage of his quest. Only when he has succeeded in the task of withdrawal and has perfected himself in the work of contemplation, is the mood likely to change and his whole development to complete itself by ascending to the philosophical level. There, he will feel the urge to give out what he has gained and there he will comprehend that, although the world is in God's hands, there is something in man which has been made in God's image and that therefore he may participate in God's work.

128

Quietism, the smug doctrine that it is enough for the mystic to give himself up to passivity and ecstasy, refraining from personal activity or social service, from intellectual improvement and aesthetic culture, was medieval Europe's counterpart of India's yoga. Philosophy walks all the way with quietists and yogis when they would have us go into retreat from the world and when they would have us learn the art of meditation. But it turns off their road when they would make retreat the business of an entire lifetime, when they proclaim a specific virtue in physical or intellectual lethargy, and when they debar positive effort in meditation in favour of a limp waiting on God. Their enjoyment of this inward rest is legitimate, but their enjoyment of it to excess—to the point where every other duty is dropped for its sake—is not. The intellect degenerates, the morals stultify, the heart shrivels. Idleness, whether of the body or the mind, is not holiness.

129

This study must be prefixed by the study of self, and a knowledge of the springs which actuate human actions and human motives must be obtained.

130

"What am I?" The formula is excellent for novices, who are naturally and legitimately interested more in themselves than in the world at large. But it will not do for the advanced seeker, who has outgrown this narrowness and has begun to vex his head as much with universal questions as with personal ones.

131

He will have achieved what is a goal for himself but what is only the starting point of a further path for the philosophical student. If, preoccupied with the Part (himself), he ignores the Whole (the sensuous universe) when his retracted attention returns to his external environment, he will be a mystic—a perfect mystic indeed, but not more.

132

The mystic is forced by the tempo of formidable events into a new usefulness and practicality. He is having to bring society into his purview, the State into his scheme of things, ephemeral history into his contemplations of eternity, and hard economics into his spiritual problems. He is being made to surrender amateurish dabbling in meditation or neurotic playing with it. He is being compelled to forgo the tea-table treatment of the mystical experience as though it were mere embroidery on life instead of being the very core of life itself.

133

There is an elusive horizon in mystical studies, researches, and experiments. The farther one advances the more it recedes. There is no end to them in this lifetime. The present great crisis in humanity's history, with its war and upheaval, has provided the opportunity to delve into, and glean revelations about, a field which the advanced mystic might never have touched in normal times. The result leads him to conclude that this troubled and misunderstood world must be considered, however more attractive other, higher realms may be. The former mystical attitude of mere escapism and sheer indifference is false, meaningless, and selfish today. The correct attitude must be to wish to spiritualize life *in* the world—not to ignore, deny, or run away from it. This requires a certain mental equilibrium, but it is quite attainable.

134

Those who cannot demonstrate by their achievements what they can do for themselves—whether spiritually or materially—will never be able to do anything worthwhile for humanity. Yet the irony is that so many visionary people who talk about service belong to this ineffective class.

135

Philosophic mystics are those who are not satisfied with the feeling of inner peace alone, although they enjoy it, and want to understand the world in which they live sufficiently to know how to live with more good health and less avoidable suffering. That is, they not only want to know God, as all mystics do, but also God's workings in the environment in which they find themselves—in the world of physical Nature, which includes their physical bodies. They want to know the way the divine World-Idea is expressed outside and inside those bodies so that they can cooperate with it, obey its laws, and live in harmony with it.

136

Whatever ordinary mysticism may be, philosophical mysticism seeks to escape, not from, but *into* reality.

137

The first vital difference is that whereas ordinary mysticism uses only the mental pictures of spiritual leaders for its meditations, philosophic mysticism uses their mind, character, and realization along with, and ultimately in place of, the pictures. That is, it replaces form by essence. The second shows the philosophic insistence on developing a compassionate attitude and helping others through special meditations.

138

Philosophic mysticism has a higher object than merely tranquillizing the passions or peaceably sitting in trance. These are excellent attainments, but they are not enough. For they tend by themselves to lead to a cessation of active life. They cannot constitute a sufficient and complete goal for human beings. We are here to live. Is our life to end in dreams alone, not deeds? We find ourselves among other human beings; have we no duty to them? Can we rest content in self-absorption and, as a mystical friend once remarked, "Let the world go to the dogs!" He justified in his own mind his indifference to the world-wide butchery of war, which was raging at the time, but will this justify it in humanity's mind?

139

Speaking of the mystic who has attained this highest degree, and speaking with the authority of personal experience, Saint Teresa uttered a similar warning: "You may think, my daughters, that the soul in this state should be so absorbed that she can occupy herself with nothing. You deceive yourselves. She turns with greater ease and ardour than before to all that which belongs to the service of God."

140

However exalted their experiences, the latter are all of a self-centered character. Is it not nobler to seek similar experiences but to seek them against a background of the social concepts of compassion duty and service?

141

It is impossible for the human being to separate itself from the outside world in which it lives and with which it has an inescapable relationship. How can it truly know itself if it refuses to learn about this relationship?

Rational mysticism

142

The developed mystic needs but neglects the undeveloped thinker within himself, just as the thinker needs but neglects the mystic. It is not enough to arrive at truth through mystical feelings; we must also arrive at it through metaphysical thinking. The liability to strive for unrealizable ends, as well as the tendency to mistake in his hurry mere reflection of reality for the Real itself, will then be eliminated. Truth can never suffer from the proper activity of human reason and experiment, but only from their improper or unbalanced activity. The moment the mystic seeks to convey his experience to others, when his trance, ecstasy, or inspiration is over, that moment he has to begin to analyse it. If he lacks the proper intellectual equipment to do this with scientific objectivity and precision, he will convey it faultily, insufficiently, and to some extent ineffectively. This is most often the case, unfortunately, because the distaste for intellectual activity is one of the customary reasons why a number of men have taken to mysticism. Without such equipment, the aspirant will be unable to extract the precise significance of his own mystical experiences, as he will be unable to check the correctness of his opinions upon them; whereas with it in his possession, he will be able to examine any such experience and any such opinion by the light of a systematic, thoroughly tested world view. The vagueness of his concepts, the looseness of his thinking, the confusion of his facts, and the partisan character of his conception of life all combine to render the average mystic's understanding of the truth about his own inner experience often unsatisfactory and his evaluation of other men's vaunted occult claims often untenable. We must distinguish between ebullient emotion and deep love. Those whose aspirations are still in the region of the first may sneer at any other spiritual path than the devotional one, yet if an aspirant is really devoted to the Divine, as he says, he ought not to object to learning all he can about his beloved, which is to say that he ought not to be averse to study of the metaphysics of truth, however difficult and strange it is likely to be.(P)

143

We may make ourselves deeply sensitive to mystical feelings and thoroughly convince our intellects of mystical truths, without falling into mystical superstitions or foolishness.

144

The hypnosis of the wakeful consciousness is pleasant, but it is no substitute for the enlightenment of the wakeful consciousness. A yoga-path which merely stills the mind, but does not instruct it, is a help on the way, not the end of the way.

145

Why may I not be satisfied with the peace gained in meditation? This is a question which may justly be asked. The best answer to it is that those who have realized the Overself, and know whereof they speak, themselves declare that this study is essential. It is only through such study that the mystic can learn what the Overself cannot be. This negative result is not therefore to be deemed unimportant. For if he learns that it is utterly without form, he will no longer be deceived by visions or abnormal occult experiences.

146

The mistake of the mystic is to seek in immediate feeling a reality through which the reason has not worked its way, instead of boldly renouncing that feeling for the higher work of reflection and thus eventually attaining a loftier form of realization which preserves the results of that reflection whilst outgrowing its limitation.

147

A man may be quite advanced mystically but yet quite in error intellectually.

148

When the triumph of emotional unbalance over calm reason is announced and accepted as a heaven-sent inspiration, when error is asserted in the name of mystical communion with God, we can only stand aside thoughtfully and note the dangers of unphilosophic mysticism.

149

He must beware of making glandular satisfaction a sufficient criterion of philosophical truth. Philosophy need not object to his having such satisfactions, but it must vigorously object to his setting them up in the seat of judgement upon itself. For a physiological state, however ecstatic it be, is not to be equated with the faculty of reason or with the power to penetrate reality.

150

The demand is twofold. I want a scientific as well as a metaphysical mysticism. I want mystics to become rationally minded and scientifically observant.

151

So long as the mystic is unable to function fully in his intellect, why should he expect to function clearly in what is beyond intellect?(P)

152

The mystic who overbalances himself with ephemeral ecstasies pays for them by deep moods of depression. This is worth noting, but it is not all. If there is not a rationally thought-out metaphysical foundation to give constant and steady support to his intuitions of truth, he may find these intuitions telling him one thing this year and the opposite next year. But this foundation must be a scientific and not merely a speculative metaphysics, which means that it must itself be irrefragable, gathering its facts not with the critical intellect alone, but also with the spontaneous intuition and above all with the insight. Such a system exists only in the metaphysics of truth.(P)

153

A mysticism ennobled by service and fortified by science could attract and help many more persons, but a mysticism indifferent to service and opposed to science will continue to eke out a lethargic life in an obscure corner.

154

Resistances are set up by the average mystic simply because of his metaphysical ignorance. He is somewhat like a person who has never studied the theory of music nor learned to read a musical manuscript but who can play two or three tunes on a violin solely by ear. The comprehension of what he is doing during meditation is missing. The ability to play any tune whatsoever and not merely two or three is lacking.

155

The untrained mystic's understanding of his own inner experiences is often superficial and generally confused. This is because it lacks a metaphysical foundation. Again because it starts usually from the standpoint of personal emotion it develops various vagaries. A common example is that the bad habit of attributing everything he does not understand to something supernatural or of finding the mysterious hand of God in the most ordinary happenings, becomes an ingrained one.

156

An intelligent mysticism may not have been so necessary in the olden days when a mystic was almost always a monk, an anchorite, a begging hermit, or a wandering friar. It is necessary in these days when he may have to be a business executive.

157

There are too many people who mistake a confused mass of unrelated assertions, unrefined terms, and unproven statements for mysticism. They do so because they think that mysticism is beyond logical proof, above scientific demonstration, and out of reach of mathematical exposition. They consider mysticism to be entirely a matter of feeling and not of thinking. These are the people who fall victim to the charlatans and the impostors. The kind of mysticism they espouse is a bemused one.

158

Those who call themselves "pure mystics" because they will not "adulterate" mysticism with rational, practical, altruistic, and other activities naturally adopt a contemptuous attitude toward philosophical teaching. This often happens because they are not usually conscious of the intellectual and demonistic pitfalls which beset their journey. Therefore we protest against such a partial view. Those who are sincere but lack judgement will not be saved by their sincerity alone from the sufferings into which their errors may lead them. If this, the practical reason, were the only one for adding a philosophical background it would surely be enough. The mystics who throw away the use of reason, throw away one of the chief tools which Nature has given them to adjust themselves successfully to their environment. It is strange how they are so shy of this fact and actually flee from it. It is only in the hard school of bitter experience that their hallucinations may begin to fade. Those who use their mysticism to become confirmed in their foolishness are welcome to do so. But not all of us can afford to do so. Life's leaden tread sooner or later comes down on the foolish and makes them suffer for the unwisdom of their deeds. It is not an accident but a consequence that misty vagueness prevails in such circles whereas definite clarity prevails in the philosophical ones. Spiritual progress may free itself from these delusions and dangers only on the basis of a clear understanding of what spirituality really means.

159

So long as the mind pursues satisfaction and not truth, it will never attain truth. Yogic *samadhi* is a form of satisfaction. Therefore the successful yogi may feel happy. But he does not know the meaning of life. The craving for gratification of some desire—whether it be the desire of flesh, fame, or God—enslaves man, makes him a dependent, and sets up a stone wall 'twixt him and truth.

160

Mental alertness and not mental death is the characteristic of this farther road.

161

The mysticism which the twentieth century needs is not a drug to enervate reason and paralyse activity. It is a way of combining useful life in the world with intelligent search for the soul.

162

The medieval mystic gave himself the unnecessary choice between following reason's thinking *or* following the soul's intuition. The modern mystic cannot afford such a narrow outlook. For him, it is thinking *and* intuition, reason *and* the soul.

163

Without this philosophical exploration of what lies behind religion and mysticism, there will often be a confusion of levels of reference in the minds of students and believers.

164

If so much spiritual doctrine has been at the mercy of megalomaniac teachers and demented prophets in the past, that has partly been due to lack of education, inability to adopt a more scientific attitude, and insufficient balance, experience, or study. But the opportunity to counteract these causes is becoming more and more a feature of this century.

165

The philosophic student seeks peace of mind just as much and just as personally as the others do. But he does not seek it at any cost; he will not pay for it with his reason. Nor does he want it as a drug, wherewith to suppress the symptoms of emotional weakness and egoistic neuroticism.

166

Both the man who has despised rational learning and the man who has applauded it have been able to attain the soul's consciousness. Let the first type of mystic not be so intolerant nor the second so conceited.

167

Mysticism will only benefit and not suffer if its intellectual basis is enlarged. It can then better meet the dominant questions of our time and better serve the kind of life which a twentieth-century individual has to live. But whether contemporary mystics understand this or not, such is the view upon which evolutionary necessity will confer forcibly in the future.

168

Jacob Boehme was a competent and advanced mystic. His little book, *Dialogues on the Supersensual Life*, would alone testify to that and his career adds further evidence. Yet, because he had not undergone the liberating process of a philosophic discipline, his mind was so confined that he would allow no other God-sent prophethood than that of Jesus.

169

"By doubting we come at truth," were the words which Cicero set down in Latin to guide the thoughtful among his fellow Romans. But our yogic friends do not care to become his disciples. Hence their strange disregard of actuality and their lofty flights into fantasy.

170

That some mystics have obtained excellent results with superstitious procedures and without any intellectual understanding of the processes employed does not mean that they would not have obtained better results had they possessed rational techniques and correct understanding.

171

The belief that the most illumined state is so rapturous that it degrades human reason to the lowest place, is a primitive one.

172

The advance in educational attainment always means the lapse in superstitious belief.

The power of rational faith

173

Religious devotion is good, mystical contemplation is far better, but when enlightened by knowledge both become immeasurably superior. Hence the mystic has nothing to fear from metaphysics. It will rob him of nothing worth keeping whilst it will present him with a clearer perception and stronger impression of the truth.

174

Those who are willing to learn the doctrines and practise the methods of scientific mysticism are few. Such an approach does not appeal to the many. This is because they are hypnotized by authority and simply cannot think for themselves; or because their experience is too narrow, too parochial; or because they prefer sentimentality, miracle-mongering, and pseudo-intuition; or that they are too ready to take as facts what are merely surmises. It will never be a popular one. Yet the mystic will lose little and gain much if he makes a scientific approach; if he places facts above speculations and does not take the unchecked play of the imaginative faculty—whether it be his own or some authority's—for ascertained data or verified observations. The scientific spirit is a proof-wanting one. It seeks certainty. The mystic may ignore or despise such a spirit, but the philosopher welcomes and incorporates it in his own. For he perceives that here is the difference between blind faith and assured knowledge. Even if there are matters that he has to take on faith, at least he takes them on a reasonable faith, not a blind one. Our appeal is against a negative misleading emotionalist mysticism. It is directed toward a rational and scientific modern mysticism, and therefore it is at the same time a crucial test of the wisdom of our readers. If they take the first and easier path, the loss in the end will only be their own. For I seek neither a single follower nor supporter for myself, and certainly not popularity. I am self-content and self-contained. If they take the second and harder path the gain will be entirely their own. They will be saved from wasting years in sterile beliefs and deceptive practices. They will learn a healthy self-reliance, of which half-blind guides or exploiting cults would have robbed them. They may even come to regard these warnings and pointers with gratitude.

175

Most mystical enlightenments arising out of religious devotion alone or aspirational meditation alone are partial ones. Mysticism needs the support of knowledge to attain self-maturation and self-completion. It does not possess an adequate understanding of itself. The intelligent mystic will sooner or later feel the want of an adequate formulation of his own inward experience. But this can only be done through a metaphysical system, and if he seeks and finds the right one, which is the metaphysic of truth, he will find something which will be both a guiding star amid all the bewildering maze of his inner experiences and a supporting hand to help him keep his balance amid their confusing alternations. It will provide him with a definite means of assessing the truth-value of doctrines, ideas, movements, or masters. It will enable him to determine the proper moral attitude to adopt in whatever kind of situation he may find himself.

176

Accurate ideas about the nature of the soul he is seeking to unite with— that is, right thinking—will not only not hinder his venture in meditation but actually promote its success.

177

Nobody is likely to be a worse mystic but, on the contrary, he is likely to be a better one if he adds to his knowledge of the laws which govern human existence a knowledge of the forces which operate in human life and the influences which affect human mind. His mystical experiences will not suffer if he develops more clarity of mind about the world in which he lives and more definite understanding about the personality through which he functions.

178

Yes, mystical experience can be rightly interpreted only by a rightly disciplined mentality. But the discipline required is so subtle, so hard, and so complex that it is rarely undergone in all its fullness.

179

He will be all the better and not worse if he brings to his mystical path a scientific method of approach, a large historical acquaintance with the comparative mysticisms of many countries, a scientific knowledge of psychology, and a practical experience of the world. He will be all the better and not worse if he learns in advance, and in theory, what every step of the way into the holy of holies will be like.(P)

180

There is hope for the seeker who wishes to recapture the joys of a past mystical experience. But the experience may be regained in a different form. The emotional excitement that accompanied its earlier phases is more likely to be balanced—as it should be—by greater intellectual understanding of what is happening and how to control it.

181

In view of the growing interest, it is more needful than ever to dispel the confusions which hang like clouds around mystic thought and practice. All who seek truth with open eyes and not with blindfolded ones must sooner or later face the same problems which then confronted us. If no ray of metaphysical understanding penetrates the minds of others, then they are practising mysticism in the dim twilight—if not altogether in the dark night. The wise aspirant will one day refuse to walk through the spiritual life without full consciousness of where each step is leading him, as he will eventually refrain from striving vaguely for aims which are not clear to him. Let others do what they wish, but he should not tolerate such confused thinking in his own mind.

182

What harm will it do the mystically inclined if they desist from shallow and unsystematic thinking? And how much good will it surely do them if they begin to deepen and systematize their thoughts! What lessening of their devotion to the Divine will result if they critically base it upon the pure truth about the Divine instead of blindly revelling in personal imaginations about it? And how far are they better off with their glorification of intellectual poverty?

183

It is not a merit to be proclaimed but a defect to be deplored when mysticism would put a taboo on modern knowledge and scientific attitudes. The medievally-disposed mystic who looks down upon the practical inventions and mental achievements of science is not really being spiritual, as he believes, but merely being foolish. And those who scorn literature and vaunt anti-intellectualism are dreamers of the dreamiest kind. Sharpness of intelligence and breadth of experience are not only at a large discount in such circles but are actually regarded with disfavour. You will not find the kingdom of heaven between the covers of a book, but you may find some ideas which could point the way to the kingdom. If so, the book has served you well. Mystical denunciations of intellectual activity find their logical conclusion in the advocacy of absolute idiocy, in futile stagnation. Moreover, we need the intellectually formulated doctrines to guide our thinking and conduct because we cannot hold for long the moods of religious reverence and mystical inspiration. They give us something to hold on to when we are bereft of inward experience. The endeavour to make a scientific analysis of the contradictory situations which arise in meditational practice or mystical doctrine and thus clarify its issues, is often avoided with horror as being blasphemous! Those who are afraid to look such shortcomings in the face—or who even deny that they exist— are not suited for philosophy. We may find in their uncritical enthusiasms and vague outlooks and anti-rational attitudes some of the grounds why mysticism has not commended itself to the educated Western mind. For the latter expects and rightly expects that what is claimed to be a higher way of life should surely raise and not lower the level of intelligence of its readers.

184

Even some of the great Christian medieval mystics began to see these truths glowing on the horizon. Saint Victor advocated ordered thinking as a preparation for the mystical experience. Saint Thomas Aquinas proclaimed that intellectual endeavour was "no less a service of God than any other" and also advised aspirants to "live like men, that is, like embodied souls and remember that souls embodied cannot behave as though they were disembodied."

185

It is unfortunate that few mystics have ever been trained in critical habits of thought and scientific habits of observation. The ordinary mystic seldom raises the question: "What is the intrinsic truth of my inner experience?" But the philosophic mystic must do so. For instance, mental inertia may be mistaken for mental peace. And the fact of experiencing a mystical vision is no guarantee of the authenticity of its revelation. It was not an utterly materialist sceptic nor a fully enlightened philosopher but one of the best and most famous mystics amongst a people who have produced Europe's greatest mystics, the Spaniard Saint John of the Cross, who dryly remarked of a certain nun's meditations: "All this that she says, 'God spoke to me, I spoke to God,' seems nonsense." Saint John could never have arrived at such a perception if he had not himself arrived at the very end of the mystical path and so come to know quite well what he was talking about. Such beliefs as this nun's can only be accepted by people whose capacity for critical judgement is very weak. Mysticism unchecked by reason may degenerate into mere superstition. That men cling to fantasies and accept absurdities merely evidences their lack of intellectual capacity—not their spirituality. It is good to be a mystic but it is better to be a critical mystic. The mystic who suffers from intellectual, muddleheaded, or emotional hysteria should not be content with these defects but should try to get rid of them. In a region where yogic aberrations and mystical excesses abound so freely, the value of scientific attitude, accuracy of statement, disciplined imagination, and broad-based learning is surely indisputable. When the scientific habit of observation is missing, when reason is under-developed and emotion over-weighted, the mystic receives his experiences in an unbalanced way or holds his views in a disproportionate relationship. Most necessary indeed is the scientific antidote to the excrescences of unbalanced mysticism, which magnifies the trivial and minifies the essential; most valuable is the rationalist counter to the impulses of shady superstitions; most helpful is prudent reserve against the exaggerations of antiquated mysteriosophy; most assuring is the mental armour against premature conclusions; and most desirable is self-criticism, too, as a safeguard against the truth's being turned by our fancies, imaginations, or desires into something quite different. The mystic must use his whole intelligence—that is, his scientific faculties of criticism, observation, and fact-finding, plus his metaphysical faculties of abstract reflection upon facts—to check his inspired emotions and spiritual experiences. Such a remorselessly critical method of approach loosens the bond of dogma and superstition and thus prepares the way for a genuine understanding which shall be as impeccable as it will be rational.

186

What the mystic fails to see is that there cannot be an adequate realization of life without an adequate ideology of life. Otherwise his practices, however emotionally satisfying they may be, will necessarily be blind ones. How much wiser and safer will be that mystic who is guided in his practices by a correct understanding of what he is about.

187

The use of intellect need not detract from the use of intuition. The mystic will be all the better for it. Only if he is unbalanced, and misuses it, will he be worse.

188

There is no sound reason why a man's critical faculty should be forced into a coma merely because he seeks to cultivate a higher faculty.

189

The mystic gazes at God with the eye of personal feeling. The eye of rational understanding remains shut. He must open it with the help of metaphysics to get a correct view.

190

There are those who believe they are spiritual because they are unpractical. This is idealism run aground, cast on the shore of folly. For even here, on this non-worldly quest, there is need of intelligence, just as few would doubt there is in their dealings with the world.

The goal of truth

191

Nature (God) has given the mystic physical eyes, and he gladly uses them. It has also given him mental eyes (reason), yet he foolishly refuses to use them. The sharpening of reason and the development of practicality constitute valuable features of the general human evolution. Scientific observation and rational thought are necessities of a higher human life. Those mystics who do not believe this to be the case, who persist in maltreating their intuition and maiming their intellects, can be quickly discerned by their neurotic attitudes and exaggerated statements. They abound in every mystical movement, cult, and society. To get at the truth we must reject their partial one-sided and oversimple approach. To repudiate or denounce reason as being unspiritual and to disdain or discard balance as being unnecessary, to follow every upsurge of fancy and to accept every claimant as intuition—this may lead the mystic further along the path he has chosen, but it will also lead him nearer to the unfortunate necessity of requiring a psychiatrist's attention. Only an incorrect metaphysical approach could contemptuously pronounce intelligence to be an enemy of intuition, just as it always pronounces "spirit" to be eternally opposed to "matter."

192

Without a complete and penetrative understanding of philosophical truth, a real union with the Overself cannot be effected, but only an apparent one. This is why yoga alone is insufficient, although recommended as a help to fit the mind for such understanding.

193

All emotional realizations, with their claims to a false finality, are deceptive. They must pass; the fluctuant moods of the mystic are not reality. We have to *think* and think our way through to Truth. Such thought must be long sustained and tranquil, hence the need of yogic ability in concentrative thought. When we gain an impetus in meditation practice, we should use it not merely for gaining temporary peace (which is all the peace it can give) but for philosophical study.

194

The fact that these differences between men inevitably occur, these conflicts of interpretation leading to conflicts of bodies, does not mean that we are therefore to regard intellect as an enemy of mystical experience. For the same intellect which creates false ideas that divide and antagonize men may also create true ideas that can unite and harmonize them.

195

The aspirant who is sincere but ill-informed is always in a less secure position than one who is well-informed. This is not only because "knowledge is power," as an old thinker once said, but because the opposition of evil forces has to be encountered and mastered.

196

He will lose nothing and gain much if he tries to know scientifically why these experiences arise. And he will be a better mystic if he can relate them to the rest of life, if he can move forward to a fuller understanding of his place in the universal scheme, if he can reach an explicit and self-conscious comprehension of his own mysticism. If we grant that he can successfully attain his mystical goal without this definite knowledge, he cannot become an effective teacher and guide without it. So long as his interest is confined to himself this need not matter, but as soon as he seeks to serve mankind it does matter. For then only can he present the way and the goal in the detail and with the clarity that helps to convince others.(P)

197

Those who enter Shangri-la with prepared beliefs about its glamorous spiritual personages but without any prepared critical judgement, may find what they come to see—but only at the cost of deceiving themselves.

198

The true mystic values inward experience out of all proportion to the theories about it. This is at once a virtue and a defect. Virtue, because the inward is the reality and the intellectual its shadow. Defect, because the path to it and the manifestation of it are so subtle that without a sound rational conception of mystical practice and an accurate metaphysical conception of mystical attainments, it is immeasurably easy to go astray from the one or to distort the other.

199

Answers are sometimes so subtle and vague that critical observers might think them one way of evading questions if they did not know that the mystic was perfectly sincere. The fact is he cannot describe what he does not know.

200

The disappearance of balance from mysticism means the disappearance of intellectual self-reliance, of the validity of reason, and of the realistic attitude towards life. The heavy price which mystics pay for this loss has been revealed by history. For when superstition supplants reason, suffering follows like a shadow.

201

The seeker who has not awakened the critical faculty—and is therefore still a child in his intellectual development—is naturally unsuspicious, plastic and docile. Even the seeker who has awakened it is sometimes so overawed by exaggerated or false claims as to leave it off on the threshold when he enters the presence of spiritual charlatanry.

202

These gullible people are admittedly humble but they do not understand the immense importance of being humble before facts, of setting aside their emotional predilections and prostrating themselves at the feet of fact, of withholding belief from men or doctrines where it is not warranted by the facts yielded by prior investigation.

203

Metaphysical and scientific knowledge of the leading features of the cosmic plan for human existence and human achievement is necessary to the mystically minded; their inner experiences do not exempt them from this necessity. Without such knowledge they may become victims of self-deceived "masters" or of plausible errors or they may constantly vacillate from one belief to another.

204

Let them not court suffering by misplaced faith, or invite trouble by misguided action, when the suffering is unnecessary and the trouble unwelcome. Wisdom protects: let them seek it first.

205

The attempt to secure protection against impending evil, disaster, or misfortune by proclaiming its unreality, before proper analysis has unveiled the cause and cure, is a premature one and can end only in failure.

206

They would die for truth but they would not think for it.

207

So much wishful thinking and imaginative nonsense enters mysticism that the seeker must apply independent judgement to his study of it if he wants to find truth and keep sanity.

208

The emotional nature needs to be balanced by the intellectual faculties, in the mystic even more than in others. Otherwise mental disease can easily parade itself as spiritual experience.

209

There is a difference between transcending reason and contradicting reason. Both the foolish sceptic and the foolish mystic may not see this and thus fall into error.

210

The mystic who claims that his knowledge is verbally incommunicable and that it is useless trying to explain it intellectually, is stretching a difficulty into an impossibility.

211

It is the *thinking* mystic who can best explain mysticism to others and even to himself. And it is the *active* mystic who can best demonstrate its worth.

212

The narrow mystic who sets up for others his personal limitations in mystical development, does a dangerous thing. His justifiable fear of barren, dry intellectualism may become exaggerated into a fear of wisely discriminating reason. This can end only in over-credulous accepting of superstition and disturbance of the mind's balance. It may even lead in weak intelligences to a mild insanity.

213

If the intellectual and realistic attitude is not developed previously to coming into the mystical life, it will have to be developed afterwards. Only as it is inserted into and balanced with the psychic and intuitive attitude will the results be consistently reliable. Without it the seeker will be lost at times—through emotion, whim, theory, auto-suggestion, or prejudice—in baseless fantasies, irresponsible vacillations, and fanciful experiences.

The path beyond yoga

214

The common opinion implicit in most mystical literature places all illumined mystics on the same level, since they are all supposed to experience the same God. But the truth is that they are at different levels and have different experiences. For even within illumination itself there is a primary degree, which most remain at, and a perfected degree, which only those who master and embody the philosophic mysticism can attain. What is required for the first degree is so much less that it is easier and simpler to pass.

215

All genuine mystics who claim this God-experience may be granted their claim, if we substitute the word *Overself* for the word *God*. But what cannot be granted is that all of them have an equal awareness of the Overself. There are different degrees of this awareness.

216

The degree of enlightenment which a mystic has reached corresponds also to the degree of freedom from the ego which he or she has reached.

217

The atmosphere of muddle-headedness which is prevalent in such circles is one inevitable consequence of pouring scorn on intellectual advancement. The first step out of this fog of confused appreciation of mystical culture is to learn that the latter possesses various strata. What he has achieved through aspiration and meditation is excellent but not enough. It may even be self-deceptive if it lulls him into thinking he has done enough. He must be warned not to fall into the easy temptation of jumping prematurely to sweeping general conclusions from inadequate data but to be patient until the whole landscape can be surveyed. He must beware of comfortably believing that he has already attained the larger goal when he has merely attained a lesser goal on the way, as much as he must beware of mistaking a fitful glimpse for an abiding enlightenment. He has not reached, as he fondly believes, the end of man's possible course. He must do one thing more, without which the achievement will in the end prove unsatisfactory and imperfect.

218

Just as the infant human has to learn to balance his body, and then to walk in the physical world, so the infant mystic has to learn to balance his soul, and then to walk in the mystical world.

219

Few mystics ever achieve the ultimate of mysticism. Most live in the same field of awareness as ordinary people and only occasionally do they achieve a limited contact with the soul.

220

These early mystical experiences are representative of the divine in man; they present it to us in action, but they are not the divine itself in all its magnitude and fullness.

221

Some have succeeded in getting a hazy intuition of the soul, but they are very far from getting a vivid realization of it.

222

When the mystic comes to the end of this phase of his career but believes he has come to the end of the career itself, he falls under an illusion from which it is hard to recover.

223

Caught up by the newness and strangeness of the experience, exuberant in its delight and freedom, it is not surprising that he should refuse to heed those who tell him there is a far journey yet from this child's first acquaintance with Spirit to the adult's completed understanding of it.

224

Enlightenment is not equal in all mystics. With most it is only at its beginning, whatever they personally may believe to the contrary; with some it is more developed; with a few others it is perfect. In all cases it is proportionate to the extent to which the ego's influence is obliterated.

225

Few mystics attain an exalted condition all at once, or are able to maintain it permanently. It is reached by successive stages.

226

Whereas the ordinary yogas seek primarily to control the activities of consciousness, the higher yoga seeks in addition to bring enlightenment to its practiser both about the objects of his consciousness and about the consciousness itself. Consequently it is different from them in inward spirit as well as outward form. Thus the earlier yogas serve really as starting points whence we travel to the ultimate one. They are not ends in themselves but only means to help us reach an end. The error of most Westerners and many Orientals is to regard the various yoga paths as approaches of equal value rather than as stages of increasing importance. All other yogas prepare the aspirant to be fit to follow this philosophic and higher yoga. They do not and cannot take him to the ultimate realization. Nevertheless, although they cannot bring the full insight to birth, they are necessary prerequisites for this birth.

227

A common but wrong idea, into which some writers on mysticism fall, is that the final goal is realized by becoming one with the universe—a part of and united with Nature. That is indeed a state which often arises either on the way to the goal or on the return from it, but it is certainly not the ultimate goal itself. Man's highest source is in the infinite fullness of being whereas Nature is an expression of that being just as he is. It is the lesser thing, not the Ultimate Fact. The mystic's true goal must lie beyond it.

228

Ordinary mysticism is the intermediate state of inner development. When this phase has closed and intuitional mind powers are mature, then the truths of philosophy may be taught. They constitute the final doctrines and they do not need to deprive their predecessor of its place.

229

Their path will be determined by their object. If primarily they wish to give themselves some satisfaction, they need not go beyond ordinary yoga. If however, they seek truth as well as satisfaction, they must go beyond it.

230

To unite the ego with the Overself is the highest achievement open to the mystic whilst yet in the flesh. It is not possible for him to become one and the same identity with God, united in every possible way, and with his own separate and distinct identity utterly lost.

231

There are likely to be many who will reject these criticisms and revaluations of yoga because they emanate from one who is a Westerner and who is therefore supposed not to know what he is talking about in such an exotic matter. Let us therefore learn what some competent Indian authorities themselves say. His late Highness, The Maharaja of Baroda, who was famous for his frequent association with and patronage of the most learned Indian pundits, scholars, philosophers, and yogis, said in his inaugural address to the Third Indian Philosophical Congress held in Bombay in 1927: "The Yoga system in its essence is a series of practical means to be adopted as a preliminary to the attainment of the highest knowledge. . . . what the yoga system may have to teach us as to the preparation for the attainment of true philosophic insight needs to be disassociated from the fantastic and the magical." And at the same Congress, the general president, Sir Sarvapalli Radhakrishnan, did not hesitate to declare that "the Indian tradition gives the *first place* to the pursuit of philosophy."(P)

232

If those who have hitherto given their faith and thought to the ordinary presentations of yoga will now give further faith and more thought to the higher teaching here offered, they need lose nothing of their earlier understanding but will rather amplify it. Nor is anyone being called upon to renounce meditation; those who criticize me for this are as mistaken as they are unjust. What is really being asked for is the purging of meditation, the putting aside as of secondary and temporary interest those phases of yoga experience which are not fundamental and universal. But meditation itself should and must continue, for without it the Ultimate can never be realized. Only let it be directed rightly. Hence the inferior yogas are not for a moment to be despised, but it should be recognized that they are only relative methods useful at a particular stage only. Thus they will take their place as fit means leading towards the ultramystic practices and not be confounded with them.(P)

233

A mysticism based on the dualism of body and soul leads to passive mental emptiness, but this is not the same as the enlightened mental realization. As the Buddha put it when referring to Samkhya, one of the Indian forms of such dualistic mysticism: "This doctrine goes not to Nirvana but only to the attainment to the Realm of Nothingness."

234

Mystical meditation, like metaphysical thinking, is after all a preparatory act. Its ultimate end must be kept in sight. It must not itself be mistaken for that end. This tragic confession of Sadhu Sundur Singh is worth noting for its hard but wholesome factuality: "I have spent hours in meditation every day. That may have helped me to cultivate my spiritual faculties but I did not understand spiritual reality. It [yoga] only assisted me up to a certain point." Let nobody fail to see the full significance and tremendous gravity of this admission. The fault however does not lie with meditation. It lies with an incomplete and misconceived theory of meditation.

235

If we compare his state with the state of the crass materialist, his is certainly the better one. It is good that he feels that only when he gives himself up to meditation does he live at all. But it cannot be for this alone that his spirit was made flesh, his being brought down to earth. Life must certainly be large enough to include meditation but it cannot end with it.

236

It is only when vague misgivings begin to trouble him, only when indefensible acts begin to distress him, that he is likely to perceive that mysticism is insufficient in practical life and its revelation only partial in intellectual life.

237

Gautama learned yoga from two renowned teachers, Alara and Uddaka, passing through the successive degrees of *samapatti* (ecstatic meditation) with them but left them when he discovered it was not the way to ultimate Enlightenment.

238

It is not enough to master yoga, as this term is ordinarily understood. Something beyond it is also needed. Hence one of the texts belonging to this teaching, the *Lankavatara Sutra*, says of those who have perfected themselves in yoga: "When they reach the eighth degree they become so drunk with the bliss of inner peace that they do not grasp that they are still in the sphere of separateness and that their insight into reality is not yet perfect."

239

The search after mystical adventures can go on indefinitely and fill a whole lifetime, but one such experience can only yield another to repeat or replace it. It cannot end in the Unutterable Peace.

240

Yogic experience must be prolonged for many years before the yogi can realize that extravagant hopes of attainment will be disappointed.

241

There is a fourfold evolution in humanity and it unfolds successively—physically, emotionally, intellectually, and spiritually. Hence the mystic has to return to rebirth to complete his evolution despite his "union" which is consequently temporary. For riddance of the ego being the price of attainment, riddance of the emotional ego still leaves the intellectual ego untouched; that must be dealt with at its own level. Hence after emotional union has subsided he must cultivate his mental powers and regain it again as "intellectual union."

242

The basic efforts of the mystic, insofar as they attempt to reorient attention inwards toward the divine source of thought, are not mistaken ones. Hence, the ascent to philosophy does not require the abandonment of what we have previously learned, but it does require a shift in emphasis. It neither renounces the sublime fruits of mysticism nor liquidates the essential value of mysticism. The higher teaching does not come to destroy but to fulfil, does not seek to supplant but to augment.

243

We must arrive at a correct understanding of the place of yoga in the curriculum which leads to truth, and this can be done only by drawing a sharp distinction between what is known through experience and what is ascertained after inquiry.

244

Yoga serves as a contributory help, as a means of removing certain hindrances, and finishes tentative conceptions, to secure the proper conditions for studying Advaita. It does not lead directly to Truth.

245

Even Patanjali opens his famous classic manual by declaring that the goal of yoga is to equilibrate the agitations of *the mind*. Note that he does not say it is to cross beyond the mind altogether.

246

Mysticism, rid of its delusive fancies, purified from its wild eccentricities, freed from slavish taints of preconception and suggestion, becomes a part of philosophy.

247

The inner peace of elementary mysticism results in a satisfied personality whereas that of philosophic mysticism results in a surrendered personality.

248

The mystic must grow into the philosopher as the religionist must grow into the mystic.

The completion in knowledge

249

Students must be warned however that yoga exercise cannot of itself suffice to yield the ultimate realization of the All but only the realization of the inner self, the "soul," rare and advanced though such an attainment be.

250

The attainment of this deep state of oneness in meditation by an ordinary mystic may seem to be the end of the quest. Nevertheless the cycle of reincarnation will not end for him until he has become a philosophical mystic. For even though all earthly desires have been given a quietus, there will remain a latent desire to *know*, to understand his own experience and the world experience. To satisfy this desire, which will slowly come to the surface under the compulsion of Nature, he will have to develop intelligence to the proper degree. If he cannot do it quickly enough, then the work will have to continue into as many other births as are needed to finish it. For nature is shepherding the human race not only along the road of spiritual evolution but also of intellectual evolution.

251

Man does not exist alone, isolate. He is himself part of the universe into which he is born. Therefore he cannot obtain an adequate answer to the question "What am I?" unless he also obtains an answer to the question "What is my relationship to the universe?" Consequently the mystic who is satisfied with the answer which he discovers through meditation to the first question, is satisfied with a half-truth.

252

Mystical experience does not yield a cosmogony, hence does not tell us something new about the universe or about God's relation to the universe, even though it does tell us something gloriously new about ourselves—that is, about man. In such experience, it is not the universe that reveals the inner mysteries of its own nature, but man.(P)

253

He cannot obtain from ordinary mystical experience alone, precise information upon such matters as the universe's evolution, God's nature, or the history of man. This is because it really does lack an intellectual content. The only reliable increment of knowledge he can obtain from it is an answer to the question "What am I?"—an affirmation of the existence of man as divine soul apart from his existence as body. Apart from that his inner experience only improves the quality and increases the intensity of his life, does not constitute a way to new knowledge about what extends beyond it.(P)

254

The mystic seeks to stifle all thinking activity by a deliberate effort of willpower and thus arrive at a sense of oneness with the inner being which lies behind it. When his practice of the exercise draws to a successful end, the object upon which he concentrates vanishes from his field of focus but attention remains firmly fixed and does not wander to anything else. The consequence is that his consciousness is centered and this is true whether he feels it to be withdrawn into a pin-point within his head, as results from the commoner methods, or bathed in a blissful spot within his heart, as results from other ones.(P)

255

From the point of view of yoga practice, the yogi gradually succeeds in bringing his field of awareness to a single centre, which is at first located in the head and later in the heart. This achievement is so unusual that he experiences great peace and exaltation as a result—something utterly different from his normal condition. For him this is the soul, the kingdom of heaven, the Overself. *But from the point of view of the philosophy of Truth*, any physical localization of the Overself is impossible, because space itself is entirely within the mind, and the mind is therefore beyond any limits of here and there, and the Overself and Pure Mind (unindividualized) holds all bodies within it without being touched by them.(P)

256

The quietistic condition got by ordinary yoga is got by withdrawing from the five senses. But the hidden prenatal thought tendencies which are the secret origin of these senses still remain, and the yogi has not withdrawn from them because his attention has been directed to vacating the *body*. Thus the trance-condition he attains is only a temporary, *external* inactivity of the senses. Their *internal* roots still abide within him as mental energies which have evolved since time immemorial. Without adequate insight into the true nature of sense operations, which are fundamentally exteriorizations of interior mental ones, the yogi has only deceived himself when he thinks he has conquered them.(P)

257

The successful mystic certainly comes into contact with his real "I." But if this contact is dependent upon meditational trance, it is necessarily an intermittent one. He cannot obtain a permanent contact unless he proceeds further and widens his aspiration to achieve contact with the universal "I." There is therefore a difference between the interior "I" and the universal "I," but it is a difference only of degree, not of kind, for the latter includes the former.(P)

258

It would be a grave mistake to believe that the following of ascetic regimes and the stilling of wandering thoughts *causes* the higher consciousness to supervene. What they really do is to *permit* it to supervene. Desires and distraction are hindrances to its attainment and they merely remove the hindrances. This makes possible the recognition of what we really are beneath them. If however we do nothing more than this, which is called yoga, we get only an inferior attainment, often only a temporary one. For unless we also engage in the rooting out of the ego, which is called philosophy, we do not get the final and superior transcendental state.(P)

259

The unphilosophic mystic says: "God is in me." The philosophic mystic says simply: "God is!"

260

Regarding the mystical God-realization, its characteristic experience is not only a "mere" feeling of bliss, but an overwhelming one. This feeling may come without any vision whatsoever, but in several cases a vision does *precede* the profoundest state of bliss. In such cases it is nearly always a consequence of the devotion given by the devotee either to a living teacher or to a historical saviour. However it is only the accompaniment to the goal and not necessarily a part of the goal itself. Apart from this vision of some human or divine personage, the only other vision which may be experienced at this stage is of an ocean of light surrounding and permeating the mystic. This is only the case in the penultimate stage and vanishes when the highest goal is reached. Along with the bliss, there is a certain intuitive knowledge which may best be described as the knowledge that a divine power is present within the heart and that this power is beneficent, immaterial, and righteous. This knowledge is overwhelming in its certitude to the mystic. However, he must note at this point that this experience concerns the mystic himself, that the realization associates him with God, and does not concern itself with the rest of the world. Whatever else he believes he experiences, or in whichever way he understands these experiences, there will be added the workings of his own intellect or imagination or the unconscious agency of his tendencies. To put the matter briefly, the mystic attains intuitive knowledge that *he* is a divine self or soul, but the knowledge does not extend beyond that. It gives him no certitude or knowledge about the world outside of his self.

261

The visions seen by mystics who have not made the return-to-earth journey and who have not understood God as the world movement, will always be unreliable—sometimes correct but often wrong—in the same way that dreams are often jumbled and irrational. The ultimate path gives knowledge, yields only correct, truthful vision, and alone completes realization of the All. Mystical experience is incomplete because it is the experience of withdrawal only. It shows one aspect of divinity, not the whole of it.

262

The entry into objectless thought-free contemplation may be made year after year and a wonderful state it is too. But however pleasant and peaceful it is, the seeds of negative feelings are not made sterile but are only rendered inactive until new outer circumstances appear which bring them back to life—although the longer their suppression the weaker they become. Only knowledge of the truth and application of its understanding can end the bondage to ego where these tendencies lurk. Hence if the practice of contemplation is accompanied or followed or, although not usual, preceded by the path of knowledge, a real rooting-out of ego-bondage is possible. This alone leads to permanent reform of character and transformation of outlook. It is done by stages, or rather depths of insight, but the final one is quite abrupt.

263

Ordinary meditation exercises aim in their earlier phases at rendering the mind concentrated and undistracted, and in their higher phases at resting in the Spiritual Self or in God—which usually means in a concept of God. Philosophic meditation exercises do this too but refuse to stop with a concept and seek to exclude all preconceptions from the mystical experience. They go farther still because they also expand the aim into contemplation of the infinity of being, the universality of consciousness, and the illusoriness of ego.

3

PHILOSOPHY, MYSTICISM, AND THE OCCULT

A criticism of the mystic

Humanity needs yoga, yes, but it must be a yoga that is workable under twentieth-century conditions. It needs mystical ideals, certainly, but they must be realizable in London and New York, not only in Shangri-la. It needs profoundly to kindle the spark of mystical experience within dull mechanized lives, but it does not need to kindle the historical errors and traditional excesses of such experience. There is need for mystical practices to spread but there is no need for mystical absurdities to spread with them. We personally do not want this restoration of the art of mental quiet to be accompanied by a restoration of the art of out-of-date views, blind super-stitions, impracticable or unnecessarily harsh rules, and unethical exploita-tions. Hence nobody should be so foolish as to misunderstand this effort to purify yoga as being an effort to denounce yoga altogether. That would be a profound error.

Much of what I have written will sound like heresy to the unreflective among the mystically minded. But they have their guides and I do not write for them. More intelligent mystics ought not to take exception to what has here been written but ought to probe fearlessly into the true significance of their own experiences. Let it not be said that they cannot bear the truth. In encouraging them to independent or even heretical thinking, and in pointing out the perils of travelling down a mental blind alley, I seek to serve and not to harm the mystically minded. The discern-ing reader will see that I have all along tried to explain mysticism. The prejudiced reader may however see erroneously that I have tried to expose it. If I have challenged and criticized the validity of certain assumptions common in half-baked yogic circles, if I have impartially showed up some of the insufficiencies of yoga and mysticism as well as corrected their commoner errors, if I have criticized wrong mystical attitudes, all this has been done only to save right mystical ideas from being perverted or lost. I know from personal experience just as much as most Western mystics and Eastern yogis the valuable and attractive benefits resulting from this practice. It is this appreciation which has helped to support me in undertaking the unpleasant task of purifying the theories about it. The weeding-out of errors from such theories is a better service to yoga than their superstitious support. After all, it is not the man who flatters us when we are making mistakes but the man who is courageously outspoken and tells us the bitter but wholesome truth who is a real friend. If, therefore, these critical studies have helped a few mystics to think clearly about their mysticism, and to think of it in terms of the larger background of life itself, then they have rendered them a service. If they have influenced some readers to think and rethink their mystical beliefs, I have rendered them a service, whether they are aware of it or not. If they have persuaded other readers even to consider that the philosophical approach to their own experiences will fulfil and not deny their deepest aspiration, then I have rendered them a service.

2

I do not criticize such men and such practices for any other reason than the protection of earnest seekers, and I may not desist from doing so because their path is beset with psychological dangers, fantastic experiences, worldly harm, and grotesque beliefs. An unhealthy inner life is often the consequence, one filled with strange phantasmagoria. From all this they may be saved by wise guidance, just as they may be plunged into it by the pseudo-guidance which they usually find. So far as I am aware—and I have travelled the wide world—all the available guidance which such seekers are likely to obtain will lead them to everything else except the one thing that really matters, namely, fulfilling the real purpose of our human existence here on earth, and not an illusory one. Where such guidance is honest, sincere, and unselfish—which is rare indeed—it is likely to be imperfect, inadequate, and incomplete. In the written statements of these blind leaders of the blind, as in their uttered ravings, the sage can quickly discern—by such signs as the terminology and syntax used—how unregulated and how unbalanced is their course of thought and experience. I set myself seriously to ponder the question: "How can these earnest seekers avoid the abundant dangers and satanic deceptions to which they are exposed?" Hence my published and private warnings.

3

It is most important that I make it clear that I do not teach the *error* that *all* mystic experience is merely private opinion, judgement, or prejudice, solely personal imagination, belief, or wish-fulfilment, but rather that I hold it to be a private interpretation of a general experience, a personal response to a universal event. On the first and erroneous view, mysticism would merely tell us something about the feelings and ideas of the person having the experience. On the second view, it tells us all this, undoubtedly, but it also tells us much about something which is itself quite independent of the individual's feelings about mystical reality and the divine soul in humanity. Whereas the first view denies any truth to mystical experience, the second one vindicates, even if it qualifies, it. The difference between the two views is most important. Mystical experience emphatically refers to something over and above the projection of man's wishes or the draping of man's opinions. Whatever interpretation he places upon his experience or whatever imagination he projects upon it, the possibility of such experience is undeniable.

4

Mysticism is a Step—Not a Goal

Point out that it is the seeking of experiences exclusively, making them central, that I criticize—and not the value of the experience itself. Experience is necessary and important. But the young, devaluing the other components of the quest, are going to extremes in seeking experiences alone. For then, in the end any means will do, so—drugs and sex. These are manifestations of the impatient desire for quick results, results at any cost, results here meaning getting experiences, which has become such a mania today. This impatience affects even foods, where instant processing robs them of nourishment and ruins their flavour.

Whirling, as practised so artistically by the Mevlevi dervishes, is another way of losing the everyday consciousness and gaining the mystic experience. It is comparable to the more elementary forms of yoga like mantram-muttering. But its value is as limited as the latter's. It gives no wisdom.

Balance requires all the other quest components; experience is then put in its proper place as their associate. It then becomes healthy, being kept in equilibrium by them. Otherwise there is no discrimination between good experiences and evil ones, no protection against the misleading, the dangerous, or the insane. Cults appearing in the last thirty-six years have emphasized experience and were bemused by the raptures of drugs and sex. Gerald Heard started Trabujo Monastery, which collapsed. D. Goddard tried to start the first Buddhist monastery in Vermont and failed. His friend and near disciple Aldous Huxley wrote on mescaline—all were seeking experience.

In non-mystic circles among the youth and younger adults, the same over-concentration on experience occurred. In this case experience of sex led to an explosion of having sex continuously and promiscuously. If bare walls and a monastic cell appeal to him he may find peace there. If celibate single existence appeals without experience in the world, there too he may find it.

5

"Why do you contradict yourself by advocating meditation in your earlier books and then criticizing it in *The Hidden Teaching Beyond Yoga?*" One answer to this question which I am sometimes asked is that there is some misunderstanding here. It is not meditation but the abuse and misuse of it that was criticized. It is a necessary part of the philosophic quest, but this does not mean that the laws which govern it can be recklessly ignored by those who think their enthusiasm for it a sufficient equipment for it. The law of life is rhythm.

6

He may angrily dissent from the truth of my conclusions but he can hardly contest their value. For they are not formed from an outside view of both the Orient and mysticism but from an inside one.

7

These categorical statements should put an end to all doubts about my present position. Nothing would please me better than to live to witness a world-wide revival in the practice of meditation.

8

I study the various searches for God in the different religions, the various techniques of contemplation in the Oriental and European mystical systems, and the various ideas of metaphysics in the ancient and modern philosophies. It is inevitable, therefore, that in the pupilage in Comparative Spiritual Culture I should investigate contemporary gurus and their methods—which can be properly done only by putting myself on their level. But this quite temporary and quite brief activity does not in any way make me a follower, disciple, or believer. To put such a label on me would be absolutely incorrect. Yet in the past this is what unscrupulous gurus, or their assistants, have actually done. It is very regretful to note a repetition of the practice.

9

I am not prepared to continue as an agent, although hitherto an unwitting one, for their exploitation of aspiring gullibility.

10

Instead of abandoning and decrying the beatific experience of yoga, which was my life-long study and which is still my daily practice, I have actually put it on a firmer because more philosophical pedestal than before. Only, I have enlarged the common conception of this antique art, placing it in proper perspective as being a step forward beyond both materialism and religion but not being, as ordinarily known, the final phase of man-kind's journey. Aside from this revision of grade and the consequent revaluations arising therefrom, extremely important though they be in themselves, I have nothing important to retract from previous statements on the subject but only to supplement them in the light of a forward advance.

11

Nobody who has had sufficient experience of the world can deny that this is a study which is infested from fringe to core with cranks, quacks, and charlatans. Thanks to them the whole study has been brought into disrepute among well-educated people. My effort to present it in a thor-oughly scientific and philosophic manner, to free it from all superstitious nonsense and pernicious practices, to base it on reason rather than on belief is in its own best interests; and I claim to serve mysticism more faithfully by such effort than do those who blindly, stubbornly, and fool-ishly allow it to rot and perish.

12

It is because I have too large a conception of yoga and not, as some think, too small a one, that I have written in this critical strain.

13

It has been hard to speak my whole mind on such unpleasant matters. If I have made large reservations and say no more despite their importance it is only from consideration of their unpleasantness. But to look away and refuse altogether to see these unpleasant features of mysticism, to pretend that it has no such defects at all, is a silly muddleheaded procedure. It is wiser to learn all about them and from them.

The extremes of mysticism

14

When mysticism becomes a breeding ground for ridiculous illusions, the time has arrived to protect it against them; when it lets the mystic become an indifferent spectator of mankind's sufferings, the time has arrived to modify it.

15

The lack of accurate firsthand knowledge has brought about a sorry picture of the subject. Charlatans, sceptics, pseudo-mystics, and imagina-tive dreamers have together unconsciously conspired to present mysticism alternately as primitive superstition, occult humbug, glorified conjuring, and super-religion. Such is the fruit of the hazy understanding about it which is to be found in most circles today. Real mysticism is none of these things.

16

The greatest dangers to the aspirant come from the votaries of a materialism which deceives itself into believing that it is mysticism when it is merely materialism varnished with mystical paint.

17

The mystic of the past was too often a philistine, anti-cultural and anti-intellectual. Not content with his bias for asceticism on the physical level, he carried it to the mental level also.

18

Such a man may seem to outsiders to be nothing more than a dreaming loafer. And indeed he might be, for many take the name of mystic who do not know what true mysticism is.

19

It is a great pity that such an excellent discipline should have fallen, during the course of ages, into disrepute through having fallen into the hands of those who despised civilized, self-respecting society and preferred primitive, half-animal existence, who rejected the earning of an honest livelihood in favour of undignified begging, who exiled the faculty of intellect in favour of unthinking adherence to absurd superstitions, who did violence to natural functions of the body by atrocious asceticism and traded on the gullibility of the masses by pretending to marvellous powers.

20

The puritanical view of life has been mixed up too often with the religious view. The philosopher is not concerned with that. But it has equally been mixed up with the mystical view. Here he is concerned, enough to declare that they do *not* necessarily go together.

21

The lack of a sense of humour in certain mystics has exposed them to the charge of being superstitious and credulous. It has caused the writings of other mystics to be laughed at, their ideas to be ridiculed. The lack of aesthetic taste in still other mystics has caused them to offer fanatical opposition to the decoration of rooms with pictures, or to the playing of musical instruments.

22

His superior development as a mystic does not thereby endow him with superior development as a man or bestow on him a larger capacity to make right decisions than that of other men.

23

The history of modern mysticism has indeed become a history of gradual declension from the fine disinterestedness of teachers like Emerson and from the firm truths of mystics like Eckhart. I speak here only of the West, of the Europe and America whose evidences are most readily available to readers; but I know from study and experience how true this is also of the Orient.

24

The conventional ethical codes which regulate human relations are transcended only in the sense that an even higher, more austere code is now imposed upon him *from within*. Those would-be mystical sects which history has recorded not infrequently—ones that claim a wider moral freedom than others because they claim to be nearer God, and then proceed to actions which bespeak the gratification of unloosed baser desires—deceive themselves, betray mysticism, and lead others astray.

25

Pseudo-mysticism tempts the ego in the mind or the beast in the flesh with its doctrine of man's divinity requiring no control, no discipline, and no obedience to ascetic rules.

26

The paths of mysticism are waylaid with destruction for weak minds. The light is too strong for their eyes and they emerge with egoism strengthened under the cloud of spirituality.

27

In an exhibition of old historical paintings once seen in Amsterdam, there hung on one wall a portrait of Sabattai Zevi, the wild dreamer, self-appointed Messiah, and fantastic leader of a cult whose career along with his own was abruptly ended by disillusionment and disaster. On the opposite wall there hung a portrait of Baruch Spinoza, philosopher and ethicist, whose career brought the fruits of wisdom to humanity. There they were, these two portraits facing each other—the one a type illustrating the defects of an unbalanced and unphilosophic kind of mysticism, the other a type of spiritual intuition and rational intellect active in man, yet balancing each other and benefiting each other.

28

Since men are liable to err, and since even the best of mystics are still men, we must not be too awed by their attainments to believe that they could not make such serious mistakes.

29

In ordinary religion and unphilosophic mysticism everyone is at liberty to build up his own heaven and hell, to create his own picture of God, and to invent his own method of reaching God, as he wishes. Who can disprove his statements? Such disproof is utterly impossible. We may disbelieve them but we cannot disprove them, for they deal with factors beyond our experience and hence beyond universal verification.

30

Why are so many mystics mediocrities in their careers and misfits in life generally? Why is so much mystical literature and history an imaginative projection of wishful thinking and rarely recognizable in its all-too-human materialization in the flesh? Here is an indication that something is wrong.

31

The monk who gets too wrapped up in himself and his moods, too locked up inside other-worldly experiences, too cut off from the facts and realities of everyday living, and unable to test by them the illusions and hallucinations which his imagination produces and his meditation confirms may tread the edge of a precipice over which he may topple into insanity.

32

It was not levity alone which made Oscar Wilde say that "most modern mysticism seems to me to be simply a method of imparting useless knowledge in a form no one can understand." It was not irony alone which made him remark of a book devoted to saintly and ascetic mystics, "It is thoroughly well-intentioned and eminently suitable for invalids."

33

I was struck by the truth of a criticism in Jawaharlal Nehru's autobiography. Nehru wrote: "The mystic tries to rid himself of self and in the process usually becomes obsessed with it." Nehru ought to know. For he has been surrounded by the society of Indian mystics for half a lifetime.

34

We appreciate the dangers and obstacles that beset the medievals but it must be said with regret that many of them belonged to the "Mysticism Made Difficult" school.

35

This lack of balance shows itself in the idolization of inertia which, regarded as a regrettable defect by most normal people, is regarded as a mystical virtue by these supposedly supernormal people!

36

The mystics and yogis would have others toil and labour to make bread and draw water while they pray and meditate. This distinction would be all right if they did not make the mistake of asserting that the kingdom of heaven lay only at the end of their path.

37

The more intelligent and better balanced aspirants should try to lead the mystical thought of their contacts into higher personal channels or wider usefulness and away from the charlatans, the recluses and escapists, the neurotics and hysterics.

38

Those who like the atmosphere of laziness which hangs over so much mystical thought and writing are welcome to it.

39

The right kind of mystical experience enriches life; the wrong kind impoverishes it.

40

They can see the truth, but only with one eye at a time.

41

Because it has been adopted by fanatics, poseurs, and fools, the contrary fact that it has also been adopted by executives, geniuses, and highly esteemed persons tends to be ignored and overlooked.

42

Sir Richard Burton, who lived long in the Orient, met and studied the Sufis. He came to the conclusion that the *extreme* mystic was a near madman. There is some truth in this view.

43

The passage from seeing visions frequently to being subject to delusions is not a long one, if the person concerned has not been disciplined in the philosophic manner.

44

There is a foolish mysticism which ignorantly follows ways that lead to madness. Those ways usually start with feeling as the essence of the matter and seek the death of reason because it too often refuses to go along with feeling. "I am God in a body," poor Nijinsky proclaimed; but he got himself confined in a madhouse as well as a body.

45

If the world has no place for mysticism this is because mysticism has no place for the world.

46

Mysticism must be saved from the hot embraces of emotionally diseased neurotics, intellectually unbalanced fanatics, and credulously naïve simpletons. It will find its best support in those who appreciate it without losing their mental equilibrium; in those who show in their own persons that it has nothing to do with hysteria, neuroticism, credulity, sensation-seeking, and pathological states. Only by avoiding extravagant claims and uncritical appraisals can it get the attention and deserve the respect of the intellectual classes.

47

At a time like the present when the world is passing though a critical phase of wholesale reconstruction, every opponent of reason and proponent of superstition is rendering a serious disservice to mankind.(P)

48

Is it not delicately ironical that Shangri-la should be more and more giving the West a mysticism for which she is finding less and less use herself?—that she is foisting upon us a solution which is increasingly failing to solve her own problems?

49

It is not that I complain of the unintellectual atmosphere of mysticism or the unintellectual attitude of its Eastern and Western devotees. The fact may be deplored but it ought not be laid as a fault against those who cannot help it. I complain of their *anti*-intellectual atmosphere and attitude.

50

Those mystics who hastily scorn science as being anti-spiritual and condemn modern civilization as being pro-materialist should stop to think how much wider service to mankind men like Jesus and Buddha could have rendered had the radio, the newspaper, the inexpensive book, the cinema, and the railway train been at their command. Let them consider how, with the airplane to travel in, Jesus could have brought thousands of disciples in each European and North African country under his immediate personal influence and Buddha could have brought hundreds of thousands more throughout Asia under his own. The inventions of man's ingenuity can be directed to give an upward trend to his spiritual evolution just as they have been directed to give a downward trend to it. All life bears this twofold possibility. We do not refuse light because it also brings shadows. We also should not refuse inventions merely because they increase the tempo of our existence too quickly.

51

Those who rightly fear fanaticism or charlatanry will not find one or the other in philosophy. Yet they will not have to go far to do so—no farther than the religio-mystical fringe which hangs on one side of it.

52

It is very questionable as to whether a spiritual renaissance which led us into the wake of fake mystics and pseudo-scientific occultists would be any better than the following of hidebound religionists drained of the vitality of truth and reality.

53

It is easy to parade incompetence and inefficiency as mystical superiority above mere earthly life, and thus deceive both oneself and others. It is hard to take oneself uncompromisingly in hand and triumph over these defects of one's very virtues.

54

This kind of mysticism, which stews truth in the same pot with absurd fantasy, may attract those who seek the dramatic but often repels those who appreciate the scientific.

55

Many so-called spiritual persons of this modern era are rightly regarded by society as neurotics, cranks, eccentrics, useless, or unpractical. They have, however, felt genuine promptings from the Overself; but because of the lack of proper instruction, or because of the defect of improper instruction, they have not also felt the need to integrate this prompting with the rest of their life—or, even if they have felt it, they have not been shown how to do it simply because their own teachers had not succeeded in doing it themselves.

56

He may feel the truth for himself but be unable to explain it adequately to others.

57

Many mystical cults present teachings which contain some sublime truths but which, because of their incompleteness or their ignorance of other truths or their wrong attitude towards the body, do not tend towards balanced living. As a result, when they over-emphasize the particular feature which most interests them, they become unbalanced. The need today is for the balanced mystic.

58

The excessive self-centeredness of ascetic mysticism, its passive enmity to an integral human life, its unworthy praise of pious indolence, its oyster-like indifference to human interests, and its narrow disparagement of the married state make it unfit to become a perfect ideal suited to our own times. What modern intelligence can accept and what modern heart can approve such an attitude? Asceticism is an important phase but it is not everything.

Philosophy attracts the few

59

The smallest understanding of philosophy will show that, although it holds a mystical core, it is quite different in approach and atmosphere from those mystical cults which breed superstition and encourage charlatanism. The understanding enthusiasts and uncritical panegyrists who are the professed followers of such cults would feel uneasy in the purer and finer air breathed by the true student of philosophy.

60

The cramped, ascetical, and intolerant virtue of the ashrams is not enough. Philosophy prefers a more spacious, more generous and kindlier virtue.

61

If we try to compute the number of those who are not overawed by the prestige, the success, and the organization of a religion, sect, cult, or group, and who seek truth with a better measure than these things, we shall find only a small remnant is left out of all those who profess an interest in the things of spirit.

62

Those who are making a determined search for truth fall into a very tiny segment of humanity. Most self-styled seekers are motivated by half-hidden desires for different kinds of ego satisfaction rather than the egoless truth.

63

The loftiness of this teaching is not to be measured by the trumpery standards of recent so-called spiritual movements.

64

To study and understand these sects, to explain the inner dynamic which draws people to them, is not necessarily to agree with their teachings or condone their practices.

65

Let outsiders not blame philosophy for shortcomings which exist only in untrained and uninstructed followers.

66

Those who have deformed their minds by vehement fanaticism or befuddled them by dangerous drugs will find the sanctity of philosophy unattractive.

67

Most organizations tend to give the impression of cults, which are the very antitheses of our objectives as well as irreconcilable with the Hidden Teaching.

68

It is regrettable that a subject so interesting—and formerly such a little-visited byway—should become infested with maniacal ideas and should attract ill-balanced persons who fall easily into superstition. The higher levels, where religion moves into mysticism and metaphysics, need a well-informed, well-poised mind for their proper appreciation.

69

Those who flock to these cults often dislike philosophy. They rightly fear its threat to their superstitious dreams and correctly comprehend that it would destroy their egoistic fantasies.

70

How many who have seen the foolishness of these cults pardonably react against it by rejecting them, but unpardonably reject the wisdom which is overshadowed by it.

71

Philosophy may not appeal to the weak-minded followers of such cults, since it would force them to acknowledge their deficiencies and to set about remedying them.

72

Where is the spiritual movement which has not deteriorated into a religious sect, with passive followers and unquestioning members?

73

No sect is important but every sect is significant. None is particularly influential but all are unquestionably evidential. For the indication here of a trend toward heterodoxy is quite plain and its cause quite meaningful.

Distinguishing the spiritual and psychic

74

Philosophy accepts part of the tenets of occultism—the part which its own seers and sages have handed down—and does not deny them. But it places emphasis on that which rests on a higher level and which is much more significant. It refuses to allow its students to be involved in the practices, the bypaths, and the dangers of occultism.

75

The *psychical* is concerned with imaginations, visions, voices, thoughts, and feelings which originate beneath the surface of the ego's mind, whereas the *spiritual* is concerned with the higher self. The two are not the same but utterly different in quality and character. Aspirants often confuse them although the first is still within the realm of personal things whereas the second is within the impersonal. A still greater confusion concerns the *mediumistic*. This is the same as the psychical but influenced or possessed by what purports to be someone else's ego, often someone unknown and usually unseen, or even by what purports to be from the realm of the spiritual itself.

76

Intuition need not be the only manifestation of this deeper layer of mind. There are indeed other and stranger signs of its existence, which belong to a classification variously called occult, magical, or psychic. They include thought-transference and clairvoyance. The history of yoga has always been associated with stories of such thaumaturgic marvels, and few advanced yogis fail to manifest these powers at some period or other of their careers.

Such are some of the extraordinary mental powers which may be unfolded by man, but they are of secondary consequence to the sage. He holds to and values most the remaining constantly fixed within that universal being which transcends all forms and changes.

Nevertheless the average scientist who used to sneer at their existence has since become much more cautious, although a remnant of materialistic scientists still continue to sneer. Such people represent a type of mind which dreads superstition to the point of making its dread a superstition! These supernormal powers of the mind lose much of their mystery when their rationale is understood.

When the entire world itself is mentally constructed—that is, a kind of magical show—why should we be incredulous of the possibility of magical powers? All of us have these powers in vestigial form. Evolution will make them grow anyway, and effort will make them grow more quickly. However surprising to beginners, they are realizable facts to an adept.

Telepathy is perhaps the first, simplest, and most easily explicable of these powers.

77

What they seldom see is that spiritual illumination and psychical error can and do exist in the same mind at the same time.(P)

78

All occult and psychic powers are extensions either of man's human capacity or of his animal senses. They are still semi-materialistic, because connected with his ego or his body. All truly spiritual powers are on a far higher and quite different plane. They belong to his divine self.(P)

79

A witch's brew of mystery, compounded of ancient sorceries and modern pseudo-sciences, philosophic smatterings and monstrous claims, lies and deception—that, stripped of all its high-sounding verbiage, is a fair description of occultism.

80

It is an error, and one commonly made, to confound occult phenomena with spiritual experience. It is true that, at certain times or in certain phases of the inner life, the two may accompany one another. But they do not do so on equal levels. Spiritual experience certifies itself but psychic experience proves little because it is always open to doubt. A philosopher may be and often is a psychic, but few psychics are ever philosophers. We do not need to be purified to witness occult phenomena, and therein lies their danger.

81

Much incorrect knowledge is today offered the seeker intent on an understanding of the psychic and spiritual laws of the universe.

82

Confronted by the discoveries of science, the inventions of technology, the marvels of Nature, and the mystery of mind, one would be foolish to assert what is possible and what is not possible.

83

A man who works in a scientific laboratory can provide proofs for his discoveries which any other scientist in any part of the world can test and confirm. But a mystic, a seer, or a prophet who communicates a revelation of what he has learned by intuition, vision, or meditation can provide no such proofs. His audience is compelled to take his words with little direct or immediate means of testing their worth.

84

The finished product of a carpenter's work can be tried in use and tested by examination. His chairs can be sat upon, his table legs measured, and faults or inaccuracies will soon reveal themselves. But how are the mystic's intuitions, inspirations, visions, and teachings to be appraised, measured, tested with complete certainty? How much in them can be fully trusted, how much suspected as being the undivine part? The metaphysician's concepts and the religionist's beliefs come into the same category; they cannot at once be checked for faults, tried by results, or measured for accuracy, whereas the craftsman's productions can. Religion, mysticism, and metaphysics cannot immediately offer their proofs, if at all.

85

There are certain unusual occurrences which are often a source of astonishment to those involved in them, as well as to others learning about them. The powers to bring these into being are much sought after in some circles and are generally termed "occult powers."

86

Occultism is concerned with the unseen working of nature, and with phenomena, forms, messages of the nonphysical side of the ego's being, including visions and voices experienced inwardly. It is on a lower level than pure Spirit, not dealing with the body and not dealing with spirit, but somewhere in between. It's easy to be led astray by it, since it is close to fantasy and imagination. Try to avoid seeking it, but if it comes by itself try to judge it critically and understand it. On the highest level there are no occult phenomena which keep you in your ego.

87

Today Mechanics rules where once Magic held its sway. We do not dream that there is room in life for both.

88

As much nonsense has been written about the mystic and the occult as about politics, or any other subject where appearances do not coincide with realities.

The lure of occultism

89

We were not born to perform magical stunts, nor were we born to be able to remember past lives or to foretell the future. We were born for one thing only and that is to discover what we really are in our deepest, innermost being, not just the crest of it.

90

Philosophy rejects such psychic, occult, mediumistic, or trance experiences when imagination runs unbraked into them, or emotion heaves hysterically in them. It is then time to stop the dangerous tendency by applying a firm will and cold reason. Philosophy welcomes only a single mystic experience—that of the Void (*Nirvikalpa Samadhi*), where every separate form and individual consciousness vanishes, whereas all other mystic experiences retain them. This is the difference.(P)

91

The spiritualists, the occultists, and the psychic groups are far from the purest thought, for they are still preoccupied with the ego and with a subtle materialism which substitutes a subtler body for the material one but is just as illusory. However, they are steps on the way for spiritual children—stages to be passed through and outgrown.

92

Philosophy has no use for empty fancies, no time for mere self-deceptions. Therefore it refuses to dally in this illusory region which the inward-moving mind must cross through until it reaches solid ground. It will not give itself to psychism, occultism, or spiritism.

93

How simple is the path itself, how complex is the pseudo-path offered by occultism and exaggerated asceticism. "All that God asks of them," writes Thomas Merton, "is to be quiet and keep themselves at peace, attentive to the secret work that He is beginning in their souls."(P)

94

You must learn to discriminate between what is psychic and what is spiritual. You will tend to lose power if you yield to that popular hankering after psychic and occult experiences. It is fascinating to have psychic claims, sensational experiences. Keep them in their place, however, which is second and subordinate. They have nothing to do with the Quest, which is to lead you above the realm of mind into spirit. Mind goes down deep into the subconscious and the Overmind; there psychic and occult experiences take place—not in the normal mind, certainly, but in the region of the planetary mind, the Overmind. Occult experiences will not give you any more peace, or reality. Do you want these? Then do not over-emphasize your occult experiences. Just observe them, but attach little importance to them. The important thing is to arrive at that state of being which never changes, which is eternal, which is God.

95

The mystic is on a loftier plane than the occultist and psychic. The various systems of occultism, theosophy, and psychism are all objective to the true Self of man, and hence distract him from the straight and narrow path. Yet they are useful and necessary for those egoistic and over-intellectualized natures who cannot aspire to the rarefied reaches of the real Truth. Everything—including the fascinating systems of knowledge and practice that comprise ancient and modern occult teachings—which distracts man from becoming the truly spiritual, distracts him from the real path. Only when all objective things and thoughts have disappeared into the subject, the self or the seer, can man achieve his highest purpose. All other activities simply cause him to stray from the highest truth. So I have abandoned the study and practice of occultism. I have given it up unwillingly, for the power it promises is not to be despised. Yet I recognize that my past is strewn with errors and mistakes. I imagined that a great personal experience of the psychic and mysterious side of Nature would bring me nearer Truth. As a fact, it has taken me farther from it. Once I enjoyed frequent glimpses of a great bliss and intense state of *samadhi*; then I was unfortunate enough to come into contact with theosophists and others of that ilk who subtly supplanted my real inward happiness with intellectual systems and theories upon which I was thenceforward to ponder. Alas! I was too young and too green to know what was happening. The bliss went before long; the *samadhis* stopped, and I was cast upon the shore of the Finite, an unhappy and problem-puzzled bit of human wreckage! No promise of wonderful initiations at some future time will lure me to trust my life into the care of a so-called guru who is either unable to or unwilling to give me a glimpse of the God-consciousness he claims to possess. I am not inclined to follow a trail which may land me somewhere out in the middle of the desert, bereft of reason, hope, and fortune.(P)

96

At its best, psychism leads us into human fancies about the holy; at its worst, to the very lair of the devilish. The spiritual alone, in its true sense, can lead us into the veritably holy.

97

The essence of the matter is that the higher ultramystic experiences are not concerned with personal clairvoyant visions or clairaudient voices but with the raising of consciousness to an impersonal transcendent state wherein none of the relative phenomena of a space-time world can enter.

98

The quest is not jugglery. The most breath-taking feat of the conjurer will not prove the least insignificant of spiritual truths.

99

People spend half their lives in darkened rooms trying to establish communication with the "spirits," with dubious and debatable results, when one-tenth of the time devoted to trying to establish communication with their OWN divine spirit would bring indubitable and delightful results.

100

There are countless thousands who, weak in faith and lacking in intuition, must perforce seek amid external things for proof of the soul. Spiritualism claims to give this proof. There are, of course, those who believe that the spiritualists have misinterpreted their experiences.

101

The seventh chapter of *The Wisdom of the Overself* contains some material which generally answers the questions of life after death. It is quite true that spiritualism has served the useful purpose of proving the existence of an afterlife. Nevertheless it is a dangerous matter to experiment with practically. It is far safer to limit investigation to a study of its literature. More specifically: (1) The quest of psychic experiences is definitely a stumbling block on the true path during the earlier stages. They are almost sure to lead the novice astray, may cause him to waste valuable years, and will sometimes harm him in various ways. Most attempts to establish contact with the astral world will end either in failure and deception or psychic injury. (2) Astral projection is neither wrong nor right but it should not be sought for its own sake. It develops naturally of itself to one who is highly advanced on the truly spiritual quest. But if novices prematurely seek it they are likely to harm themselves. In the end it will be found that spiritualism is only a stepping-stone to the higher mystical philosophy. It is of use as a halfway house for many Westerners, but one should not tarry here too long. The higher and lower teachings are like oil and water. They cannot be mixed together and one day you will have to make your choice between them if you wish to progress and not to remain stagnating.

102

These occult authors catalogue such a formidable list of necessary qualifications that it is likely to deter most people rather than attract them. One wonders whether the writers have succeeded in fulfilling their own standards. It is good however to remember that there are ways not so steep as theirs, that there are easier paths in existence in other lands than that of occultism. Genuine mysticism, true religion, or right philosophy: any of these can conduct one to the goal with less trouble and less danger than occultism.

103

There is a problem of mental unbalance and partial insanity in the modern world. Philosophy offers help, as it aims at securing complete sanity whereas most other guides cater to unbalance.

104

There is something which might be called the higher spiritualism which is on a higher level altogether than ordinary spiritualism. This has been found by an exhaustive study, both practical and theoretical. The higher spiritualism stands midway between the lower kind and mysticism proper. By mysticism is meant the endeavour to become possessed, not by any disembodied human entity, but by the divine Spirit, be it named God, Soul, Christ, Allah, Atman, or some other name which has been given to that which man knows to be the Divine. In the group of those who belong to this higher spiritualism can be included such men as Stainton Moses, who edited *Light*, the leading spiritualist journal in London, and Andrew Jackson Davis, the famous American clairvoyant. Their writings were admirable and much in *Life and Its Manifestations* is reminiscent of them in tone, idea, and atmosphere.

105

Occult or spiritistic practices which have served their purpose in convincing their student that materialism is false, should be abandoned if he wishes to make the best use of his limited period on earth. When such a point has been reached, he should turn his thoughts in the direction of seeking the Overself alone, or his life-period will be wasted.

106

If philosophy denies the authenticity of many occult, psychical, and religio-mystical experiences, it does not have to deny that they did occur. That need not be in dispute. But the danger of taking fancy for reality and a way-station for the terminus is very easy to fall into and must be pointed out. "Beware them who perceive the deep reality," warned the Buddha in a statement which recalls for us the warning of Jesus about the straightness of the way to truth and that "Few there be that find it." The prudent seeker will be on his guard not to succumb to the temptation of dallying in ego-flattering thrills.

107

Why should we surrender the simple clarity of true self-knowledge for the involved obscurity of occultism?

108

Philosophic spiritualism does not go far enough. Inspiration derived from any individual, disembodied and angelic though he might be, is not as fine as inspiration derived from the unindividuated Soul, which the best mystics seek. It is a step in the right direction, though.

109

It is as necessary to avoid pitfalls of superstition on one side as those of psychism on the other.

110

Everything that stimulates us to follow the quest is worth encouraging if its demerits be not too large; but everything which paralyses this aspiration is rendering a disservice to humanity.

111

The occult, and indeed all extraordinary happenings, attracts a far larger amount of interest than the mystical. For here the physical senses come into play and find satisfaction whereas in the mystical only the intuitive and the emotional faculties are engaged.

112

The majority are seekers after occultism. They thirst for powers that will give them an advantage over others. They seek to inflate their egos whereas the true disciples seek to flatten it.

113

Excessive addiction to supernormal mystic experiences or bizarre occult titillations leads to wrong views and draws the seeker to a wrong goal. The dignity of quiet philosophical study often appears to prove too frigid for those who revel in superstition and who seek the gaudy caricatures of truth rather than the austere truth itself.

114

Many people yearn to escape from the world of the flesh; many seek for psychic worlds full of magical half-shadows; many minds are turning into the narrow lanes of thought and wide roads of study indicated by the signposts of occultism and its kindred.

115

Many are called on the spiritual telephone exchange of life, but few get a clear connection!

116

Psychical derangements are common enough to keep the specialists busy. Mentally upset persons crop up everywhere, even on airplanes. We have seen insanity appear in high places and collect many followers. If anything can give sanity, it is the calm and balance of philosophy. But unless it is hidden behind magic and occultism, those who need it most are least attracted to it and least fit for it.

117

It is not a path suited to neurotic, weak, mentally odd, and emotionally sick persons. Such people are often attracted to mystical movements and ideas but they shrink from philosophic truth and discipline.

118

History shows that where people have had the opportunity to imbibe the highest truth, they still preferred occult sensationalism to it.

119

All this interest in and pursuit of occultism is merely an enlargement of the ego's ordinary sphere. Why should a teacher of philosophy cater to that?

120

How many persons have imprisoned themselves in their own mental creations or auto-hypnotic fabrications at the very moment when they had the chance to experience the Spirit in all its purity! This could not have happened had they been prepared in character and purified in intellect by philosophy. Without this safeguard, the ego intervenes and corrupts the truth and keeps as much of its illusions as it can hold onto under that dazzling light.

121

Philosophy is not for the thrill-seekers—there are cults and groups, "isms" and practices which will better excite and satisfy them. Even on a higher level, the mystic's, there is still a search, a longing, for "experiences." In most cases such experiences are desired as escapes from the ego's tensions and burdens, its insignificance or environment.

4

THOSE WHO SEEK

Those who seek a cult because they seek a rule by which to live and a method by which to learn are entitled to do so. They comprise the majority.

2

The defects in these techniques, the errors in these doctrines, the limitations of these cults are many and sometimes serious; but withal they represent a good beginning on the journey away from the conventional lies of civilization. The earnest persistent truth-seeker will pass through and beyond them.

3

Those who go around hunting a variety of masters or joining many cults may be passing through a useful phase for beginners which is their way of making a comparative study of religion, mysticism, or philosophy. Its usefulness is not to be derided for certain types. Or it may be a sincere quest for the one master with whom they have real affinity or the one teaching in which they can find their life's guidance. This too may serve their purpose. But they should also understand that their real progress starts only when they stop this movement and concentrate their further interest on intensive work within themselves. If they do not stop the external search when it is no longer really necessary, then its prolongation will make them too dependent. Their curiosity or instability will thus weaken them further and lead them into bewilderment in the end.

4

The public organizations and organized cults do offer help. Such help may be commended provided there is a clear understanding that it is for beginners only and of a limited nature. If any claim is made beyond that— as it often is—be sure that it is exaggerated and unwarrantable.

5

However dishonest, deluded, or even insane these pretentious fanatics and their babbling followers may be, however absurd their fallacious religions and mystical aberrations are, they have one tremendous significance. They indicate the existence of a number of people at various intellectual levels below the higher ones, who are discontented with, and not willing to limit their spiritual craving to, orthodox religion or orthodox atheism.

6

What factors are present in this credulity? There is the unconscious wish of unimportant persons for a recognized place in the world, for a boost upward in the eyes of their co-believing fellows, however few may be in the small following of believers. There is the felt need, in a time of hopeless world-crisis, to believe in anything that offers some hope, at least.

7

These other paths, processes, and standpoints are preliminary and therefore unavoidable, are preparatory and therefore necessary. They are not to be rejected, even though they do not lead directly to the highest result. But, on the other hand, they are not to be clung to obstinately when they have served their purpose and a higher way opens out.

8

No cult that despite its faults has enough good in it to help some people forward on the spiritual path, should be condemned.

9

Those who join these cults may do so through genuine aspiration, but those who remain united with them show thereby that they have no innate sense of the ridiculous.

10

People who seek a more reasonable solution of their life's spiritual problem than that offered by orthodox dogma, also turn to these eccentric cults.

11

We must recognize the fact that many people take to these fanatical cults, these nonsensical doctrines, out of blind groping reaction against the harsh prosaic materialism of their times. They clutch at the first handy rope of spiritual seeking for relief, not caring at the moment in the emotional joy of help gotten about its quality. This sharp turning of a corner in their lives is to be admired, not deplored.

12

The sincere seeker need not be ashamed of the false starts which his entry into these cults represents. For they are really his gropings after the true path, the right direction.

13

Yet these cults, however nonsensical their doctrines and untrustworthy their claims, however absurd their beliefs and dangerous their failure to see actualities, however dark their shadowy corners, must be credited with one admirable reason for existence. They are reactions—fanatic and extreme—from the conventional uninspired religious orthodoxy and the cold materialistic mechanistic science which, contrary to their promises, obstruct man from finding any higher hope in life.

14

These cults may be regrettable symptoms of weak intelligence or atavistic superstition in a number of cases, but in other cases they are praiseworthy indications of searching in all directions which lead to spiritual truth.

15

It is a common phase of their evolution for beginners to move through different cults with each new personality who impresses them. It is something which they must get out of their system and they are best left alone while doing so.

16

All this flitting from cult to cult is, in some cases, a search for the one right way, the way with which the seeker feels the most spiritual affinity.

17

The seeker may pass, in the earlier and exploratory phases of his journey, through different sects in each of which he may remain for a while until its shortcomings become too much to be borne. He may get some measure of truth from each one, will abstract some ideas which teach and help him.

18

These cults serve a useful purpose in making enquirers acquainted for the first time with the existence of unorthodox mystical tradition.

19

If he wanders from one teacher to another, if he submits himself to the ministrations of occultists or mystics, swamis or masters, he may pick up quite a variety of approaches to the subject.

20

What can he gain by adhesion to a spiritual organization? The beginner may gain a limited profit, the proficient may retrogress.

21

It is inevitable that beginners should develop into partisans but they need not develop into fanatics.

22

The struggle for truth, the search for reality, may draw him to some cult and keep him in its folds for a while as he learns some elementary tenets and as he begins to develop the powers of concentration. Later, when he has become somewhat mature, he will draw away from the cult again to tread the higher path of philosophy.

23

There are metaphysical sects as well as religious ones.

24

That so many adherents to these ideas appear to be freaks or clowns, charlatans or gullibles, is painfully true. But do not stop with this criticism; go forward from it, for it is only partially true. For there were other adherents whose brains were sharp, whose practicality was unquestioned, whose places in society were high. Politicians like Georges Clemenceau and David Ben-Gurion found help in Vedantic and Buddhistic doctrine.

25

It is better to take short and flurried flights in these cults than to stay so long that the mind is enslaved by false dogmas, faith is entrapped by ambitious leaders, and emotion is held by perverted truths.

26

All such approaches including Theosophy's are useful to beginners but have to be discontinued eventually when they discover that the Quest is an individual matter.

27

If he is curious about them, he can visit these cults for a period, hear what their leaders and read what their teachers have to say, but he should not make any commitment to them.

28

Ashrams could be useful places where one can retreat for the time being only, where one can refresh the inner man for a particular period. But this is so only if they are properly conducted and if this purpose is kept in view.

29

We must necessarily be tolerant towards those who sample many teachings and many cults before they find the one which holds most truth or best suits their temperament.

30

It is true that California has produced a multitude of sects—good, bad, and merely eccentric. It is also true that some bring interesting uplifting or strange doctrines to their followers, but others spoil lives and disturb minds. But on balance it might even be a desirable state of affairs to have such a large variety of points of view, doctrines, groups, and creeds all conveniently put together in a single state of the Union. Seekers could then look at their leisure to find one that may suit them.

31

Even those who rightly object to the fanatical extremes in practice and exaggerated ideas in theory of these cults cannot deny that the effects are in part quite good, that cheerfulness and self-improvement are sought and got.

32

Why do these people run after new sects, strange cults, and heretical movements? Why are they not content to remain in orthodox religion? It can only be that the latter has been given up, and there is a vacuum in their hearts and minds demanding to be filled.

33

There are two types of seekers who wander the world of cults and societies. The first is mentally unstable and like the grasshopper which jumps from plant to plant but gathers nothing; the second is like the bee, which flies from flower to flower and sucks the honey at every halt.

The wanderers

34

Those who float from cult to cult may be engaged in a genuine progression or they may not. In the second case the thirst for novelty is either mistaken for the thirst for truth or else frankly avowed.

35

So these aspirants wander from one teacher to another, from one institution to another, but always end in disappointment. They could get from available books and with less heartburning most of what these teachers and institutions merely claim to give.

36

Under the magical glamour of these promised supernatural attainments, uncritical minds pursue the hope of evading the restrictions which life's tough realities place on them. When they fail, as fail they must, they do not put the blame upon their own fantastic beliefs, but try a different angle of approach by following a different cult.

37

They possess unlimited faith in the powers of a master. Indeed, if faith alone could bestow enlightenment they should soon get it. Even when they do cease to believe in a particular man, it is only to transfer their allegiance in the same degree to another master. Because of their initial error they may keep transferring it from one master to another. But as they do not give to the reform of their own lives the fervour they give to him, they show no results.

38

They merely pass from one set of opinions to a different set, and this they call "finding the truth!"

39

These misguided people imagine they move from a shallow thought to a deeper one, but merely move from one folly to another.

40

The true quest is not for those who flit from cult to cult, teacher to teacher, in short-lived enthusiasms that turn to long-lived aversions. They follow only the hallucination of a quest. Their ideals are as brittle as glass.

41

They repeat the same situation with each successive teacher, seeking the impossible and suffering a series of deceptions in consequence.

42

Their loyalty is unstable and depends on whim more than on intuition or reason. They adopt or discard several cults in their lifetime.

43

One reason why so many of these credulous followers are neither discouraged by their recurring disappointments nor stopped by the crash of disillusionments from joining the next foolish cult which comes their way, is because they find no place for reason in their attitude toward life.

44

Wandering from one cult or school to another, from one teacher to another, happens often enough on the religio-mystic level but cannot happen on the philosophic level. Where it seems to do so that is only because the person concerned never reached a correct understanding of philosophy and never properly applied it.

45

They float around following every teacher in turn, enthusiastically eulogizing the one currently in the ascendant, only to criticize him later—and the lesson of keeping detached, unjoined, accepting truth without tying new bonds to half-truth or nonsense, remains unreceived.

46

Up to a certain level, this gleaning of knowledge from diverse and various sources enriches man but beyond that level it confuses and thus weakens him.

47

They pass from teacher to teacher—from one venal, ignorant, selfish, insane, dishonest, or obsessed guide to another—and consequently through an unending series of disillusionments.

48

Enthusiastic about a particular guru or teaching in the beginning, dissatisfied with him or it in the end, they drift or move vainly seeking the magical eradication of all their problems, the rapturous illumination of all their being.

49

The attitude which prompts an aspirant to be always hunting down a spiritual authority outside himself who is faultless and infallible, only to drop him later when a new one appears and becomes the next quarry, belongs only to beginners.

50

The mentally sick neurotics who move from cult to cult or teacher to teacher are different from the merely curious seekers after novelty.

51

The error which attracts them to the cult is primarily within themselves and only secondarily within the cult's own teaching. The illusion which they project upon the cult or its leader is also primarily within themselves, as is shown by their habit of simply withdrawing it when unable to endure disappointment any longer and projecting it upon another cult or leader just as faulty.

52

These self-duped people rarely come to see the truth about themselves and come to no discouragement from their many disappointments. As each new leader is cast down from the pedestal as an ideal, they start at once to look for another instead of starting to look at themselves for a change. Thus they spare themselves the ordeal of discovering their own deficiencies and of facing their own defeats.

The innocents

53

Those who gather emotional security or personal companionship from membership in a group are gathering something which they need. They are not yet ready for the higher stage.

54

If we examine the membership of a sample cult we find those who, having more leisure than they can cope with, seek sensation, thrill; others, who are old and lonely, seek gregarious companionship; still others, suffering from physical malady or emotional maladjustment or environmental frustration, seek a near-miracle cure.

55

The impulse which brings them into these dubious cults is not a mistaken one, but the actual translation of it into action is.

56

Most beginners feel uncertain of themselves in these highly unfamiliar mental, emotional, and psychic surroundings. So they join a smug self-centered group, a cult, an organization. This gives them the feeling of gregarious support. They are no longer alone. They lack the courage to be alone.

57

People get the spiritual teaching they deserve. A person who is lying, deceitful, prone to exaggeration, emotionalist and credulous, accepts faith which contains extravagant interpretations, exaggerated personal claims, wild prophecies, unjustified inferences, and is riddled with inconsistencies. Thus the cult matches the character and capacities of its adherents. All are the victims of fancies—the followers of their leader's fancies, and the leader of his own.

58

The members of these cults not only possess untrained minds but also bewildered ones. Ignorant, as they are, of the laws of reasoning and the facts of science, incapable of testing doctrines and judging people correctly, they are easy dupes. Because of their impossible wishes and impractical natures, they inhabit a mental world that breeds self-cheating illusions and attracts them to self-deceived creators of illusions. Thus they find false roads more attractive than true ones and imaginary goals better than real ones.

59

Why do people join these bizarre cults? There is the feeling of spiritual loneliness, the need of social companionship with kindred minds.

60

Human dependence and human exploitation have produced between them a number of cults and sects, mostly organized but some not.

61

The incapacity to observe facts, or the refusal to accept them when observed, marks many of the followers of these cults.

62

They are weak or they are leaners. They want someone to whom they can take their worldly troubles, their emotional turmoils, or their domestic distresses.

63

It is true that these bereaved or bewildered souls get a kind of comfort from these leaders or their teachings. But it is a false comfort.

64

Many beginners are not really on this quest of the Overself at all, although they tell themselves and others that they are. Their quest is for a group to which they can belong—an organization they can join or a sect with which they can affiliate.

65

The sad, the defeated, and the frustrated who attach themselves to a devotional-path Master not seldom do so because they want the personal cheer and encouragement he offers, not because they want Truth.

66

The neurotics come to the mystical cult in the belief that it will solve some, or all, of their personal problems; heal some, or all, of their emotional disturbances; dissolve some, or all, of the conflicts which torment them. They do not come seeking for Truth. But they are entitled to seek such relief.

67

It is the ignorant who divide themselves up into sects.

68

These mythical masters, dreamed up by some highly imaginative neurotics living in isolation totally out of touch with the real world in accordance with ideas picked up from books written by similar neurotics, appeal to the naïve and gullible.

69

The theatrical figure with long hair down to his shoulders, a long beard to match, a wide flowing cloak, who makes big claims and seeks a bigger following, gets a crowd of devotees without too much difficulty. For such dupes look to, and are impressed by, externals.

70

They are very earnest but this does not prevent them from being very naïve.

71

The lack of proper education explains some of the credulousness of these followers; inexperience in the world of mysticism and ignorance of its past history explain more of it; but failure to command competent personal guidance or to obey competent literary guidance explains the remainder.

72

The innocent unsophisticated people who are attracted to such cults, the gullible inexperienced people who follow false Christs, undergo experiences which illustrate the folly of mankind and the diseases of imagination, while warning others of some dangers in religious seeking.

73

The man who gives his faith to a spiritual doctrine or a spiritual leader all of a sudden, and without examination or investigation, is either highly intuitive or highly gullible.

74

Like eyeless creatures they grope, this way and that, in one direction after another, toward a life that is higher, better, and more serene than the prosaic one which is all they know. This explains some, the smaller number, of cult-joiners.

75

These followers of cults which take the ravings of an unsound mind for the utterances of prophetic inspiration are mostly drawn from those who have not yet evolved the qualities of intellect which modern science engenders.

76

They band themselves together in groups because they lack the strength to look far enough within themselves to know how to belong to themselves.

77

In this wild extravagance of faith, with its dreams of Messianic intervention and utopian organization, credulous people find an illusory refuge from current troubles or world disasters.

78

Muddled minds seeking definite direction will always flock around the teacher prophet or leader who seems doubt-free, unhesitant, and certain.

79

Whether among the founders, leaders, or followers, some are certainly liars and others are lunatics. But there is a third group, which is quite sincere yet the victim of its own obsessive delusions.

80

The truth is that they are on the quest only in their personal supposition, and in the supposition of those to whom they talk about it. The actuality is that they have yet to find the entrance to the quest.

81

However small be the following of a cult, it gives to each member the sense of belonging.

82

Those who are easily dominated by theories, saturated by dogmas, and ruled by opinions, who are exploited by pseudo-intellectuals or pseudo-mystics, are so because of being incapable of thinking for themselves.

83

A superstitious mind will shout, "A God incarnate!" where a developed mind will turn smilingly, if not disdainfully, aside from a pinchbeck aspirant to deific honour.

84

Their leanings toward mysticism start and finish with tea-table talks about it.

85

Mysticism has inevitably attracted weak minds who seek its seeming magic, its occult powers, who hope to get through it what neither scientific procedures nor practical methods can give them.

86

Adolescent in mind even though adult in body, they find their comfortable level in such teachings.

87

Indulgence in utopianism is a great temptation—but only to the young and inexperienced, or the credulous and impractical, or the superstitious and uninformed.

88

There are the gullible ones, who believe too much that is false. There are the sceptical ones who believe too little that is true.

89

The thrill of contact with such seemingly great beings is too much for obscure persons. In its seething agitation all critical judgement is washed away.

90

Such aspirants are always at the mercy of the contrary currents of other people's opinion.

91

There is a satisfaction for those of gregarious temperaments in merging with a crowd of other people. Why is this? It may be the emotional support they feel they are getting from the presence of these others sharing a like mood at the same time. It may be a kind of emotional drunkenness brought about by the sense of camaraderie of all belonging together, but it may also be that the ego is momentarily lost in the crowd's ego and to that extent lost to the person temporarily—although not attuned, of course, to any high level. Nevertheless it is a kind of liberation from the ego.

The dreamers

92

People may become so desperate in their search for a spiritual refuge that, without the slightest critical scrutiny, they will accept romantic nonsense which promises them supernormal help. Or their level of formal education or real self-education may be so low as to leave their intelligence untrained in sound judgement.

93

It is not a matter of running after the showy, the exotic, the sensational, although there are many who, attracted to this sort of thing, fall into self-deception and miss the true way.

94

People who will not discipline their seeking, who expect to walk into the kingdom of heaven at someone else's "Open Sesame" and remain there forever, who want something for nothing, are often attracted to these self-deceptions and charlatanries, these utter idiocies and ridiculous pretensions served up with a mystical sauce or religious dressing.

95

We go to the meeting halls to hear the latest lecture with the hope that perchance we shall discover a shortcut to heaven. We wade through volume after volume of strange jargon. We listen to every new bird of charlatanry as it flies into our ken and flaps its unbalanced wings.

96

Many of their followers ardently look for, and constantly expect, some sudden magic to operate in their favour and dissolve their personal problems, or some sudden illumination to give them all knowledge and power. In both cases they believe no disciplinary struggle will be required of them in return, no special effort commensurate with the reward. They are, in short, wanting something for nothing.

97

Those whose experience of the world is limited to a single set of human and spiritual values, miss much.

98

It is the sense-bound, form-regarding type of mind which foolishly looks for verification of a true spiritual teaching by the worthless legerdemain of a country-fair exhibitionist.

99

Too many seekers come anxiously to mysticism in the hope and belief that it will solve their personal problems for them in some miraculous way and by some overnight method. They are in real or fancied trouble, in emotional distress or worldly entanglement, and feel unable to cope with it. So they look for the kind of assistance which primitive people look for from witch doctors—something that will bring results without any effort of their own being called for.

100

Balance in the spiritual life is a quality which they have seldom sought and therefore seldom found.

101

They congregate in little cliques and imagine their narrow dogmatism to be wide idealism, their occult superstition to be true spirituality.

102

The wise aspirant will not hanker after manifestations of the marvellous. He wants the highest life has to offer, and he knows that nothing could be more marvellous than the realization of God as his own self.

103

Such doctrine can only find a following among those who are literally unbalanced because they look at a few facts through mental magnifying glasses which allow them to see nothing else. It is always possible by such a process to mesmerize themselves into the most erroneous beliefs. It is always possible to paralyse the brain's power to consider facts which collide with these beliefs.

104

An insane teacher may be accepted by a sane aspirant merely because he happens to come into the latter's life just when the mystical urge has itself come uppermost.

105

Each adventure with a false or incompetent teacher was the result of impatience in seeking the true one. Each straying from the path into misguided cults and coteries was due to a lack of faith in the saying, "When the pupil is ready the master appears."

106

Those who make a fetish of their quest, more especially the "drop-outs," the escapists to Indian ashrams, and the guru-worshippers, will in no long time become narrow sectarians, still on the religio-mystic level.

107

If it is his purpose to come into contact with oracular teachers or holy saints, in the belief that he will possibly receive a permanent enlightenment or radical experience of self-transformation—that is, in the belief that he will get something for nothing—he would do better to save his time.

108

He thinks he can shed personal responsibility by taking shelter under the aegis of a group or organization.

109

Do they come to have the truth shatter their long-held, long-hugged fictions, or do they come to have these fictions approved and commended?

110

Young and inexperienced persons, as well as old and gullible ones, have been led to believe that some small closed esoteric organized group has a monopoly on truth. This is not so, as those who have been properly instructed and those who have travelled widely and investigated *thoroughly* confirm.

111

Those who seek the absolutely perfect—whether in a human love or a spiritual leader—will never find it.

112

As long ago as 1896, Swami Vivekananda wrote in a letter, half-jocularly, about the shiploads of "Mahatma-seekers" arriving in India.

113

There are temperaments which benefit by the mental effect of taking part in impressive rituals, especially initiations and inductions. They will find their way to cults suited to them. But nothing of the kind exists on this quest.

114

By surrendering to the sect he relieves himself of the burden of thinking for himself.

115

They enclose their minds in memories, confine them in ideas derived from a very limited experience, entangle them in desires, or intimidate them with fears. To expect Truth to penetrate such conditions, still more to penetrate them instantly, without first making a passageway for it, is to expect what is logically unwarranted and morally unjustified.

116

Those impatient persons who want the higher truth completely un-rolled for their gaze during a single talk and regardless of their readiness for it will necessarily be disappointed.

117

Tempted by magic formulas for instant enlightenment such as drugs or easy systems of mantric meditation now widely offered, they try to bypass the more difficult methods.

118

They demand the truth in all its purity while remaining unwilling to purge themselves of their own impurities. They claim the right to receive the most precious of all treasures while paying only a trivial price in return. Nowhere in Nature or among men can we witness such an unequal transaction.

119

If these studies attract genuine seekers after truth, they also attract foolish seekers after sensational thrills and freakish seekers after weird eccentricity.

120

Those who complain afterward about being deceived by these occultists complain about what they deserve for their childish credulity.

121

Where the enquirer is eager to become convinced and the master is eager to acquire disciples, it will not be long before both achieve their desires.

122

Those who want to remain at the nursery stage in mystical seeking are certainly entitled to do so. But they ought not to try to impose their limitations on others who want to go farther.

123

They do not see that the universe gives only what is self-earned.

124

This current interest in Zen Buddhism is mainly an experimental one, that is, a fad. It is merely a symptom of the neurotic's quest for novelty, or a sign that he is driven by instability—seldom by a quest of the Overself. He wants to receive surprise and to feel excitement, which is ironical because the real kingdom of heaven is devoid of both. Zen is also taken up as the next fad in line by the young intelligentsia, the self-conscious poets, the broken-down Bohemians, the fashionable patrons and the thrill-seekers of the theatre and the studio, by whom it is doomed—doomed to be intellectualized. The Spirit is squeezed out, the letter remains. The latter was let in, in a very real sense. Here was something new for them, something that decried their ego yet flattered it extravagantly. Above all, it was magic, witch-doctor stuff that offered a speedy exaggerated reward quite disproportionate to the effort required.

125

It would be wonderful if all men could cast off their temperament and renovate their character just by a simple contact with an inspired person. Jesus and Buddha would surely have been glad to perform this service for vast multitudes, but even they were not able to do so. Why should a Subud "Helper" be able to succeed where they failed?

126

Too many parrot phrases circulate among the followers of gurus and the members of movements.

127

The followers of these cults believe what they want to believe.

128

The character which is apt to display a sudden enthusiastic interest in a subject but not a continuous and persistent one, the seekers who possess a queer talent for joining some movement today—not because it is better but because it is new—only to drop it tomorrow or for espousing some idea merely because it happened to be the latest in time, such tend to carry neither the interest nor the espousal through to the bitter end.

129

They make demands of the quest, and bring expectations to it, which could never be fulfilled.

130

Those who follow illusory goals and impracticable techniques waste energy and invite disillusionment. In the end they become indifferent to true ideals, or cynical about them, or even antagonistic towards them.

131

The process of bringing men to engage in the quest is too slow to suit the enthusiastic neophyte.

132

They expect to find a copy of their mental image but the actuality proves to be quite different.

133

They are attracted by a doctrine if it is exotic, but remain untroubled by the question of its Truth.

134

The extravagance of faith, imagination, and expectation which has injured their judgement must be clipped short if the judgement itself is to be corrected.

135

A tendency to accept false beliefs is the product of defective intelligence and defective character: gullibility is merely its outward sign.

136

These are the dreamers who seek, as a first step towards founding an ideal society, the founding of an ideal community. So they join some group whose leadership or doctrine promises the realization of their dream and live among other seekers with a like hope. But—man is a mixture: the good and the bad find their home in him. In the end they are usually partially disenchanted.

The unbalanced

137

Those who suffer in estate or mind because they fall victim to deception and charlatanry or to incompetence and ignorance, often complain at being given such a grievous reward for their spiritual seeking. But they were never told to seek foolishly. The reward for their aspiration does come in the form of crumbs of truth and moments of peace, but the retribution of their foolishness must also come. And if the pain leads them to perceive their own faults or insufficiencies at its root, and if they work earnestly to correct them, they will gain permanently. To have averted their suffering would have robbed them of this gain.

138

Many seekers are simply looking for a modern version of the ancient witch-doctor, wizard, or magician when they look for a teacher. The thirst for occult powers or for the demonstration thereof—a thirst doomed in nearly every case to disappointment—rather than the thirst for truth is their dominant motive.

139

Those who join these cults to seek occult powers or phenomena, although with the least likelihood of attaining them, and who seldom avoid self-deception and delusions, are often those who take to these studies because they are misfits in society or because they are disappointed with the experience of life or because they hope it will bring some colour into their drab existences. But unbridled enthusiasm cannot save these fanatics from failure in achieving the new ambitions.

140

The path of black magic fascinates—or at least attracts—unbalanced, neurotic young people, whose naïveté and lack of experience make it easier for them to fall victim to it than for older persons.

141

They get a certain ego-inflating thrill from these psychical experiences, a vague feeling of uniqueness that carries the suggestion of superiority.

142

It is at once laughable and pathetic, this spectacle of those who misemploy their faculties and seek to become supermen when they have proved to be incapable as men.

143

They mostly follow "misty-cism" rather than mysticism because unfortunately they have not learned sufficiently the difference between the two.

144

Why is it that so many of these seekers sway dangerously on the brink of schizophrenia? The fact is that they are poor human material for the quest. They have not shown the requisite qualifications, despite several years of talk about it, and it is unlikely that they ever will. Some aspirants aim too high for their capacities, others aim in an altogether wrong direction.

145

What is it that attracts the spiritual fealty of eager and trusting people to such aberrations? Why do they mistake the strange for the holy? Admittedly they are without balance, without proportion, and without experience.

146

They hold the curious beliefs that to be spiritual one must be a simpleton, that the path to wisdom goes through foolishness, and that the advocacy of delusions is the enlightenment of mankind.

147

Those who enter mysticism with weak minds may become sponsors or dupes of fantastic revelations, while those who enter it with diseased minds may become similarly positioned with evil ones.

148

Others take to mysticism because they are neurotically unfit to cope with this world or because they are afraid to cope with it or because they are pathological invalids or because they want a faith as queer, cranky, and credulous as they themselves are.

149

They imagine that the Quest will take their life beyond everyday common things or that it will bring them dramatic occult powers that can be shown off to their friends. In some cases, it is mere vanity which is the source of these beliefs, but in others it is simple misunderstanding or ignorance.

150

So long as their ideas of what constitutes the goal most worth seeking are incomplete or unbalanced, so long will their procedures and results be of the same inadequate kind.

151

It is a fact which experience proclaims but which personal feeling ignores, that most people are, in some way and to some extent, emotionally, mentally, or physically unbalanced or diseased. It is a further fact that they lack self-control in one of these departments, or in most of them; their unattractive neurotic compulsions and irritating obsessional conduct plainly reveal this.

152

All kinds of fools follow all kinds of other fools along these fringe tracks. They may be labelled religious, mystic, occult, psychological, psychiatric, or even philosophic.

153

The motive which attracts many to these practices may be psychical self-aggrandizement to compensate for their ordinariness or obscurity or powerlessness in personal life. They want to be able to perform miraculous feats or to possess spectacular supernormal faculties, chiefly because of the influence, authority, and applause which can follow. But they easily deceive themselves into believing that their motives are noble, unselfish, exalted.

154

Those who succumb to the dubious influence of these cult-founders, half-baked gurus, and pseudo-masters are usually highly suggestible men or highly gullible women. Usually the teacher's personality is made the subject of gushing rapture and his words the subject of hysterical homage.

155

They flirt with the occult, seeking neither their true essence nor to have their personal egoism lifted from them, but to satisfy a dangerous curiosity or a dubious sensationalism or, worse, a thirst for conceit-breeding or temptation-bringing powers.

156

The naïve may be duped by absurd exaggerations, others by a pretentious occultism; both have yet to find the true quest.

157

Individuals who, through their own faulty characters, have failed to adjust their ordinary human problems have the temerity to add extraordinary mystical ones to them. They plunge recklessly into yoga, meditation, and occultism. They seek psychical powers when they ought to be seeking intellectual balance.

158

A large part of this interest in mystical subjects is attributable not to spiritual progressiveness but to intellectual backwardness.

159

These ill-balanced followers, who walk precipitous trails that overlook the deep ravines of lunacy, cannot be brought into philosophy and cannot be made into mystics.

160

It is natural for a woman to cling to a man; that is why we see that the male gurus have such a high proportion of women among their followers.

161

It seems inevitable that there should be so heavy a sprinkling of neurotics, fanatics, psychotics, dogmatics, and borderline cases among those attracted to these studies. The first thing they have to learn is not how to develop occult powers, but that lunacy is not philosophy, and that what they mistake for spiritual development is too often spiritual decadence.

162

The lunatic fringe surround the halls and vestibules of mysticism, the incorrigible cranks infest its ascetic disciplines and physical regimes. The morons are there, too, gullibly swallowing every tale and addicted to every superstition, and unaffected by logic, science, common sense, practicality, or facts. But the account is not finished with them: there are the sensible, the educated, and the thoughtful, the genuine seekers after truth or peace.

163

For too long these subjects have been the preserve of many who, it must be regrettably confessed, are a little shaky in the upper story and a little undisciplined in the emotional region.

164

It would be ludicrous, if it were not also pathetic, how often inspired lunacy is mistaken for inspired wisdom in these circles. They are quickly attracted to unspiritual interpreters of spirituality, provided the claims made are big enough or the doctrines taught are sensational enough. Prophets who are partly insane and partly bogus will not lack for a following, so long as there are seekers who are too ill-equipped in mind and experience to recognize such characteristics for what they are.

165

Some take up the quest because there is something wrong with them; it is not because they hope to have it put right, but because they hope that this is a medium which encourages the expression of their wrongness. In a sense they are correct, and they usually gravitate to the lunatic fringes and occultistic demesnes which abound at the quest's entrance and along its first stages. Here their egos can get full satisfaction, their craziness can find camaraderie, and their hallucinations can be strengthened and supported. The quest as it really is is not for them—for it would give short shrift to their belief that their wrongness is rightness.

166

The hysteric type should stringently avoid psychism and its phenomena, occultism and its powers, if she does not want to make a bad state worse. Much more should she avoid them if she wants to gain the peace of mind which the quest alone can bring.

167

They live in a constant round of excited expectations. They await a weekly revelation of the Infinite, a monthly meeting with an adept, a bi-monthly intervention of supernatural forces in their personal affairs, and so on.

168

When these people are not looking for witch doctors and wizards to cure their ills or mend their fortunes with quackery, they are looking for swamis and messiahs to fly them to romantic dreamlands or other planes with rhetoric. The fact is that they are not merely simple souls: they are also hungry ones. Their hunger is for the irrational, the fantastic, the unreal, the absurd, and the glamorously deceptive. They are seeking something for nothing, want to achieve their goals without working for them. They seek wonder-working panaceas or hunt formulas for magic dressed up in modern words, or sit at the feet of suave, mildly insane freaks and fanatics.

169

If materialism is to be displaced by mysticism, and if every fantastic doctrine is to be labelled and accepted as mysticism and any crackpot who claims them is to receive mystical honours, then the so-called advance will really be a retrogression. Those who accept enthusiastically any doctrine merely because it is unorthodox are not truth-seekers. They are eccentrics. And those who follow any guide merely because he wears a turban are also not truth-seekers. They are exotics. The first group may be victimized by crackpots, the second by charlatans.

170

The too narrow and too prolonged concentration upon one's own personal emotions creates the neurotic. This still remains true whether the man be a sceptical materialist or an aspiring mystic.

171

The whole horde of futile seekers, with their impotent attitudes and pale mimicries, talking constantly of a goal too distant for their feeble powers, babbling in pretentious esoteric jargon of mystical states they know only in imagination and never in experience, are heavy-lidded with hallucinations and remain sterile dreamers and neurotic egocentrics.

172

Instability and restlessness are features of the psycho-neurotic type of person. He changes his job or even his work too often to be able ever to succeed at anything. And he moves his allegiance from cult to cult too quickly to plead truth-seeking. His imbalance is also expressed physically, for the eyes are often dilated and nervous.

173

The neurotic says: "I am *going* to do it." Never does he *do* it, but remains always dreaming of these great things in the future. This is the story of his unbalanced life.

174

They all came into mystic cults, they all needed its promise of magic, truth, consolation, power—the lonely, the half-mad, the neurotic, the solemn, the over-thoughtful, the bizarre, the crushed, the despairing.

175

The presence of eccentric behaviour, dress, and appearance does not show the presence of philosophy but its absence. The signs of neurotic, hysteric, or psychotic personality point everywhere else except to a philosophic origin.

176

Too many ill-adjusted, ego-wrapped neurotics attach themselves to psychical, occult, mystical, Oriental, and religious movements not to get their unhealthy condition remedied but to get acceptance and sympathy or, if "inner experiences" are retold, admiration. Or, if their personal relationships or careers have failed, they hope a sudden transformation of their lives will be brought about by magical occult powers and enable them to succeed.

177

They have serious distortions within their own minds which are then reflected into their aims, principles, and methods. They have become pathological cases and need psychiatric treatment.

178

I am not too happy about my own role in helping to bring on this explosion of interest in mystical and Oriental ways. Hysterics, lunatics, simpletons, the mindless, the exploiters, and half-charlatans have stepped into this field. For when the truth gets into the hands of the unready and unfit, they first misconceive it, then adulterate and corrode it, finally embody it for foolish or egotistic purposes in pseudo-truths.

179

The groups and cults which young people have formed or follow— wearing clothes, head-hair, and beards of a highly exhibitionist sort, speaking a jargon about which the less said the better—are not likely to appreciate the philosophy of truth. Yet they glibly chatter of Nirvana and seek easy ways of achieving it instantly. They have tried drugs, mantrams and mandalas, Zen meditation and Art, drink and sex, as part of these ways. Needless to write that their egos remain as strong as ever, or rather, stronger. They like to gather in "loving" groups. Now and then a genius appears among them but soon finds that solitude is better for his work than these work-shy ever-talking crowds.

180

When psychopaths are attracted to these studies, it is the occult, the spiritistic, and the psychical that hold their interest. When neurotics are attracted, it is the religious and mystical which hold it. Before either can enter the portals of philosophy he has to part, to a sufficient extent, with some of his faults: the psychopath with his violence, fanaticism, hatreds, exaggerations, distortions, destructiveness, and hysteria; the neurotic with his impulsive urges, his extreme tensions, his emotional moodiness and disturbances, and his egocentricities.

181

Anyone who cares to look around in these circles will find that aberrations from the true Quest abound. They attract those who are ignorant or ill-informed about such matters, or those who need (but do not see that they need) some psychological straightening-out before pure philosophy and the correct philosophical life are acceptable.

182

Various forms of dementia may be recognized among these misguided seekers, but the cases differ widely from the extremely mild to the severely dangerous.

183

On the margins of religio-mysticism there is a recurring type which you may identify by its freakish appearance and exaggerated behaviour. It is a type which never penetrates to the true heart of mysticism but only moves over its surface. It takes the mere incidentals and makes them major affairs.

184

It is a deplorable fact that an unstable emotional temperament and an undeveloped intellectual faculty, when conjoined with mystical enthusiasm, easily lead to religious mania, psychopathic states, or mental unbalance. Whether they are really serious or merely borderline cases, those who become victims of such conditions cannot make authentic spiritual advancement but can only revolve within the circle of their own hallucinations.

185

Neurotics who know only the two extremes of licence and asceticism, who spend their lives in one or the other, or in jumping from one to the other, will be intolerant of the philosophic attitude to these matters.

186

Unfortunately their feelings are hopelessly confused with their beliefs.

187

The neurotic type acts as if its own emotions are all that matter in the world, its own beliefs the last word in wisdom. This is its danger—that it cannot climb out of itself and get a proper perspective.

188

The neurotic instability does not belong to the quest itself but to a *personal* unbalance of temperament.

189

Those who fall most easily enter the masses of the negative side of occultism if they are working alone, or fall into the hands of exploiting teachers and cults if they are among those with weak minds without education of any quality who seek after sensational experiences.

190

What has philosophy to do with these half-maniacs who pester its fringes and never enter its solid sanity, who go around half-dizzy from reading about notions too big for their small minds?

191

If half-demented persons take up these studies, it is because either the occult attracts them or they fall under the spell of a teacher who is more demented than they are. But they are not attracted to pure philosophy and could not get it taught to them anyway.

192

There are mentally disturbed persons who have aggravated their condition by taking to the quest in the wrong way, by extreme forms of asceticism, by blind naïve spiritistic mediumship, or by improper, ego-worshipping meditation.

193

There are psychological types—the lazy, the foolish expecters of something for nothing, the unbalanced—who are attracted to those who promise to satisfy their cravings for "instant peace": the purveyors of mind-expanding drugs and plants, the gurus who make large claims for themselves or their methods. The seekers get what they pay for—they end up with adventures in hallucination or insanity.

PSEUDO AND IMPERFECT
TEACHERS

The prevalence of charlatans

There is not a little sham mysticism, specious religion, and false philosophy in these days. This is why seekers must approach such topics warily.

2

Quacks and charlatans prey on uncritical questing. This warning is no theoretical one; it is based on the knowledge of many cases which have been observed during travels in Asia, Europe, and America. Many a good-living, kindly, sincere, if simple, church-goer and temple-worshipper is in safer hands and more spiritually advanced than the pseudo-mystics and so-called occultists who are being wrecked on the tragic shores of semi-insanity and worldly ruin, their egoism exaggerated, their ethics jumbled, their minds muddled or drugged by extravagances, their emotions neurotically confused, and their finances reduced.

3

The public and private cults of occultism today make a sea in which you will find ten bad fish for every good one that you take out of it. Nor from such cheap and charlatanic sources is truth to be *safely* netted.

4

The sources of spiritual help are many, but of reliable help, few. Superstition, self-aggrandizement, or semi-charlatanry taints much of what is offered to the public.

5

Have we not witnessed in our own times how, on the pretext of doing good, great evil has been wrought? But it is not only in worldly circles that this is possible, for the same thing can be witnessed in spiritual circles, especially their organizations and institutions.

6

That this is a field where psychopaths and charlatans pose as teachers is correct. That the beginning seeker should be wary of them is also correct.

7

He will find himself in a field which, both in past history and present event, is infested with megalomaniacs who have messianic complexes, paranoiacs who hunger for disciples to command or exploit, hallucinators who recklessly mingle imagined fantasies with actual facts, and melancholics who insist on putting an ascetic blight on every human joy.

8

How many false teachers have led their flocks into more misery instead of less without leading them at the same time into the promised Nirvana!

9

Not even a loose-living saviour of mankind will fail to capture a devoted and obedient group of followers among these gullible people. Can such a situation be looked at without disquiet by those who care for the influence and dignity of mysticism?

10

The fraudulent guides who have fattened on the spiritual yearnings of inexperienced women have brought disrepute on the subject in England and America.

11

These charlatans invite all and sundry on plausible pretexts to put reason under the guillotine. A sensible aspirant will close his ears and turn away from such an invitation, for he will detect its danger from its very mode and manner.

12

One deplorable result of this wealth of knowledge and revelation which has poured into common accessibility during the past hundred and fifty years is increased charlatanry and confused sincerity.

13

Quack teachers take advantage of the misery and unsettlement of a transition period like ours to offer quack panaceas for disease and alleged magical methods of getting what we want.

Difficulty of recognizing them

14

He does right to keep away from charlatans, with their feigned powers and imagined revelations; but he is not always right as to who is or is not a charlatan.

15

All religious occupations lend themselves to hypocrisy, and this is no exception. The twentieth-century mystics are often pious impostors, playing upon the credulity of their ignorant following. There exists among them a solid, saving remnant of noble men who are making arduous and genuine efforts to attain the superhuman wisdom which mysticism promises to devotees.(P)

16

Between these two poles the unwary, unsophisticated, and uncritical seeker often has to run the gauntlet of deluders and deceivers—mostly of others but sometimes of themselves. He will be lucky indeed if they take nothing more than his faith from him.

17

The refusal of the real adepts to appear publicly as such has opened the door for the cupidity and charlatanry of their counterfeits to enter all too easily.

18

The superior silence and quizzical smile with which certain mystics avoid affirming or negating a straightforward question, may certainly be the indicator of a higher knowledge—but then, it may also be mere charlatanry.

19

A trustworthy honest accurate and full history of a leader or of his sect is almost unobtainable. Significant bias or significant omission flaws all such records.

20

It is unfair to take these charlatans as characteristic of all mystics, much less of the few sages, and even more unfair to condemn all mystical and philosophical doctrines because some of them have been taught by the charlatans.

21

Such teachings are more widely given out today than ever before, but remember: there are teachings which bring out support for the evil in man just as there are teachings which support the good.

22

The beginner does not usually know how to distinguish what is true from what is false in the various personal cults or impersonal teachings which compete for his allegiance.

23

The teaching, the cult, or the teacher may appear authentic, sublime, inspiring, and true to the naïve, the inexperienced, or the gullible seeker but they will appear as a caricature of authenticity, a degradation of sublimity, a counterfeit of inspiration, and a falsification of truth to the proficient mystic.

24

Some of the presentations of doctrine and claim are plausible enough to deceive even those who are not entirely inexperienced beginners.

25

The result of a carpenter's work stares him in the face. It cannot lie. If the table's legs are of unequal length, the table's top will be wobbly. If the chair's seat is of too frail material, it will collapse when anyone sits down in it. But the religio-mystic teacher can propound any idea or suggest any practice that comes into his brain, and the truth of the one or the result of the other will either not be known at all, or only after the passage of years. The person of trained and balanced mind, who is expert or experienced in these matters, will of course detect falsity, distortion, hallucination, or imposture very quickly but the beginner has no such advantage.

26

Most people are incompetent to know whether a man has really arrived at the highest goal or not. Hence comes their misguided worship of holy men who are still working out their salvation but who prematurely announce their attainment of it. The result is foreseen by Jalaluddin Rumi, the Persian dervish poet: "To say I AM HE at the wrong moment is a curse. But to say I AM HE at the right moment is a blessing."

27

The common kind of teacher, with no real inspiration and no complete realization, but with a commercialistic attitude or a beggar's instinct, is not worth considering. But the uncommon kind, with nothing to sell and not even the willingness to accept voluntary contributions, is well worth considering.

28

The antique method, whereby a master's teachings are made compulsory upon the student, is unsuited to the modern man who is now beginning to come of intellectual age. Today the student is advised to keep mentally free and open, weighing and judging the worth of all teachings—including his master's—by every means of appraisal known to him.

29

Let us not mistake the true mystic for the false one who gathers to himself a credulous following by spectacular claims and who passes the counterfeit of necromancy for the real coin of spirituality. He still mistakes the phenomena of the senses for the fact of the Holy Spirit. He is the victim of delusions whereas the true mystic is the vanquisher of them.

30

Anyway, where is the man who can expound truth satisfactorily and who expresses in action the doctrines which he has embraced? Self-anointed babbling gurus exist in the flesh; long-distance Tibetan Mahatmas exist in books.

31

These teachers are like a crowd of blind men. The pupil believes what the teacher says, and the teacher believes what he has heard from other teachers. So he who stands in front sees nothing, and he who stands in the midst sees nothing—nor does he who stands at the back see anything. "The faith of these teachers is worthless," says a writer, on Buddha.

32

The spiritual exhibitionism which often accompanies the leadership and following of these cults, is another feature absent from the philosophic school.

33

An imposter, clever at simulating mystical insight, will nevertheless invariably fail to match his conduct with his pretensions. This is only one of the tests, but perhaps the chief one.

34

The pseudo-masters are full of demerits. The imperfect masters show both merits and demerits. The perfect masters reveal merits and values only.

35

The teacher himself must be the best advertisement of his teaching. Where there is no congruity between the two, the seeker should be cautious.

36

Seek truth from a suitable source. What can you gather from a man whose actions condemn him?

37

Many mouth what they have read in books or what they have heard said, but few have any real knowledge of the soul.

38

Has he personally employed the methods he teaches others? Has he tested their value in this way?

39

A teacher of the higher philosophy will not assist a pupil in the development of clairvoyance because this only increases the troubles and dangers from which he may be suffering already. The best advice that can be given in such a case is to refrain from endeavours in that direction and to apply his efforts to the development of his character and spiritual nature. Remember the words of Jesus: "Seek ye first the kingdom of heaven and all these things shall be added unto you." Only after he has become established in high ideals and self-discipline will he be fit for the instruction he desires.

40

It would be useful to learn how few of these lecturers and teachers have done any original and independent research work on this subject, how many are merely repeating others' opinions like parrots.

41

There is this difference between the philosophic and the foolish mystic: whereas the first will always seek to clarify your mind, the second will often seek to mystify it.

42

The genuine mystic is always sympathetically interested in the achievement of Realization by others. However, his interest is continuously balanced by reason and intuition.

43

Those who merely read his reported sayings, which run so smoothly and upon so elevated a rail, will begin to fear that I have done this cult-founder an injustice and one which will appear doubly so to the serious-minded flock which follows him—for I doubt whether they can differentiate between the light irreverent treatment of my pen and mere personal maliciousness. But when I remember his acts by the light of the maxim that we best prove the attainment of lofty consciousness by lofty conduct, I know that there is no other treatment which can suit him so comfortably.

44

Instead of trying to clear life's mysteries for his followers, he increases their number or obscurity, or both.

45

The adroit imaginativeness of these imposters, paranoids, and exhibitionists, their facility in inventing Masters whom they have probably never seen, is helped by the inability of their followers to check the veracity of their pretensions about pilgrimages to Tibet.

46

They speak or write not what they have experienced inwardly but what they would like to have experienced.

Domination and narrowness

47

In a proper relationship, no true master would seek to create a dependence on him which would cause the pupil to be unable to progress alone. Yet this is exactly what happens in so many Oriental circles today and so many Occidental pseudo-mystical circles also. The pupils become less and less able to handle their own problems, less and less fit for responsible living, less and less willing to struggle to find an adjustment to life. They will not find the path of true progress by extending the delay in effecting such needful adjustment until they become chronically incapable of making any at all.

48

Just as the true teacher will widen the circle of a student's mental contacts, so the false one will plunge him in intellectual isolation, will keep him wholly under his own influence and prevent the enrichment of ideas and expansion of outlook necessary to his progress.

49

Expert advice is always useful, often essential, in several lines of activity. But advising someone is not the same as dominating or tyrannizing over him.

50

The guru can easily persuade his followers to believe anything or to submit to any suggestion because he previously persuades them to think rationally only from the premises he supplies.

51

What this posturing leader gives his disciples is nothing less than a hypnotic performance through which he lures them to moral destruction and intellectual deformity.

52

If we are to believe the high priests and chief representatives of these pretentious cults, there is no salvation for misguided humanity outside their own little folds.

53

False guides put the seeker's mind into handcuffs whereas true guides free him.

54

Men must begin to know such truths for themselves. The age of patriarchal domination over their minds is vanishing.

55

Instead of segregating his disciples and followers into monasteries, the

Persian prophet Baha'u'llah told them they ought to disperse themselves throughout the world and help to enlighten others.

56

The psychoanalyst who keeps on turning over his patients' complexes for exhibition and discussion, as well as the guru who encourages his disciples to talk of their achievement or non-achievement of spiritual progress, is merely helping the unfortunate follower to build up his ego still more strongly.

57

The spiritual guide who encourages his pupils to speak openly to others of their occult experiences is acting dangerously. The more he continues to do so, the more are they likely to fall into the foolishness of personal vanity and to commit the error of placing a higher value on these things than they deserve. The next step is for them, and others, to regard their advancement up the ladder of perfection as being greater than it really is. All this leads the disciples astray from the true mystical path and creates confusion as to what constitutes true mysticism.

58

The quest is a mysterious enterprise. To engage in it with success, it must be engaged in mysteriously. The disciple should not make public announcement of every moral move, every psychical experience, every spiritual rapture.

59

The quest is so much an individual affair that although all questers must arrive at the same destination, each will do so by his own separate way, by his own special experiences. Any spiritual guide who ignores this fact merely tries to make his disciples mere copies of himself. This cannot possibly happen although both may exhaust themselves in the attempt. There are no two things, no two creatures, and no two quests identically alike anywhere in Nature.

60

He who arrogates to himself the right to decide what his disciples shall or shall not think read say and do, is not progressing but rather converting them into gramophone records.

61

The spiritual guide who does not try ceaselessly to get his followers to stand on their own feet is not the best guide for them.

62

A true teacher does not want to direct anyone's life. He may offer suggestions but he would never insist on their being carried out.

63

An unqualified teacher's own personal wish to impose his will on others is misconstrued into the wish to obey the will of God.

64

So-called masters who suffer from such limitations cannot set others free. Those who themselves worship the flesh-born idols of nationality race colour and status can only keep their devotees imprisoned in the same illusions.

65

Such pseudo-teachers do not want to enhance the self-reliance of their students, do not want to increase their strength but rather to diminish it. They prefer to have people around them to act like blotting-paper and merely absorb first, ideas, in order to reproduce them without thinking and second, commands, in order to obey them without hesitation.

66

The guru who intimidates, forces, compels, and tyrannizes over his followers may or may not be indefensible, but he must be regarded with some hesitation and even caution before acceptance.

67

There is a place for the guru; he has his services to render and only he can render them as with all specialists. But in giving this service he is not entitled to cripple the individuality of the disciple, nor is the disciple entitled to ascribe imaginary attributes and powers to the guru.

68

If the guru fails to lead his disciple to greater and greater freedom, he fails to encourage healthy growth, to help him find his own potentialities and to realize them.

69

There is a type of guru, common enough, who likes to keep his disciples as disciples always. It is an unpleasant shock for him to find them outgrowing the relationship (which has become irksome) and claiming freedom.

70

It is sometimes needful to remind those who emotionally exaggerate the office and service, the power and knowledge of their master and display this trait in their relationship with him, of Jesus' words: "It is good for you that I go away," and also of Ramana Maharshi's words to Swami Dandapani when he was expelled by the ashram: "This is the best thing to have happened for you now."

71

That these cults can attract apparently intelligent people or spiritually ardent people says little for the truth of their teaching but much for the mesmeric power of their founders. The temperament and tendency of some of these men make them dangerous teachers.

72

The teacher who requires absolute submission from another human being, and demands the surrender—partial or complete—of that person's property, is likely to be doing so out of selfish motives.

73

The mistake of men like Swami Ramdas is to prescribe for all seekers the particular way which suits only some seekers. The Swami successfully used mantra yoga and offers it to all alike. The grand Quest of man has been reduced to a simple kindergarten affair, a mere babbling of God's name with no attempt to understand God's purposes and workings. It makes the Overself too cheap and the nature of it too childish.

74

His suave impressive bearing, his completely assured pontifical talk, do not fail to have their effect on those whose intuition is lacking.

75

Their terrified followers are led to believe that if they stray away from his teaching, they stray away from God.

76

These fanatics propagate their opinions with such intense conviction that they mesmerize weaker minds into a similar wild, undiscriminating, and unbalanced state.

77

Neurotic flamboyant gurus who try to "hold" their disciples on the strength of their own alleged personal attainments instead of letting them free to receive truth from all sides, all eras, all media, exist in the East as well as in the West.

Incomplete teachers

78

Too many persons have assumed the role of a teacher without sufficient justification for it. Too many want to show others the way to a previously unknown cosmic experience which they have failed to attain themselves.

79

Too many have set up as teachers when their own stage of development was only a partial and unbalanced one. Consequently they can lead their people only to an incomplete goal and, which is worse, do them harm as well as good.

80

The time comes, after some years of this excessive worship by disciples, when he lets it affect him and destroy his sincerity. Then he assumes a pose to suit their idea of what a master should be. Then he is not only no longer himself, a seeker after truth, but one who has lost the possibility of truth's visitation to him.

81

When a man plays the role of guru without having reached the enlightenment of the true guru, the years of adulation and slavish obedience by disciples will affect his mind and alter his character. The more his power becomes absolute, the more will he suffer from paranoia and develop a belief in his own infallibility.

82

Those who provide quick and facile answers to such hard questions about man's lot and life merely act as unwitting purveyors of deception.

83

I am afraid that many occult teachers suffer from what Socrates called "the conceit of knowledge without the reality."

84

There are weaknesses in the thinking of these reformers, prophets, or guides, as well as serious deficiencies in their facts. They are walking in fields which not only need a deeper exploration than they were able to give but also, if they are to be walked safely, a better balance of the faculties.

85

It is an error to believe that they are necessarily attained. Most are still striving.

86

Only he who has himself been lifted up can uplift others.

87

Those in this category can inspire themselves but not others. They cannot give, or even be given through.

88

The pure truth cannot come out of human vessels which are crooked, deformed, enraged, destructive, insane, exasperated, extremist, perceiving nothing good or true or beautiful in the past, and fanatically believing they alone hold such values. But such people may still be vessels for a partial, confused, and mixed-up truth. This is where the young—naïve, inexperienced but adventurous, courageous, fresh, idealistic, utopian—may fall into traps, marshes, or illusions.

89

They have some kind of mystical knowledge but it is so small in quantity, so vague and blurred in quality, that it is unreliable.

90

What they know and teach still comes from within the limits of their own little ego-consciousness, although transferred to a psychical level. It does not come from the infinite Overself—the sole source of authentic truth.

91

Those prophets who have not undergone the purificatory discipline of the mind and emotions often see the truth in a false light and communicate this caricature of it to their followers.

92

Rather than search their subconscious carefully, or face their conscious frankly, they continue to dispense error, hallucination, and superstition. For this is their way of escape from the humiliation of publicly admitting either that they had been grossly mistaken or grossly deceived.

93

How many contemporary mystics have gained from all their work in meditation nothing but illusion, self-aggrandizement, or giddy hallucination? One claiming communication every day with the Buddha drips nonsense, propagates fear, and repeats the profound metaphysic read in Buddhist books; another while professing to be Jesus reincarnated and announcing his own Messiahship makes extensive financial demands on his disciples every year.

94

One of the great mistakes to be found in mystical circles is that which fails to recognize that most glimpses fade away. They come for a time only, not for all time. Out of this mistake there are born cults and sects, teachings and doctrines, practices and methods which merely reflect human opinion, guesses, theories, prejudices, and preferences, and not at all divine enlightenment.

95

The guru, sitting on his lonely eminence and surrounded by his disciples' awe, is a mystical, not a philosophical, figure.

96

They do not make any real contact with the Overself but only imagine that they do. For they are still enclosed within the field of the ego.

97

We may admire a man for his holiness and yet reject his ideas for their wrongness.

98

In those mystical and pseudo-mystical circles, where fanaticism is not seldom pushed to the point of madness, it is not easy to find a guide who is not only competent but also sane.

99

It is conceit for the mystic and an error for his followers to take his personal colouring of truth as being the infallible inspiration of truth.

The ego's ambition

100

If he sees himself appointed to lead a spiritual movement or in the limelight at the centre of a large group of fervent followers, he ought to exercise extreme prudence. For it may be nothing more than his own fantasy, the play of his own secret ambition. The need for protection against his own vanity is essential. The temptation of self-exaltation is a common trap for unwary occultists. The way to keep out of it is to keep humble: let others oppose him and criticize him or belittle his mystic experiences and ridicule them; if he can bear this without anger, without resentment, and with coolness, he will not fall into the trap and exploit the manifestation to glorify himself. So important is this virtue of humility that it may be labelled both first and final. The asserted spirituality which lacks this quality but which makes its own personality occupy a prominent position ought to be regarded with suspicion. That is why upon those who really do aspire to the very highest there descends the dread phenomenon of the dark night of the soul. When later they emerge from this awful experience, they emerge with all vanity ground down to powder and all pride burnt down to ash: it is better in the frail state of human nature to have nothing to burn, to hide our occult experiences from the knowledge of others.

101

The charlatanism which accompanies several of these cults need not necessarily be deliberate; it may also be unconscious. This is possible in cases where their founder's earnest efforts resulted in a partial mystical illumination but where his imagination was unrestrained and his speculations unguarded, his critical judgement and reasoning power undeveloped, while the ambitions of his ego were strong enough to push him into premature leadership.

102

If he is a man of ambitious nature, his predictive messages or directive intuitions will themselves reflect this. They will reveal a brilliant future of leadership and urge him to assume the robe of authority or to ascend the dais of Power. Thus a new cult will be born.

103

Few start with a pure motive, that is, with the deep and disinterested wish to assist the spiritual welfare of others without receiving any reward in return. As for the others—and they are in the majority—they are usually started with mixed motives, that is, the desire to do some good by propagating some teaching plus the desire to receive adequate financial reward for the trouble taken. These usually degenerate into forming an increasingly broadened definition of the word "adequate" until irremediable spiritual rot sets in. Finally, there are a few institutions which represent clear attempts to exploit gullible people in the basest manner—dark manifestations of an immoral greed for power. Apart from such organizations and ashrams there are always individuals who seek a purely personal following—long-armed fanatics who would gather the gullible into their clutches and over-eager proselytizers who would chain the impressionable to a ridiculous and dogmatic credo.

104

A teacher of the highest wisdom can serve his disciples only if he serves them with the highest aims. If he mixes selfish considerations, egotistic exploitations, personal desires with his interest in them, his teaching will to that extent itself become impure, ineffective, and falsified.

105

It is not necessary to deny that these hierophants honestly hold spiritual beliefs in order to point out that they are using these beliefs to subserve their personal ambitions and selfish vanity.

106

Any cult leader who pretends to be working solely for the service of humanity is either a mountebank with a following of fools or a fool with a following of greater fools.

107

The leader of a little cult, surrounded by devotees who openly and adoringly give him Himalayan rank, hearing nothing else and meeting nobody else, is conquered by their suggestions and soon begins to believe them. This puts him (and them) in danger. If he were more prudent, he would take care to reject the flatteries of disciples and welcome the fulminations of detractors.

108

No matter how he disguises these efforts under tall talk about "service to humanity," high-sounding ideals for himself, or the achievement of transcendental nirvanic goals, they are designed to gratify his own ego.

109

This eagerness to capture new disciples has too often a somewhat egotistic motive blended in with the wish to communicate teachings. The pure giving in a spirit of genuine love and selfless obedience of those simple apostles and first preachers who went forth to preach the Christian gospel seems to be absent or else adulterated.

110

The temptation to set himself up as a new prophet, acquire disciples, and gather followers will have to be met and overcome—even if it disguise itself as service to humanity.

111

He is all-too-eager to play the missionary or the apostle who will make dramatic conversions of men—a spiritual ambition in which, although he does not know it, his ego is playing a central part.

112

If only the masters of these cults could leave their pedestals and step down from time to time, both they and their flocks would benefit greatly. For the former might then get a truer perspective of themselves and the latter might lose their complacent self-congratulation.

113

If a man believes he has become enlightened and wishes to spread the Truth, he is less likely to do it if he also becomes conceited, puffed up by his knowledge, and arrogant in his attitude towards those who hold and spread other teachings. He is more likely to succeed if he shows goodwill, tolerance, and understanding towards these others.

114

When a man sets up to instruct his fellows spiritually, to guide them—still more, to *lead* them—in this way . . . it is only in the end that he discovers that he was working as much to obey his ambitions as to obey God, that it was as much because he loved his ego as because he loved his highest being that he entered and maintained all his activity.

115

The teacher who has a personal motive behind his work of teaching may give out a true doctrine, but only so far as it suits him. Consciously or unconsciously, he will mislead his pupils at the point where his own personal interest is affected.

116

Through vanity or through ambition, these teachers never allow themselves to look impartially at their teaching or honestly at its results. If they did, and if they were honest, they would renounce the one and be ashamed of the other.

117

That which makes a man set himself up as the head of a cult is usually ambition. It may however disguise itself as pious service. It is rare that such a man receives the divine mandate authentically.

118

When either pride of achievement or desire of exploitation enters into him, he will start a cult of his own.

119

Somewhere along the path they lose their way. Their good intentions become bad actions. The ideal of service disappears, the lust of exploitation replaces it.

120

The crazy visions or egoistic doctrines which float through their feverish brains and push reason from its seat, will not fail to find believers so long as they are pushed forward by ambitious, power-seeking leaders and would-be leaders.

121

The danger here of course is of spiritual megalomania, of believing that one's egoistic actions are inspired by God, that one's thoughts come straight from divinity itself and represent infallible wisdom, that one's personal interests coincide with humanity's welfare, and that one's baser motives are in fact higher ones.

122

When they present opinion as personal opinion and theory as speculative theory, no harm is done. But sooner or later the position in which they find themselves—placed on pedestals and worshipped as idols—brings on a belief in their own infallibility and a presentation of mere opinion as divine revelation. The situation is much worse when the guru is a man locked up in his own mad delusions and misleading his followers into sharing them.

123

They confuse their lust for adulation with the law that bids us give to the thirsty.

124

The teacher who becomes drunk with the wine of his disciples' adoration will soon commit egregious blunders. The power which has come to him has corrupted him. Punishment will surely follow.

125

The arousing of messianic expectations and millennial hopes is another suspicious sign. Countless unbalanced fanatics have followed this line. True mysticism has no necessary connection with it.

126

These self-anointed apostles of eccentricity prey on misguided followers, mostly women.

127

Where gurus are mainly intent on profiting personally from their work of instructing disciples, the latter may receive little benefit spiritually in return.

128

One form of delusion from which quite a number of cult-leaders have suffered is the belief that they are a reincarnation of Christ. Meher Baba, the Parsee Messiah, and Father Divine, the Negro Messiah, have shared it. Annie Besant and Charles Leadbeater attached it to the young Krishnamurti—who eventually rebelled and rejected it. Several others still hold and teach the belief. No philosophic student need be taken in by this fancied revelation.

129

The larger his following becomes, the larger his megalomania grows.

130

The so-called spiritual teacher who plays tricks on his disciples and practises deception on them, fools himself in the end and he stops his own progress.

131

When his meditations lead him to believe in his own great importance, he would do well to stop them. When his communications boastfully proclaim his own spiritual eminence, it would be better to dismiss his disciples and be content with obscurity.

132

Cult-leaders give themselves too much importance and their followers too deceptive a satisfaction.

133

They want to increase the ego's powers, disregarding the fact that if successful this must be paid for with inflated ego, thus obstructing the channel to the Overself still more.

134

Their spiritual light is no larger than the glimmer which shows under a door.

135

They expect to be worshipped by their followers as a tribal god is worshipped. The history of all such cults is full of misplaced devotion and misguided seeking.

136

Too much personal worship is not only bad for their followers but also for some spiritual guides themselves.

137

Those who pose as infallible mentors and perfect masters get the kind of gullible disciples suited to them.

6

DELUSIONS AND PAINFUL
AWAKENINGS

The illusion of perfection

It is common enough to find among seekers the illusion of perfection-ism. It shows itself in the belief that somewhere there exists a Master who is perfect in every respect: in his spiritual consciousness, his feelings, his intellect, his physical health, his appearance, and his behaviour. It shows itself also in their hopes of finding an ideal environment where they can live a fully spiritual existence, particularly in some ashram where everyone practises brotherly love and meditation all the time. Let them give up such vain dreams, for nowhere on earth will they find the one or the other.

2

The childish worship of every illumined man as if he were the World-Mind itself and the blind reception of his every utterance as if it were sacrosanct—these are defects to be regretted. And they occur not only among the Orientals, where it is to be expected, but also among the increasing number of those Occidentals who accept the doctrine of the Orientals and imitate their attitudes. They point to excessive attachment to the limited personality of their spiritual leader, so that it is disproportion-ate to the pure impersonal Spirit of which he is but the channel. They reveal the devotee to be on the religio-mystical level, to have advanced beyond popular religion but not to have travelled sufficiently far into mysticism proper to feel comfortable there. He has escaped from the crowd which is so taken in by the mere outward forms of religious obser-vance, but he cannot yet escape from the olden habit or need of depending on some outward thing or person. So, he transfers to his master's body the devotion he formerly gave to popular pieties.

3

The religio-mystical mind easily falls into cults or personality idealization and worship. The philosophic mind rises to a higher level and emphasizes the importance of Principles. For persons are ephemeral whereas principles are enduring. The cultists attribute to the worshipped one all sorts of godlike qualities, especially omniscience and omnipotence.

4

As soon as a cult is formed around a seer or prophet, fixed dogma and unalterable creed go with it. His revelation is turned into a final declaration, his inspiration into a fixed and finished tenet of faith.

5

Not only is no one perfect but also there is no one—be he husband, master, saint, or neighbour—about whom you may expect to find everything to your liking. When therefore we hear of a "Perfect Master" in Meher Baba, about whom everything was sadly imperfect, and find thousands of followers accepting him as such, including Western followers, we may understand why philosophy, not less than science, warns against credulity and gullibility.

6

It is hard to find an upright spiritual guide, easy to find his insincere imitator, easier still to find a crooked one. So long as they adoringly surround him with a halo of perpetual infallibility, so long will his disciples fail to think rationally or observe realistically.

7

If only they would give to the infinite being of God the faith they give to the finite and faulty being of some charlatan, how quickly they would progress!

8

Legends like this grow around the person of an Oriental recluse or ascetic faster than he himself knows. He could only slow the pace of this growth and not stop it even if he wanted to. And this while he is yet alive—how wildly will it progress after he is no longer alive to check it. How baseless the tales of miracles that will pass from mouth to mouth.

9

The cult of saint-worship is popular in the East both in religious and in mystical spheres. Its very foundation being a blasphemous misapprehension of the true relation between man and God no one need be surprised at learning that it teems with superstitions, abuses, and exploitations.

10

They fall into a new sectarianism when they make success solely dependent on a guru, and when they make their own guru the chosen and perfect one decreed for contemporary humanity.

11

The folly of refusing to recognize that his guru is certainly not as all-knowing as God, is a defect in this type of disciple. Nor can the guru himself stand exempt from censure if he allows the error to remain.

12

When all men are holy in the divine sight, why proclaim a few only and set them apart from others?

13

To become a disciple is to become an enthusiast, one who exaggerates, distorts, or overlooks the real facts. He will grossly misrepresent the true state of affairs because his guide is no longer reason but emotion.

14

Experience teaches us to be a little wary of those disciples who indiscriminately laud their teachers to the skies. A robust common sense is not usually accredited to mystics.

15

Just as they shamefully caricature the true Infinite Being by their personified and symbolized idea of It, so they shamefully falsify the true characteristics of a Master by their exaggerated and sentimentalized idea of him.

16

We must remember that a leader's name has acquired special meaning for his followers, that it is charged by their own minds, through the effect of suggestion, with a certain stimulus and exceptional symbolism. Hence they react to it favourably in a way in which non-followers do not.

17

They see and make no difference between the human instrument and God himself. Such exaggerated worship may be harmful both to the worshippers and to the man worshipped. It makes them too dependent on some one person, too ignorant or neglectful of the real source of his power. It may fill his head with grandiose notions and far-stretching ambitions. Simply because he *feels* that he is communing with God is not enough basis for him to claim, or for others to accept, that he is really doing so. The remedy for all this is to teach them the truth concerning such dependence as well as to show them how to establish their own direct contact with the source.

18

Idolizing followers are not concerned to know what is factual and what is imaginary: they need to have their bias satisfied.

19

It is idol worship, only they substitute a living idol for a stone figure.

20

Even the qualified teacher is no perfect man; he is fallible and mortal; indeed, he even makes mistakes. The attitude found in simple Occidentals or superstitious Orientals of regarding him as above all possible criticism, the attitude which elevates him to the status of a divine being, is ill-informed and ill-judged.

21

To set up these good and great men as being even better and greater than they are, and especially to deprive them of their humanity and replace it by some supernatural status, is to render a disservice to them as well as to truth.

22

All these gurus possess inevitable human limitations and some human deficiencies. To see any one of them under an appearance of perfection and make him into a demigod is a superstitious error which will not bring us nearer the world of truth and reality. He who is over-awed by the claims of these teachers suspends his reasoning faculty, dismisses his critical judgement, lets his intellectual integrity collapse, and falls victim at their feet.

23

To demand impossible perfection in any human being—spiritual master or wifely mate—is as silly as to make impossible idealizations.

24

The ideal master can be found only in the imagination of seekers who are either over-fanciful and unrealistic or else hypercritical and unable to understand that to be at all human is to be imperfect.

25

This guru is not a nonhuman or superhuman being. Take away the prestige, the ashram, the theatrical settings, and he is left a person, perhaps on a superior level but not infallible, still liable to make mistakes.

26

With a few exceptions, most Orientals consider the connection with an instructor rigidly necessary. But when it is made, he is turned into a deity and worshipped. Both learning and teaching may then get submerged in an emotional bath.

27

There are gurus who literally enjoy the atmosphere of devotion, exaggeration, and exploitation which surrounds them, as well as disciples who enjoy helping to make and sustain this atmosphere.

28

Just as the Renaissance brought forward brilliant minds and talents in scattered places, so we see today spiritual geniuses rising here and there. The followers of some lose their balance, get swollen with pride, and talk proudly that the avatar is here, each claiming his own leader as the avatar. Let us not be taken in by such sectarianism.

29

There is something blasphemous in placing human figures on a pedestal of the highest worship. Such worship should be reserved for the Infinite Intelligence alone. Nevertheless, as institutions of organized religion go, one may be much better conducted and far more to be recommended than most others. Undoubtedly, some conversation and companionship with a friend who attends such a superior type of place may be helpful to the seeker—if he can recognize and ignore the superstitious admixtures to be found in all religions and cults.

30

It is wiser to keep attention upon the teaching and not upon the teacher's personality.

31

The psychic structure of a person contains a light and a shadow side. It is naïve to see in him only one side, for that usually leads to an exaggerated view of it. A fantasy is then built around the person by those who fall into this error and they no longer meet, think of, or speak with a realistic person. There is also the other case where people build up fantasies about themselves even more than about others.

32

They make the mistake of affirming the divinity of man without taking the trouble to notice that this is still only in a potential state.

33

One common fault is to greet the latest master with adoring emotion, then to follow him with a strongly personal clinging attitude and to talk of him only in superlatives. In such an atmosphere the ego thrives unsuspected where it is supposed to be most absent!

34

The myth of superhumanity, even of divinity, created around the gurus will remain undeflated for their followers despite all the historical facts and psychological principles involved.

35

Though the transcendental power may be using him as a channel, he himself is still a very human human being. Only youthful, inexperienced, untravelled, or fanatical naïveté can so deceive itself as to think otherwise. The commonest error made by the guru-seekers or guru-greeters is to believe him to be perfect. The haze which surrounds their eyes prevents them from noting the flaws.

36

Most aspirants possess extremely hazy notions of the powers of a mystical adept. Many even possess quite fantastic or quite exaggerated notions about him, while few seem to realize that he has any limitations at all. This is not altogether their fault. It is largely the fault of irresponsible loose-thinking muddleheaded enthusiasts for mysticism, or incompetent half-baked exponents of it, or incorrect teaching about its goal. When an adept is supposed to have attained complete union with God Almighty, when there is supposed to be no difference between his mind or power and God's mind or power, where is the miracle we may not legitimately expect him to perform?

37

The merits are magnified out of all proportion, the drawbacks minified almost to nothing. Such is the way of enthusiastic believers with any system they adopt or any master they follow.

38

The prophet may be personally discredited, his prophecies may fail to be fulfilled, yet the blind faith of his adherents may still continue unshaken.

39

An ageing master, surrounded by a court of reverent admirers, an echoing group of disciples who behave as if they were in physical proximity to the Deity—this is the inevitable end.

40

After making all allowance for the awe and affection which, quite properly, well up in the guru's presence, it is still a fact that Oriental devotees are unduly laudatory of him.

41

None of these biographies written by overzealous disciples ever shows up the master's faults or even suggests that he had a single one.

42

The illusion that some human being has somewhere achieved perfection gives the naïve a curious kind of satisfaction.

43

The intense, unbalanced, and anti-human attitude which is so often favoured by the over-devout followers of these cults and which renders them ridiculous to the sight of sceptical outsiders, is one which will never be found among philosophers. This foolish attitude makes men morally indignant with their contemporaries, impatient, and highly charged with propagandist aggressiveness. Their wild assertions and exaggerated claims show what a startling lack of proportion exists in this attitude.

44

A famous case of the unfortunate results of excessive guru-worship was, of course, that of the Rasputin–Empress Alexandria relationship. It led in the end to loss of the throne and defeat in war.

45

These disciples assume so much, such as that the guru knows everything about them, what they should do in their particular and private situations—everything about everything.

46

They glamourize their guru, provide him with qualities and powers he does not possess and perhaps does not even claim.

47

The glamourous myth of infallibility surrounds such a person. Neither he nor his followers dare confess a blunder. Once having declared such a thing impossible, they have to cover any slur on the myth with supernatural whitewash.

48

Many people make the mistake of thinking that because someone has gone farther than they, he has gone to the end of the Way.

Superstition, imagination, and self-deception

49

Worse than failing to comprehend the truth is thinking that you comprehend it. It is harder to climb out of the pit of error than out of the pit of *illusion*.

50

Philosophy does not accept the literal inspiration of every page of scripture. It knows that human fallibility and human preferences may be present. Another important factor which broadens or narrows the nature of an individual's revelation is the breadth or narrowness of his general cultural experience.

51

A mystical interpretation may be shaped to fit almost any scriptural text. Twenty different interpretations may be shaped to fit one and the same text. For the same heightened imaginative faculty which operates during the dream state operates during certain mystical ones. That in the latter case it is conjoined with genuine revelatory insight does not alter the doubtful character of its own contribution.

52

It is pleasant to hear that so many mystics have communed with God, but if the word "God" means the ultimate principle of the universe then their words must usually represent wishful thinking rather than true statements of fact.

53

They accept such beliefs as are their own wish-fulfilments.

54

Mere chance happenings are made to hold deep esoteric significance.

55

Their pleasant belief that all cults teach substantially the same thing relates to the world of their private thoughts and wishes, not to our world. How can the results of totally different spiritual positions be other than different themselves?

56

One and the same psychical experience can be interpreted to support ten different religious tenets.

57

The occultist who sees esoteric mysteries wherever he looks, the mystic who reads allegorical meanings into every text—such a man is merely projecting his own mentality.

58

He has a peculiar capacity for self-deception, bringing himself to a point where he sincerely believes in the truth of false reasonings and egotistic promptings.

59

We must beware of those who are obsessed by fanatical delusions which walk endlessly round and round within the brain like a tiger in a cage.

60

Ignorant persons turn coincidence into miracle because they are unable and unfit to distinguish between reason and imagination.

61

It is easy for the superstitious to assign a supernatural origin to a perfectly prosaic event and see the work of a magician in a perfectly material circumstance.

62

There is a moronic credulity which too often passes for mystical faith.

63

The habit of seeing more in his words than what he says is likely to become delusional.

64

They become willing partners to their own self-deception because it flatters their vanity and panders to their conceit.

65

People throughout history have been able to think themselves into any belief or conclusion; have been able to deceive themselves into acceptance of whatever is offered them; have been susceptible to the most opposite, contradictory, and varied suggestions which the human mind can formulate.

66

Too many times he assumes that what he desires for himself must be the same as what God desires for him.

67

Charlatanic occultists and half-insane mystics take the great sayings as sanction for their misdeeds in the one case, and for their misleadings in the other.

68

It is right and necessary to seek inward guidance for each important step in life, but it is wrong and foolish to accept any and every inward impression as being divine guidance. What is taken to be the voice of the Lord can very easily be the voice of the ego.

69

They easily mistake their ego's doings for God's doings, their human ego's healing for divine healing, and their own ideas for imperishable truths. This happens, and can only happen, because they are so attached to themselves and so unable or unwilling to forsake themselves.

70

These texts and symbols, these memorials and characters, pyramids and bibles, can be construed to mean nearly anything or everything that pleases anyone's temperament or taste or to support any of the fanatical beliefs which thrive on human credulity. All such interpretations which are prejudged from the beginning are either of little worth or teach nothing at all. Whether ingenious or foolish they diminish the sum of human knowledge—the very opposite of their claim to enlarge it!

71

It is impossible for the fanatic to receive or give truth, for even in his most inspired moments he holds up a cracked mirror to truth's face.

72

Imagination can find support in any fact for what it wants to support. Faith can discover relations and connections between things, persons, events which are simply not there at all. Superstition can misinterpret statements and twist texts to mean what speaker and writer did not dream of.

73

Belief in the protective power of the Overself is valid only if it is really the Overself with which you establish a connection. Otherwise you fall into mere superstition or, worse, into the hands of lying evil spirits making false promises. In one or the other of these classes were the following instances, the first two occurring in our own century and the last two in the previous one. The Tibetan army believed that it had been made invulnerable against the howitzers of General Younghusband's British forces. Their spiritual guides, the lamas, were responsible for this pathetic error. The Moplah rebels in southwest India were told that the bullets of their Indian army would be averted by magic power. Chembrasseri Thangal, their leader, made this promise. The Boers, in South Africa, following Van Hansburg, were convinced by him that they were under special divine protection. Lastly, those Maoris of New Zealand who adopted the new religion of Hauhavism were fully persuaded by their prophet, Te Va, that the English troops would be defeated and that the Angel Gabriel would cause the English guns to have no effect.

74

They want these occult experiences so much that the smallest ones are greatly magnified, the most trivial happenings are greatly exaggerated. The results—wrong interpretations, mistaken deductions, and premature claims—are then inevitable.

75

Every piece of gibberish is not to be accepted as momentous revelation merely because it is the product of so-called mystical processes.

76

They are consoled by their imaginings, which, being completely divorced from realities, are shaped to please their egos.

77

Those who believe themselves to be in mystical communion with God do not usually admit that they may be mistaken.

78

Some of these facts of occult research and experience have no existence anywhere, no reality at all, outside of the occultist's own mind.

79

Too many have only an imaginary understanding of the truth, arising mostly from books they have read or lectures they have heard.

80

In the end almost all teaching, doctrine, and revelation is someone's interpretation, opinion, or imagination.

81

Men who delude themselves with false ideas may go on from there to impossible ideals.

Penalties of delusion

82

There are three well-defined stages in the master-disciple relationship. In the first one the master is enthusiastically loved and exaggeratedly appreciated. In the second there is revulsion of feeling against him; he is depreciated, criticized, and finally rejected. In the last stage the disciple either attaches himself to another master and repeats the entire situation or decides to walk alone without any master at all and take care of his own further development.

83

When they find that their paths do not lead to the expected results, dissatisfaction is sure to arise. This in turn will lead to some painful thinking, questioning and revision of views. They will eventually recognize their mistakes. In the effort to rectify them, they will start learning anew.

84

So long as fools allow themselves to be duped, so long is it spiritually necessary for them to be duped.

85

In brief, those who look for light where it is not, lose their labour.

86

Those who carry their faith too far and place it too foolishly must pay the penalty of their mistakes.

87

There will one day be a stupefying awakening from these superstitious dreams and these misplaced loyalties.

88

The enthusiasm, the zeal, and the fervour with which they give themselves to these cults are in many cases displaced in the end by disappointment, disillusion, and even cynicism.

89

Those who expect him to play God may get the foolishness and tyranny they deserve.

90

Those who revered him as the embodiment of spiritual sincerity may later shun him as the embodiment of spiritual quackery.

91

To idealize them and later, if one has judgement, discernment, and balance, to suffer disappointment, upsets rather than advances one's spiritual progress.

92

The failure of his predictions ought to open their eyes to the fallacy of his doctrines. But so weak-minded are many mystical believers that it fails to do so. What they will not learn from experience, what they could more easily have learned from reason, they will later have to learn from suffering.

93

Those who, in their green innocence or intellectual folly, accept such doctrines and follow their expounders will necessarily have to accept the tart fruits of their decisions.

94

The spell of black magic which such a sinister man casts over his pupils has to come to an inevitable end. Their awakening brings them to reactive mental depression and merited emotional misery.

95

Their romantic enthusiasms for false teachings and knavish masters can rarely be cooled down by forewarnings: they are usually brought to an end only by having to experience the bitter consequences of such misplaced faith.

96

They hanker after divine illumination but these lampless guides bring their feet upon the path of stony man-made enigmas.

97

I have seen criticism vaporize into discipleship as the years passed, and I have also seen other cases where discipleship has evaporated into criticism.

98

Those who attach themselves to an incompetent teacher usually pay the penalty in a double form, for they merely inflate his ego at their own expense.

99

They expect the master to support and even save them in many senses, and not only in a spiritual one. When they find that he cannot do so, they turn on him with a resentment as great as their former adulation.

100

It is a pathetic scene. They squat, sit, recline for minutes or years, serenely futile, living in their private world.

101

They are unwilling to surrender their occult dreams as their leaders are unwilling to surrender their pretensions. Both, then, must fall into the ditch.

102

Those foolish aspirants who are mulcted of their financial means by so-called masters deserve exactly what they get. In no other way can their stupidity be shown up to the outside world as a warning to others who would imitate them. For quite often they persist in stubbornly continuing their misplaced adherence despite their own bad experience and despite the good teaching of genuine master's books.

103

Those who succumb to the wiles of the cult-leaders sometimes get what they ask for, but sometimes deserve our commiseration.

104

By following such a false teacher he may become mentally disabled for years.

105

It is well known that some persons struggle for years along a quest that brings them in no way nearer to God but only nearer to mental chaos or emotional fanaticism. They are mostly to be found as members of organizations whose leaders are themselves imperfectly and incompletely developed.

106

The harm these gurus do is proportionate to the faith they arouse.

107

Experience shows that many seekers take up the position that they have been led by God to meet their "master" or "teaching" and that it is useless to reason or even expostulate with them. They *know*, and all one's longer years of wider experience count as nothing against their dangerous emotionality or conceited ignorance or misplaced stubbornness or open egotism. The dementia of the so-called master and the falsity of the supposedly inspired teaching will be able to reveal themselves only by the melancholy consequences of following them.

108

A sham mystic may deceive himself for a time and dupe his followers for a further time, but he will one day be found out and then turned out.

109

The mental world they have built up will prove a tower of Babel. They will come close to inner collapse.

110

The danger of this personal deification is that the person is expected to exhibit his perfections and when he exhibits his imperfections there is an emotional fall.

111

Those who fall for the bait of a quick and easy spiritual path get only what they have paid for—no more. I refer to the advertising methods some use. That which is bought cheaply is usually of according worth.

112

The frenetic evangelist, worked up to a state of unbalanced excitement, may incite his audience either to melodramatic holiness or to religious hysteria. They are so overwhelmed by their emotions—which in turn are prompted by hypnotic suggestion—that when the wave subsides later, they may repudiate what is now accepted.

The value of disillusionment

113

Everything is seen, on the contrary, through the spectacles of narrow intellectual preconception and biased emotional belief. They suffer from mental sleeping sickness, a dangerous lethargy from which they rarely awake; but when they do, it is only because the pain of repeated bitter disappointments and the ache of constant ugly disillusionments have become completely intolerable. A persistent capacity for throwing a romantic veil over ugly facts merely reveals an equivalent incapacity to review instructive events. In short, they lack the intelligence to recognize their errors and the courage to learn from them even when recognized.

114

It is not helping anyone's spiritual progress to let them go on living in a fantastic realm of supposed attainment. It is better to arouse them from their hallucinations, however painful to both teacher and student such an act may be.

115

He is seldom disillusioned, but merely shifts from one hallucination to another. If it be true that experience is the best teacher, he remains stubbornly untaught.

116

They dream of a perfect state or a perfect being. This is their start but not their end, which must needs be arrived at through progressive frustration and disappointment to finish in disillusionment.

117

The naïveté of many occult seekers is so evident, that only time, experience, and mental growth can supply what is lacking.

118

Both these conclusions are unpalatable to the purblind enthusiasts among such seekers and, therefore, when they subconsciously recognize the dilemma, they prefer to quell the revolt of reason and look the other way. They have neither the courage to be starkly realistic and descend from their clouds nor the capacity to be impartially reasonable and perceive aright what is happening beneath their noses.

119

Untaught by the disappointing consequences of many previous self-deceptions, they greet each new hope as though it were the absolutely certain one.

120

The self-deceived mystic may continue to nourish himself on delusions but, with time, the impact of facts becomes uncontradictable and inescapable.

121

Those who let themselves be taken from the true path by grand words or great promises or colossal claims show by that a certain mental incapacity, a lack of discrimination. This will have to be adjusted by their own efforts. But they will neither become aware of this need nor be willing to put forth such efforts until forced to do so by disappointment or by being awakened by calamity. Meanwhile they will live as dreamers, without respect for actualities and without being able to look at everyday happenings just as they are.

122

They take a long way to reach, in the end, a recognition which they ought to have reached in the first encounter.

123

If he were to put aside all this fancy and jargon, all this suggestion which others have put into his head, he would come back to sobering sanity with a bump. Alas, it is unlikely that this will happen while he is thoroughly mesmerized both from outside and from inside.

7

THE PATH OF INDIVIDUALITY

Dangers of dependence

We would all like to learn quick ways of achieving Nirvana; we would all like to realize the Overself overnight. Spiritual teachers are often asked for some magical formula whose use would turn man into Overman.

2

The less advanced an aspirant is, the more help he wants to receive from outside himself. That is why a beginner exaggerates the role of a master. The more advanced disciple seeks and finds more sustaining help inside himself.

3

The worst of this guru-chela relationship is that, by exploiting one another, both are prevented from having a free growth.

4

Those who have never grown up, who cannot cope with the problems of adult life, substitute the master for their mother and run, like children, to him for the solution of their problems or for the making of their decisions. If he yields to their importunity, he hinders their true development.

5

The idea of total submission to a guru is widely prevalent among Oriental seekers but does not appeal so much to Occidental ones. They fear demands may be made on them, because of their loss of autonomy, that would involve them in unpleasant sacrifices, deprivations, or renunciations.

6

There is a similarity in nature and results on a number of points between the dictator-worship which has appalled us in recent times and the guru-worship which still runs riot in ashrams. The attitude of these followers to their guru is psychologically fascistic. Such pitiful self-surrender will not promote a man's spiritual progress. On the contrary, it will only cheat him out of establishing conscious contact with his own higher self.

7

When they reach a stage where they are overwhelmed with joy at his praise and ready to commit suicide at his criticism, they are in an unhealthy condition.

8

In the earlier stages of growth such an attitude of servile submission or unthinking imitation may be both adequate and helpful. But in the middle and later stages it is a hindrance.

9

If the aspirant develops the habit of relying only upon this outside support and does nothing to develop his own self-sufficiency, he will become weaker and weaker instead of stronger and stronger.

10

At best they can become mere reproductions of the master—at worst, inferior imitations. For they have nothing else to do than make themselves passive and absorb all they can from him.

11

The disciples who turn themselves into copies of their guru do well for themselves up to a certain point. But after that their aping actually retards their growth.

12

They expect a guru to be not only a teacher, friend, moral supporter, and whatnot, but also a magician who can make things happen, by his mere wish, for their spiritual or material benefit.

13

Of what advantage to him is it to become a puppet on a string pulled by the master?

14

So many who look for, or have, a guru do so because they come with personal problems and expect him to enable them to handle these problems or even to handle them himself. This entirely misses the higher purpose of the quest.

15

What they expect and look for in a master is a kind of personal friendship exaggerated to such an extreme degree that he interests himself in every little detail of their personal lives.

16

In some cases this dependence is merely pathetic but in other cases it is actually desperate.

17

The relationship with the guru is made an excuse for want of effort in the disciple.

18

The disciple who tries to live in the image of his guru becomes a copy of him. This may be good or bad or a mixture of both but it is still only a copy.

Independence

19

The path is an individual not a corporate enterprise. You do not tread it by joining a mystical society any more than by joining an orthodox church.

20

Whoever seeks this intimate awareness of the Overself-presence does not need to seek anywhere outside his own heart and mind, does not really need to go to any distant land nor try to find some other person to become his "Master." Yet such is the power of suggestion that because he hears or reads that the one or the other is an essential prerequisite, he fills himself with unnecessary anxieties, frustrated yearning, or futile speculations as a result.

21

It is absolutely necessary for the person who has attained the highly sensitive and highly advanced state of mysticism to keep away from all Western cults and teachers because only with the completion of his training through the fuller initiation in the Ultimate Path will he become strong enough to have any contact with these movements without injuring himself.

22

He needs someone who can pilot him through these rocky unfamiliar seas. But if he can only find someone who misdirects him, he had better travel alone.

23

Any attempt to heal the breach between the various mystical societies is doomed to failure. They have degenerated into narrow and dogmatic religious sects. Seek rather to deal with ideas and not organizations, principles rather than persons. Here independence is praiseworthy.

24

We do not need to walk into new captivities.

25

But there are also elements of danger here. There is a path downwards into the abyss which is being trod by some leaders who have succumbed to greeds and lusts. They begin by exciting unsuspicious curiosity and end by obtaining foolish credence. They end by betraying their followers with unfulfilled predictions and unredeemed promises, and themselves with travelling at an ever-wider tangent from the path of assured peace. Better by far to walk alone than walk into such pitfalls and snares in the company of others.

26

As soon as the feeling of being tightly enclosed by a sect arises, it is time to put on one's shoes and take leave of it.

27

Let him avoid the spread-out nets of organized cults and hold on to the freedom to take his mind through the best thought of mankind and the deepest findings of seers and sages. Independent search has its difficulties but also its rewards.

28

The quest is a lonely enterprise. Those who join cults, groups, societies, ashrams, or sects in order to escape this loneliness do so only in appearance, not in reality.

29

To be herded together may be the only way out for those who lack capacity to find a measure of spirituality. But it is not the way for an independent mind.

30

The want of inner affinity may make it advisable, after a time, to be content with what one has learned from a teaching, a school, a sect, even a religion, and move on elsewhere.

31

Those who look for salvation on group lines, that is to say on mass-product lines, look for self-deception.

32

It is not by sedulously aping other questers that one follows the quest, not by conforming to a rigid pattern. Its requirements must change with each individual and even with his circumstances.

33

When a teaching is turned into a cult and congealed into a sect, it is time to get up and go away.

34

He can recognize the usefulness of an institution or an organization or a group without wishing to identify himself with it. For he knows at the same time that there is also a limitation in it which would stop the freedom of his search for truth.

35

The disciple who entrusts himself to a guru has, in Bacon's phrase, given a hostage to fortune.

36

If people only knew what they could do for themselves, they would not run hither and thither looking for vicarious salvation through another person.

37

It is unwise to make oneself join any group or society, or force discipleship with any teacher where no affinity is felt, however much others—relatives, friends, or acquaintances—try persuasion.

38

The hope that by joining sects or following leaders they can develop their own inner resources is a vain one. To go inwards they must stop going outwards.

39

Why should a man have to associate himself formally with any particular cult or organization if he wants truth? Why should he not follow his private and independent judgement, feeling, or interests?

40

It is completely unnecessary for aspirants to seek out each others' company or join together into groups or societies. This can do as much harm as good.

41

Those who feel tempted to do so may study the public cults and listen to the public teachers, but it would be imprudent to join any of the first or follow any of the second. It would be wiser to remain free and independent or they may be led astray from the philosophical path.

Be responsible

42

There is no substitute for personal effort, no gratuitous presentation of the divine consciousness by a master, no escape from the hard necessity of unfaltering practice of the exercises, no way of being absolved from the need of patience.

43

Since all things have come out of the primal Source, all that I really need can directly come out of it to me if I put myself in perfect harmony with the Source and stay therein. This is the truth behind the fallacy of these cults. For to put myself into such harmony, it is not enough to pronounce the words, or to hold the thought, or to visualize the things themselves. More than this must be done—no less a thing than all that labour of overcoming the ego which is comprised in the Quest. How many of the followers of the cults have even understood that, and all its implications in connection with their desires? How many of them have tried to overcome the ego? If they have not succeeded in understanding and complying with the divine law governing this matter, why should the divine power be at their beck and call to bring what they want? If they have not sought and largely attained that mastery of the animal propensities and that deep concentration in the centre of consciousness which the Quest seeks, is it not impertinent to expect to reach that power with their voice?(P)

44

In the end he has to be his own teacher. It is a comforting kind of escapism to imagine that someone else is going to save him, but this will happen only in his wishful imagination and excited emotion. Such a tremendous saving of effort would be welcome indeed but it would be contrary to Nature's law of growth. Those who are "saved" in return for their fervent faith are mostly victims of suggestion, whether it be their own or others'. Yet such dependence is an inevitable stage of their inner life at the religious level.

45

Given enough time or rather lifetimes, the master may lead him to peace and wisdom—but they can never be unearned gifts. They can come to him only through his own deserving. If people accept a spurious or a shoddy mysticism as the real thing, it can only be because they are not yet ready for it.

46

Because it can be turned into an escape, turning over responsibility for a decision to a group's leader is easier than accepting it oneself.

47

He was not put here to live on other men's spiritual experience but on his own.

48

Do not make any other man responsible for your happiness. He cannot really carry you even if he wanted. Assertions, claims, promises, made to the contrary by gurus or their disciples, are the fruit of imagination in the one or wishful thinking in the other.

49

The passive following of some leader in thought is not enough. The positive working on one's own character and consciousness, using the weight of one's own will, is also required.

50

The teacher who takes from a pupil the responsibility for his own spiritual growth, prevents that growth.

51

The responsibility must be placed where it belongs—on the aspirant himself, not on his guide whatever the latter claims.

52

He will not find true security by depending on another man for it—even if that man be his spiritual master. He must build it within himself, by himself, for himself. The genuine master can contribute toward this work but cannot perform it for him.

53

Even in the case of those who take the guidance of a guru, it should not be forgotten that if development advances sufficiently the pupil must start somewhere to be his own teacher, must start looking for, and finding, the inner guru—his own soul. A sincere *competent* guru would demand this.

54

When a certain famous yogi died, a number of his disciples fell into negative conditions for months or years. Some had nervous breakdowns, others became physically very sick, others suffered from melancholia. All these cases were observed only among resident disciples, living in ashrams, not distant ones.

55

The service of a guide is helpful to beginners to direct their way, to point out where it lies, and—if the guide is inspired, if the students are sufficiently receptive, if their personal karma is favourable, and if the World-Mind uses the guide for the purpose—to give them the important experience of a Glimpse. Beyond this the guide cannot go, despite all the gross exaggerations which surround this subject in most Oriental circles and which, if believed and followed, actually keep aspirants back from making real rather than fictitious advance. They themselves *must* do the travelling.

56

Too much dependence on another person—even if he be a guru—develops an inferiority complex, a feeling of unworthiness or of weakness.

57

It is a superstition to believe that salvation can be *given* by any other man, be he priest, guru, or whatever. The notion that it can be derived from some man's grace is a mirage.

58

Without labour, sacrifice, exertion, or training, but merely for the asking, the rare fruit of enlightenment is to fall into their mouths. How illogical and unreasonable is such a demand! How can any sound and lasting growth come in such a way?

59

The mere belief that anyone can hand over permanent salvation or freedom from the series of earthly re-embodiments is offensive to the sense of justice and fairness. Such a consciousness is not a material thing to be ladled out in charity like soup. It has to be worked for.

60

The labour of discovering and realizing the soul is something no other person can vicariously take over from you. You alone must do it because it is precisely through such labour that you can *grow* into soul-consciousness.

Use your judgement

61

Independence in spiritual seeking, a mind kept wide open for new and true ideas, discrimination between appearances and reality behind them— these are what will lead a man in the end to discover and know things for himself. Let him keep his common sense and keep outside all fantastic religious cults, with their hocus-pocus. Let him avoid the sheer lunacy which masquerades in certain circles as mysticism. There is nothing to be gained from the grotesque characters who form the membership of certain cults nor from the self-appointed Masters or Messiahs who lead them.

62

The student of comparative mysticism may examine the various doctrines without necessarily accepting them. His approach should be dispassionate, unbiased, and open-minded no less than discerning, cautious, and questioning. He should remember that they are not only sources of enlightenment but also of obfuscation. In this way he may pass intellectually through the region of fanatical superstitions and psychic delusions to the truth.

63

It is possible that the membership of such a cult or the following of such a teacher will still benefit him if he takes care not to make the mistake of asking more than the one or the other can give. That is, he should not ask for the truth which only perfectly equilibrated, fully developed philosophy can give. He should accept the fact that the sect has its limitations, the leader his errors. But if this safeguard is not taken, if he fails to resist the doubtful enthusiasm untempered by reality which will surround him, or the wild eccentricity into which weak persons are swept away, then the group or the guide may bog down his progress or even harm him.

64

It is unfortunate that the printed page democratically levels all alike; that it puts on terms of a flat plane of equality the vital convincing speech of a Jesus with the speech of a nonentity; that it invests a man or an idea with a dignity which in actuality they may not at all possess; that all words when set in type look more or less equally imposing and important, no matter by whose lips they are spoken or by whose hand they are written. Were we all gifted with profounder mental percipiency, the fool in philosopher's clothing would then be plainly revealed for what he is; the scratcher of Truth's surface would no longer be able to bawl successfully that he had solved the secrets of the universe; and even the brainless idiot who stumbles on a momentary ecstasy would not be able to assert to an admiring audience of devotees that he had become a Master. Then, too, we would be able to penetrate the disguises of some humble ones and raise them high up on the pedestals of respect which they deserve; we would bend the knee in reverence before the figures of those who really do possess truth but do not possess the gift for personal publicity, who know the Infinite reality but who know not how to turn it to finite profit.

65

It does not really matter that there are cults, creeds, and teachings stretching all the way in quality from the lowest and most primitive up through the mediocre and most orthodox to the theosophic and mystical. The limited range of human mentality and character puts limits on its spiritual satisfactions, demands, and expectations. What does matter is that anyone should confuse them, should regard the worst as the best, the commonplace as the inspired, the false as the true—that good judgement is so lacking that there is hardly any recognition of the best as the best.

66

Overcoming the ego does not consist of replacing one's own by some other man's. When we leave science (so far as it consists of recognizing or discovering facts, not putting forward theories) and enter the world of occult/mystic studies, we have to be wary of unproved assertions, of statements for which no reliable evidence is offered, of revelations which are compounded from inventions and imaginations as well as from inspirations.

67

The seeker should beware of cults masking their commercialistic motive under the guise of an earnest purpose.

68

When its assertions become mystical to the point of being quite mysterious and the reader can no longer follow it along these obscure paths of thought, it is time to be cautious.

69

All this does not render his message valueless. It is merely an indication that the recipient should not paralyse his critical faculties merely because the message does unquestionably spring from an inspired source.

70

Doubt is the spearhead of hope for believers deceived in their quest of spiritual life, as is discontent for those deceived in their quest of pupilship.

71

It would be a blunder to accept all mystically derived messages as divinely given and specially revealed. They may be wholly so but it is much more likely that they are only partially so, and even that they have no divine origin at all. It is wise and needful to examine them carefully, sympathetically if we wish, but critically thereafter. We should note where personal limitations have insidiously or blatantly crept in and where pure universality has let the divine stream flow clear.

72

The important thing is the kind of mentality which produces such ideas. Is it alive with goodwill, alight with wisdom? Or is it the opposite?

73

We should apply the test of reason to these revelations, however lofty their human sources, for we must recognize that no human mind is infallible. The failure to make this recognition, the refusal to see the contradictions between revelations, can only work to our own detriment in the search after truth.

74

The statements of prophets and reformers, teachers and exponents, who have shown themselves irresponsible in behaviour and unpoised in consciousness, cannot be trusted. Yet there may be some measure of truth behind the exaggeration or the fallacy.

75

Embrace what is sound and progressive in these systems while rejecting their absurdities, falsities, and tyrannies.

76

Psychical delusions and imaginary experiences borrowed from these cults should not be imposed on the true quest.

77

Selfish hypnotists pose as spiritual teachers. They usually attempt to suborn their pupil's intellect, in order to make him their obedient slave. When the latter is frightened to use his reasoning and critical faculties upon the claims made, he readily becomes a mere puppet in the hands of his mental "Master." Intellect is not to be abandoned, but to be rightly understood. Its doubts of the divine are to be cast aside; its scepticism of the Ineffable may be discarded; but its powers of reason and logic are not therefore to be destroyed at the unscrupulous bidding of some pseudo-sage.

78

To adapt certain selected ideas and practices to our own thought and use is wise, to adopt them wholesale is foolish.

79

Everybody makes a judgement, acts as a judge, even where he seems not to do so at all; merely by accepting an organization's view, or a religion's creed, he actually judges the organization or religion and the view. He may seem to depend on authority, to submit to the hierarchy of the organization or religion with its supposedly superior knowledge or power, but in actuality he unwittingly pronounces judgement in its favour. In the end, the responsibility for this decision is primarily his own.

An ancient Sanskrit work, The *Yoga Vasistha Ramayana* by Valmiki, pertinently says: "Judgement is the sole resource of seekers; they have no other way for their intellect to shun evil and attain good. The state of spiritual release which is boundless freedom is brought about by the help of judgement."

80

He makes choices whether or not to adhere to a certain moral code, belong to a particular organized group or institution, follow some spiritual guide or teaching. This is the fact, whatever he may assume, believe, or assert to escape personal responsibility.

81

Before he joins the crowd pressing down the road, he wants to inquire where they are going, and whether it is right or reasonable, and then to choose whether he wants to go their way at all.

82

The prudent seeker will not be swept off his feet by the impressive but theatrical appearance of a proclaimed master, nor stupefied by the grandiose claims, titles, organization, and theories which accompany the proclamation.

83

While they are trying to get rid of old faults, the very procedure they are using leads to the birth of new ones. The more they use this procedure, the more they unwittingly nurture these fresh evils. What good is it in the final balancing of accounts to be continually curing one disease at the cost of creating another? The harmful effects of the procedure are inherent in it and can be avoided only by using it with critical judgement, and not with blind partisanship.

84

Philosophic training protects him from falling into the nets spread by those who arrogate to themselves extravagant titles in order to play God. He will be in a position correctly to evaluate them and their procedures.

85

Not only novices but even others ask, in the agony of their disillusionment or the shock of their discovery, why, when they are so sincere, the higher power permits them to make these mistakes, why it lets them fall into the traps and pitfalls set along the way, why it does not save them from getting into the hands of deluded, unscrupulous, evil, or demented prophets.

86

Too many believe that because they have become interested in mysticism, they must join one of the minor or major cults which use it as a background. Too often their bubble of romantic delusions needs pricking. Life will have to be cruel to them so as to be kind in the ultimate purpose.

87

It is understandable that the earnest aspirant who is willing to consecrate his life to following the quest wherever it leads him, will give himself enthusiastically and obediently to the discipline of conduct and the personal re-arrangement demanded from him. But if these are strange, morally dubious, or ignorant fanaticisms, he has a right to question them and a need for caution concerning their sponsors.

88

To get behind the scenes of these small cults and to find out what their origin and history really is, may shatter as many idols as doing the same to the great old-established religions does. For the human ego's self-worship manifests in both, although in different degrees. The informed seeker need not be dismayed by his discoveries, for they will serve him well if they turn him away to final and firmer reliance on the Overself alone.

89

They need philosophy not only to lead them to truth but also to protect them from the fools and frauds, the hallucinated teachers and mercenary guides who infest the approaches to it.

90

The aspirant who is the frequent victim of his own or other people's false beliefs and suffers the consequences, would be foolish to abandon his search for truth. That would be an emotional reaction. He would do better to probe into the mental weaknesses which render him so liable to such deception, and to put himself on guard against them in the future.

91

A teaching cannot always be judged accurately by its effects on those who follow it. For some, by their own inferior character, give it a worse reputation than it deserves while others, by their superior character, exalt its apparent value beyond its own merits.

92

He could easily become half-cynical about what these groups and movements, institutions and organizations are doing but, as a good philosophic apprentice, he turns aside from them and from the negatives they arouse to collect and keep the positives he has uncovered, the verities, grand or exciting, that he has discovered.

93

Pretension to such wisdom and power is one thing but possession of them is another. Where enthusiasm is not counterweighted by discernment, this difference remains unseen.

94

We may bring to the pages of these mystical writers all our intellectual sympathy and general faith but we ought also bring to them some of our critical judgement.

95

The earnest but innocent aspirant should beware of teachings which are outwardly attractive but inwardly destructive, which are subtle forms of egoism or materialism disguised as spiritual paths.

96

To detect those who know Truth is hard; but it is even harder, among so many conflicting teachings, to detect the true one.

97

What is sane in these cults must be separated from what is not. The followers do not, and can not, do so. A fair evaluation can come only from outside.

98

The attitude towards cultism should be precisely the same as that towards all other religions with organized institutions. One may learn what they have to offer without joining them. It is needful to use one's critical judgement and try to see clearly their limitations, deficiencies, and weaknesses along with their truths and services.

99

A doctrine may be false even though it is given in good faith, even though the teachers believe it to be true.

100

Experience is the acid test which proves the real worth of a theory. If a teaching appeals to both the heart and mind, if it seems rational and feels right, then I am willing to adopt it tentatively. But when later I discover that the result of practical application of the teaching is negative and that the facts cannot be made to square with the claims, then I must unhesitatingly reject that teaching no matter how great be the repute of the man who has promulgated it, nor however holy he be regarded.

101

How many have felt their faith shaken, their mind worried, their intelligence puzzled by these contradictions between claim and result, between theory and practice? They may suppress their doubts for years, hide their fears in their most secret heart, but time will only increase rather than lessen their torment.

102

The moment must come, in the end, when the consequences of false belief show themselves in unavoidable form and must be faced.

103

It is a valuable practice to judge a theory by its everyday results, to measure its truth by its personal effects, and to test its correctness in one's own experience. Such a course, however, is valid only if accompanied by other and non-practical assessments.

104

It is questionable whether these masters have led more pupils astray than aright. But the final test is: Do these years of membership leave the aspirant where he was before he joined? Have they availed him nothing?

105

He projects all his hopes of a higher knowledge and experience upon such an inferior teaching and imagines that he has found the truth. It may be many years before the painful awakening happens.

106

The way to test such an argument is to push it out farther and farther until it reaches its ridiculous ultimate.

107

It is said, and believed, that time will sort out the charlatans from the true seers.

Be discriminating

108

It is easy to understand that it is not necessary to accept the gibberings of absurd quacks merely because one is willing to accept the revelations of true mystics. But it is not generally known that even these revelations need also to be screened by critical judgement.

109

The mystic has begun to feel the presence of the Mind within his mind but he has not begun to understand it. This is because the first is much easier than the second.

110

A "pure" intuition is a rarity in our experience because wishes and desires, fancies and fears interfere with it, maul it, and even kill it.

111

Philosophy fully admits and believes in the possibility of revelations, be they religious, mystical, or even psychical, but it points out that to the extent that the seer mixes in the picturizations of his own imaginative faculty or the ratiocinations of his own thinking process, to that extent what he receives or gives out is no longer a revelation. It is only an ordinary idea. Philosophy goes even farther than that and asserts that his human ego may interfere unconsciously with the very process whereby he becomes aware of the revelation. When that happens his awareness is tinged by inherited traits or by suggested beliefs or by personal wishes.

112

If the personality has been unevenly developed, if its forces have not been properly harmonized with each other and defects remain in thinking, feeling, and willing, then at the threshold of illumination these defects will become magnified and overstimulated by the upwelling soul power and lead to adverse psychical results.(P)

113

If, however, anyone were to believe that a genuine mystic experience is only a product of the mystic's own subconscious mind and conscious tendencies, and nothing more, he would be gravely mistaken.

114

The man who looks within his own consciousness may eventually find impeccable truth. But he may also find inane fantasy. Thus the mystical path has its attendant dangers.

115

The authentic inspirations of the Overself and the human illusions of the ego will often be mingled together in his mystical intuitions and experiences. Both factors being present, the result may confuse his mind if he is discriminating enough as well as exhilarated; sometimes it will misguide his mind if he is conceited enough. Only when the ego makes and keeps its fullest union with the Overself can he be sure of an unerringly true intuition or a perfectly transcendental experience.

116

Their interpretive world-views often reveal the limitations of their intellectual knowledge and general backgrounds—indeed are sometimes quite out of accord with indisputable historical or scientific fact. It is only when they describe such matters which have actually come within their own inward experience, such as the opening into the higher consciousness and the way thereto, that their accounts possess elements of permanent and universal value.

117

The revelations that come out of the purity of man's Overself contrast definitely with those that come out of the fancies of his ego. Clear and authentic are the tones of the first; but diffused are the vaporings of the second. In the one case the end is more light, in the other more fog.

118

The proportions vary widely with individual mystics. Some messages have enough inspiration and little adulteration, others have less of the one and more of the other.

119

When inquiring into the genuineness of the teachings of one who claims to have received direct guidance and revelation, a seeker must remember that subconscious complexes are very important in this connection. If he inquires into the background and associations of the seer or mystic he will doubtless find the seeds out of which many of the revelations have grown— with or without the seer's conscious assistance.

120

We are all too familiar with mystical revelations which lack substance, abound with old clichés, lose themselves in a woolly vagueness, and are even slightly sickly to the mental taste because of over-sentimental cloying sweetness.

121

This tendency to bring up from below the mystical experience elements which mingle intimately with those that come into it from above is innate in all disciples until they have passed through the purifying fire of philosophic discipline.

122

Messages very often contain genuine guidance plus some contribution from the personal ego. Naturally, when the ego attempts to enter the pure atmosphere of the Impersonal, the possibility of misinterpretation becomes far greater.

123

That visionaries often suffer from hallucinations is lamentably true, and I spend much of my time dodging such persons! It was an important part of my training in *philosophical* mysticism to study them, to understand how it is that these experiences arise and why, and then to develop all the necessary safeguards.

124

Few people are on so high a level that they are able to have both genuine mystical experiences and the right reflections arising out of them.

125

The mystic who has reached some point of truth in his consciousness, but not the farthest point, may easily fall into the fallacy of believing (and teaching) that the way whereby he came to it is the best way, probably the only way.

126

It is a picture of personal feelings and human opinions posing as impersonal truths and divine revelations. The consequences are worse than what they would otherwise be because the prophet is unable to believe that he could be so fallible.

127

What is not possible for the ego-expressing man becomes easy for the divine-expressing man. This shift, from the lesser consciousness to the greater, opens the gates of power. But it must be divine, or in the result the ego will merely become fatter.

128

A man's inner experience may reach far and yet be commingled with a character only partially purified. His mystical attainment may or may not confer a total transformation of his nature, a total subjugation of its lower part to the higher—that depends on Grace. This explains the moral weaknesses of some mystics who have given us great teachings. Only the very few who have taken the pains to undergo a thorough re-education of their whole being, and to bring it into proper equilibrium, involving its development and its discipline, are likely to receive the Grace which will make them morally faultless as well as scrupulous practitioners of their own preachment.

129

Most mystics communicate in their teaching or revelation a mixture of reality and fiction; the reality comes from the Overself, the fiction from their own limited mind. Few are able to reproduce the reality alone and to exclude the other.

CHRISTIAN SCIENCE, OTHER
SPIRITUAL MOVEMENTS

Virtues and faults

Christian Science is a useful anticipator of the fuller philosophic teaching.

2

Because we must refuse to follow the Christian Scientists all the way, because we must refuse to regard Christian Science as the one and only thing that matters—this is no excuse for not following them part of the way.

3

The essential difference between the Christian Science method and the one which has been explained here is that the former *asserts* that man is divine whereas the latter *asks* what man is and then awaits the answer. The first method may, and often does, easily fail by remaining a mental statement and not becoming a spiritual experience.

4

Mrs. Eddy, I regret to say, made these and other errors but it is not my purpose to evaluate either the merits or demerits of her cult. She had her part to play in the spiritual instruction of the Western world, and if she made serious mistakes, she nevertheless brought to birth a widespread movement which, as she says, has done much good. The system which she founded contains elements of the highest truth, and if her followers will only have the courage to remove the fetters which have been placed upon their independent thought, if they will not hesitate to utilize the powers of free inquiry which God has bestowed upon them, and if they will not shut their eyes but adopt an attitude of wider sympathy and less intolerance towards other systems, they may avoid the fate which overtakes most spiritual movements, when growing numbers kill the spirit and adhere to the letter. I have introduced Mary Baker Eddy's name into this book to render some small service of correction for the sake of her large following, if not for the benefit of the world at large. I cannot conceal a certain admiration for the dignified way in which Christian Science is doing its work in the world, much as I deplore its fanatical narrowness and intellectual mistakes. It contains truths which are sorely needed by ignorant humanity today.(P)

5

The New Thought or Christian Science claims, where correct, are true only of the adept, for he alone has fully aligned himself with the Spirit.(P)

6

With a little perception of the metaphysical truth in mentalism but a large application of it, the Christian Scientists have healed sickness and banished anxiety.

7

Theosophic misunderstanding of Indian wisdom is not surprising in view of the fact that the majority of Hindu Vedantins have misunderstood the tenets of their own doctrine.

8

Theosophy is often helpful in serving as a means of information to some seekers of spiritual truth. But it also contains elements which can lead them woefully astray.

9

Is life's purpose in us to add new experience to the old ones, as the Western theosophist thinks, or to shed all experience entirely, as the Eastern ascetic asserts?

10

The thought service of teachers like H.P. Blavatsky and Mary Baker Eddy was to help those people who were ready to move away from the materialistic view of Nature which prevailed in the nineteenth century, and which was created by the scientific activities of that century. Theosophy and Christian Science helped to arouse such people to question their materialistic beliefs and provided them with the necessary higher faith to which they could step across. These cults provoked new ideas and gave new points of view.

11

The defect in all this "New Thought" type of teaching is the arrogance and absurdity, the unpracticality and unreality incorporated along with its undeniable wisdom and usefulness. Its advocates, insofar as they defend and propagate this defect, are self-hypnotized and thus self-deluded, or have little experience of practical human affairs, or are carried away by intemperate enthusiasm into unbalance.

12

The historians of New Thought point to Emerson as their first prophet, but he himself would deny the honour. What he thought of George Muller's autobiography, an early book which is made much of by the movement, was indicative of what he would have thought of the movement as a whole had it existed then. It pulled piety into the shoe-closet and left it suffocating there, was his first criticism. It could not stand close cross-examination, was his second. It lacked philosophic depth, was his third. Nevertheless, he was fair enough to praise the piety which it did contain.

13

One of the disadvantages of Theosophy is that it invariably leads to a confusion of paths. The quest, on the other hand, being an individual rather than a group affair, offers an unobstructed view that is free from confusion.

14

My attitude toward Theosophy is certainly neither hostile nor prejudiced: while intensive and sympathetic study of its history, as well as long-range observance, makes its limitations and defects clearly obvious, I am nevertheless fully aware and appreciative of the valuable part it has played in human evolution.

15

We hope no one will misunderstand us to be supporting the enemies of Christian Science and taking sides against it when we state—without ill feeling and quite as a matter of scientific observation—certain facts. We are not here judging these facts but only stating them. These paragraphs are intended to explain, and not to justify, a point of view which we do not hold. It is an unreasonable point of view, but anyway it is an intelligent one. Although we do not accept it, at least we understand how and why others come to accept it. But we do not stand on the same platform with them. It is not that we are hostile to their attitudes. It is simply that we feel we cannot participate in them. Christian Science has its virtues and faults. It contains a number of needed truths, but it also contains a number of dangerous errors. Hence it cannot be accepted as it stands. Nevertheless we are always glad to give our blessing and not our opposition to a genuine spiritual movement. Therefore we give it to Christian Science.

16

During her lifetime, Mrs. Eddy became one of the spiritual illuminators of the Western world. Her work began on the American continent, yet the organization she founded has spread across Europe. In spite of the fierce light of publicity which beat down upon her, she remained an enigmatic figure to the end—partly because her followers permitted no whisper of criticism to disturb their placid regard, and partly because the scoffing world outside her church could obtain practically no access to her. The result was that her believers came to look upon her as a goddess who never erred, when in reality she was but a human being possessed of certain failings, yet one who also attained a mixed illumination.

17

Mrs. Eddy's fundamental contribution of importance was the teaching that the world is Mind, and thus she paved the way for the higher truth which is based on this doctrine and which has yet to be unfolded to the Western world. But it is a truth which is purely spiritual, that does not attempt to bribe people with material benefits to enter the Kingdom of Heaven—a thing which can't be done. That is why I criticized her doctrine in my book.

We are all working in our different ways—Christian Science people and myself—for the spiritualization of the world; but that need not cause one to confuse the issues. There are different grades of perception and consequently different grades of truth.

18

Studies in Christian Science and Unity will also have been useful in preparing you for the metaphysical studies.

19

Mary Baker Eddy must still receive the tribute and credit due to her for grasping anew and developing in a modern way these fundamental age-old truths, which are so important to the well-being of mankind. I say this although I am not a Christian Scientist in the narrow sense of being one who holds this faith and no other. Her system enshrines deep truth, but even in her own lifetime she altered her teaching from time to time.

20

Christian Science has taken up this great truth of mentalism. For this it must be praised and respected. But, in important ways, it has also misunderstood and misapplied it. Moreover, it is not enough simply to make the affirmation, "Divine Mind is the only reality." It is also necessary to adopt the practical course of self-discipline and mental re-education which will enable one to realize this truth.

21

The progress of Christian Science students and the success of the movement itself does, however, afford some encouragement, some hope that mentalism will not be entirely a voice in the wilderness but will also find a few receptive hearers.

22

Some cults come close to this truth when they assert that there is in reality but one true consciousness—the activity of divine Mind. We are in sympathy with much of their theory but less with their practice. For we admire their propaganda of mentalistic truth—obscurely understood though it be—but dislike their degradation to commercial methods.

23

It is regrettable to have to make strictures on the logical side, for Mrs. Eddy followed a trail of original thinking and deserves commendation on this account. Christian Science comes close to the philosophy expounded in my books at several points, and consequently I am interested in it and rejoice at its spread. Nevertheless, there are points where it flies off at a tangent, partly due to some confusion of thought on the part of its founder. Those critics who say that it is based principally on emotion and not on reasoning are not correct; rather, it is based on both, but, as I have said, its reasoning becomes faulty at times and its emotion attempts, not quite successfully, to mix the highest aspirations with self-centered human ones. In any case, it does not offer a complete answer to the questions "Who am I?" and "Why am I here on this earth?"

24

What is true in her message will endure; the rest will inevitably succumb under the severe testing of Time.

25

If the orthodox religionist seriously takes up Christian Science, this would be an excellent advance on the old standpoint. He ought, therefore, to be encouraged to travel in such a direction. Christian Science makes greatly exaggerated claims about its practical results and physical possibilities, but on the whole its metaphysical and religious aspects especially are to be approved for people of this mentality.

26

Although we have ventured to disagree with Christian Science on a number of points, we recognize the valuable truths it certainly contains. Our criticisms do not despoil its genuine merits, and there are many— enough to overbalance the account in its favour. Despite all difference of view, it is propagating the foundational doctrine of mentalism in the world of theory, as it is inculcating the casting out of negatives in the world of thinking.

27

The Christian Science doctrine is only partly true and its claim only partly tenable. This is because the human mind is only the part-maker of the world of its experience.

28

"Astronomy, optics, acoustics, and hydraulics are all at war with the testimony of the physical senses. This fact intimates that the laws of science are mental, not material," wrote Mary Baker Eddy. This shows her acceptance of Mentalism as the basis of her teaching.

29

The Christian Science Church achieved success not at all because it taught mentalism, which is too hard and too subtle for most to grasp, but for two reasons. First, it gave visible results in the healing of sick people. If some of the cases were quite trivial, others were spectacular. Second, it taught a practical method of not letting the ego's "mortal mind" manage its own affairs (since it is so faulty and so limited) but of turning them over or surrendering them to the Overself for management. This is similar to the Ramana Maharshi's story of a passenger in a railway carriage who was advised to put his parcel down from his shoulder and let the train carry it.

30

New Thought would be better titled Muddled Thought. It is an amazing amalgam of the divinest truths with the stupidest errors. People can often see the golden reef in it and then proceed towards the unwarrantable conclusion that it is ALL gold. It is not. A mixture of right and wrong has never yet produced all right, nor can it.

31

One may admire Rudolf Steiner without wanting to be grouped with his disciples and without agreeing with all he wrote!

32

The Shaker sect built very successful communities which mainly grew and preserved fruit, medicinal herbs, and garden seeds.

33

Mary Baker Eddy was an inspired woman, an illumined teacher. She had a great mission but she muddled it. And this faulty execution derived, as it often derives, from the interference of the lower ego, with its earthly desires, in both her inward receptivity and her outward activity.

34

If H.P. Blavatsky got some things wrong, it is pardonable in a work of vast dimensions. She got many new unfamiliar things amazingly right.

35

New Thought and kindred cults may, if *rightly* used, prepare and control, refine and thin out the ego. But this is only the first stage. After that comes the work of surrendering the ego. Few followers of these success and cheerfulness cults are taught this second stage, or would be willing to go on to it.

36

Those New Thought cults which make the seeking of health, wealth, and worldly happiness their real objective, and which do not hesitate to use the spiritual techniques of prayer, meditation, and affirmation to achieve this objective, are entitled to do so. But they are not entitled to practise the deception that their methods can achieve entry to and naturalization in the kingdom of heaven. For with all their lofty talk they still love the ego sufficiently to prevent this from happening.

37

The great error of all these worldly-happiness Spiritual teachings like New Thought, Unity, Christian Science, and especially Dr. Peale's "Power of Positive Thinking" is that they have no place for pain, sorrow, adversity, and misfortune in their idea of God's world. They are utterly ignorant of the tremendous truth, voiced by *every* great prophet, that by divine decree the human lot mixes good and bad fortune, health, events, situations, and conditions; that suffering has been incorporated into the scheme of things to prevent man from becoming fully satisfied with a sensual existence. They demand only the pleasant side of experience. If this demand were granted, they would be deprived of the chance to learn all those valuable and necessary lessons which the unpleasant side affords and thus deprived of the chance ever to attain a full knowledge of spiritual truth. It is the ego which is the real source of such a limited teaching. Its desire to indulge itself rather than surrender itself is at the bottom of the appeal which these cults have for their unwary followers. These cults keep the aspirant tied captive within his personal ego, limit him to its desires. Of course, the ego in this case is disguised under a mask of spirituality.(P)

38

The fallacies of Christian Science arise not only from its ignorance of the law of karma but also from its ignorance of the law of opposites. Every kind of experience in this space-time world is conditioned by its opposite kind. Thus light appears to us only because darkness also appears. We can call some things large only because we are able to call others small. We are accessible to joy only because we are also accessible to misery. We live only because we die. Consequently, in claiming the right and power of mankind to physical immortality, unbroken prosperity, and continuous good health, in wanting pleasure without the pain which it rests upon, Christian Science claims what is contrary to universal law; and when it believes it has succeeded in making a demonstration of truth, it has merely succeeded in making a demonstration of self-delusion.

39

The reformer who thinks that the kingdom of heaven will be inaugurated on earth when men will accept his pet idea or proposed change, does not understand the kingdom of heaven. Firstly, if it comes at all it will come individually, man by man. Secondly, it will come as a presence within one's own heart, as a state of being and not as a social organism.

40

With her faulty mental development, it was not surprising that Mrs. Eddy's version of mentalism was equally faulty—and not the same as philosophy's. In denying disease she perforce denied the body—a procedure which even philosophy dares not do. In making man God's idea but refusing to make the universe God's idea too, she showed her lamentable self-contradiction. In dismissing the world as illusion but failing to see that she ought to explain the origin of this illusion, her attempts to explain the origin of matter, sickness, evil, and error as beliefs of mortal mind, which was nothing, became pointless.

41

The greatest limitation of these cults, whether Christian Science or New Thought, is their refusal to admit any limitations at all. They would part the universe from God's control and put it under their own.

42

Those members of New Thought schools who take it upon themselves to instruct the Almighty as to how he is to arrange the future course of their lives do not, of course, understand either the temerity or the foolishness of their action.

43

New Thought at times degenerates into unconscious black magic. Mysticism itself even degenerates at times into necromantic spiritism.

44

Too many people use New Thought to deceive themselves, to evade their responsibilities, and to shirk their duties. This is because they think it promises them something for nothing, results without working for them.

45

The failure of cults like New Thought and Christian Science, which make so much of the power of thought, is that they make so little of the power of will.

46

Too many "New Thought" books contain little of verbal sense, and even less of the common kind.

47

The craving for Utopias of brotherly love and social sharing is common among the religiously or mystically inclined but not among the philosophically inclined. It can be nurtured only by those who refuse to believe the facts of human existence and who long to believe that their wishes are equivalent to these facts.

48

The term "universal brotherhood" is idealistic but vague, pleasant-sounding but windy. An attempt to form a society whose main object was to become the nucleus of a universal brotherhood was made by the Theosophists, and by less-known cults. Moreover, they added constant talk about "the service of humanity" to their other prattle. Not only did all such groups end in failure to actualize their ideal and in inability to influence the remainder of mankind, but most ended in bitter disputes, harsh quarrels, and internal fission. There are several different factors behind such failures. The two which concern us here are first, lack of any practical workable method to implement the ideal, and second, belief in the delusion that a group can do better what only an individual can do for himself. This is where philosophy shows its superiority. In reference to the first of these factors, it teaches us exactly what we can do with our bodies, our feelings, our thoughts, and our intuitions to bridge the wide gap between ideals and their actualization. In reference to the second factor, it proves that to practise individualism, self-reliance, is essential to real progress.

49

Rudolf Steiner's metaphysical ideas lack subtlety and depth, partly because his addiction to science—which deals after all with the *form* side of things—was so excessive as to disturb his natural balance, and partly because the kind of science in which he had steeped himself was that which may roughly be called "Victorian," and "mechanistic," and is now wholly outdated by the new science of today which is so much less materialist. The "impasse" between science and religion, the blank wall terminating scientific materialism of which Steiner made so much and to which he addressed so many pages, is hardly a serious issue today. After all, three-quarters of a century have passed since it really was one. Rudolf Steiner was too much a creature of his own period to be considered our contemporary today; his work is too dated. His agricultural ideas, however, are excellent and are now being taken up with great benefit by farmers.

50

When World-Mind withdraws the entire cosmos into itself and there is literally nothing at all, it only then fulfils the Christian Science teaching of having no existence whatsoever.

51

A sister cult is that which teaches them to surrender to the higher divine power that rules the world, saying that the more they surrender the more prosperous they will become. This is a misunderstanding of the wiser notion that surrender can only be actual and justified *after* they have done everything humanly possible to get what they need and that they are here to *strive* for it, thereafter leaving ultimate results to destiny.

In an age when economic troubles are widespread, we need not be surprised at the prevalence of another type of cult, more particularly in the Occident, which believes that merely by thinking frequently in meditation of desired possessions, the latter will fall somehow into one's life.

52

There are misguided Christian Scientists who believe that the existence of poverty is an outward sign of inner failure, of inability to comprehend and apply the spiritual purport of life!

53

Another defect of its technique is that it makes attainment too cheap and too easy. The notion that anyone can attain the Real without paying the requisite price, and especially without a purification and ennoblement of character, is a deceptive one. It is a bubble that not a few mystics harbour, but it will be pricked in the end.

54

A proper argument possesses steps and must move by logical jumps. But here Christian Science's first facts do not justify its last conclusions.

55

It is as easy for Christian Science to dismiss sin, sickness, and death as unreal and erroneous as it is for Vedanta to dismiss not only them, but also their contraries, as non-existent. But the thinking mind of man will still continue to ask these cults, "How did the human race even begin to hold, and to hold so firmly, such unreal, erroneous, and non-existent ideas?" There will come no answer, for in both these dogmatic theologies there is no answer.

56

The evasion of a problem is not the solution of it. This is a truth beyond the mind of the mystic who is unable to reconcile life in the soul with life in the world and flees from the one to seek the other.

57

Why deny, for the sake of wishful thinking or to satisfy a speculative theory, facts which we find in nature? Such are the denials of Christian Science. Thinking can make such concessions to human weakness and such violations of its own integrity only at the cost of failing to arrive at Truth.

58

Those cults which remove suffering from their conception of human life and believe that the latter could and should consist solely of health, wealth, success, and joy are the fruits partly of wishful thinking and partly of misapplied intuition. They ascribe to Deity what are merely the desires of humanity. They accept what they wish to be true, and reject what is unpleasant if true.

59

The fallacy of Christian Science on its practical side is its overestimation of the powers of man. It turns him into a veritable god.

60

However much the Christian Scientist may deny the world, or the Eastern/Western ascetic reject it, the world is still there, with its experiences and conditionings. He must still live with it. Is it not better to accept it but to transform its meaning in his own mind?

61

The fallacious self-deification of New Thought, this human audacity "thrusting insolently beyond what our nature warrants," as Plotinus called it, is not new; Plotinus had to ridicule its folly at Rome in the third century with the scathing sentence: "Imbeciles are to be found who accept this teaching as soon as they have heard it uttered!"

62

A problem is not solved, a disease not spirited away by denying that it exists.

63

Their total optimism is immune to the shocks and disturbances, the thrusts and disappointments of experience. It sees only what it wants to see: not the world in which it actually has to live, but the one in which it would like to live. The lessons of suffering are not assimilated; each adverse experience leaves them exactly where it found them.

64

When life's situations prove too hard for them to bear or deal with or adjust to, or when a battle occurring within themselves finally ends in defeat, such a simple faith-doctrine sets them free from the need of doing. But does it really? Or does it only give them the illusion of being set free?

65

Nothing could be more certain than the fact that not a single person in historic times has conquered death, that not a single irrefutable record exists of that tremendous event. Yet, in the nineteenth century, when science established its world-wide celebrity and dominance, a woman arose in America and established a religion which spread rapidly and asserted that it had found the way to eliminate death! The founder herself died, and not one of her followers has yet succeeded. In spite of such grandiose failure, this woman-prophet also propounded a second astonishing tenet, which is remarkably true, that of mentalism. And this despite the fact that she used the only basis she was capable of using—a religio-metaphysic one alone rather than what would be called a strictly scientific one.

66

A justifiable criticism of de Waters' teachings which mix Advaita with Christian Science is that they represent a magnificent but a one-sided and hence unbalanced position; consequently her brilliant conclusions can never be the perfect impeccable truth. They are necessary to offset the other form of unbalance which arises from the step-by-step self-improvement school. But the latter's teachings are just as necessary to offset her own. Philosophy, by accepting both the immediate and the ultimate, by keeping them always together to compensate and balance each other, alone offers an adequate and faultless teaching.

67

Whatever defects exist in Christian Science exist partly because of the confusion which existed in the mind of its founder, partly because she was fond of using impressive words even though she often did not know their meaning, partly because she habitually used the appearance of scientific thinking without being able to attain the reality. Mystics have often used announcement for argument, fantasy for fact, and they have the right to do so. But they do not have the right to label their pseudo-science as science.

68

Margot Asquilth once wittily observed that if the practice of Christian Science is pushed to a logical conclusion, you could jump off a roof without being hurt!

69

To drug the mind with the idea that pain, poverty, suffering, and sickness do not exist because, finding them unpleasant, we do not want them to exist, is not a heroic act nor even so spiritual as it seems. Behind it lies physical fear and prompting it is personal desire.

70

The foolish cult which denies the existence of disease and then gives "treatments" to cure it is caught in confusion.

71

It is pitiful to witness these naïve persons rise from their prayers or affirmations in the belief that what they want is already theirs, that their particular desires are already accomplished.

72

The idea that anybody can get what he wants simply by thinking of it is an exciting one. Who would not like it to be true? But observation of results shows that although not wholly false, the truth in it is greatly exaggerated.

73

The danger of New Thought–Christian Science affirmations about our divine power and of Vedantic meditations on our identity with God is that they may merely swell the ego with spiritual arrogance and grandiose babble. And because humility is both the first step and the inescapable price demanded of us, such exercises may remove us farther from, and not bring us nearer to, the Quest's goal.

74

The differences in character and tendencies and values among people make for natural class divisions. No amount of Vedantic tall talk will produce a real equality among people, nor even a fundamental sameness. Each class, each of Nature's groupings and gradings has its limitations. They do not vanish merely by asserting inner oneness. How can we love our neighbour when he differs from us in so many ways? Vedanta would be closer to fact if it shifted the emphasis to unity with our higher being rather than with our neighbour. It fosters illusions about a non-existent brotherhood of man. Its disciples swim in vague idealistic abstractions which they are forced to betray in actual living. If "babble" Vedanta shows itself in the end as impracticable, this is only because it applies itself in the wrong direction. That end is theory and words.

75

A system of assertion is not the same as a science of observation. When Christian Science ceases to deny facts or avoid realities, it will have the chance to become a science in the true sense of that term.

The hidden materialism

76

Some of these visionaries, strangely enough, deal in the art of attracting earthly things. A good deal of New Thought and Christian Science is like the ostrich. It buries it head in the sand, holding the thought of prosperity the while, and refuses to see the slum in which God compels it to live. It becomes excited to the point of purple ecstasy with its vision of riches yet to come. But alas! When that vision fades down the years through the hard refusal of facts to accommodate themselves to our theories, bewilderment comes like a blasting wind, yet brings an aftermath of enlightenment to those who have been forced to think.

It seems to me that the average New Thoughtist wants to deal himself *all* the aces of life, leaving the poorer sort of cards for the lesser and unfortunate mortals.

77

The truth in these New Thought and Christian Science doctrines can be known only by clipping and correcting the extravagances from which they suffer. The largest one is the belief the the body's health and the bank's balance must always and necessarily increase and improve to the extent that one's spirituality increases and improves. What really happens is that one is brought into increased and improved awareness of the higher self's leading, love, and protective care. It leads one toward those acts and decisions or into those situations and events which best promote the purpose of one's existence. It exists for the ordinary unenlightened man too and would do the same to him, but, not being on the Quest, he unwittingly frustrates its guidance and thwarts its moves. As for the material help it gives the Quester, this is a fact, for, as Jesus mentioned, "The Father knoweth that you have need of these things." But what the Father understands as one's need is viewed in the light of life's true purpose, whereas what the unenlightened man understands is dictated by the ego's desires. The New Thought teachings fail to make this distinction.

78

How distant are these votaries of New Thought from the real goal may be judged by the fact that not until they are as aware of the Overself as clearly and positively as they are aware of any object experienced by the senses, and not until this awareness is as firmly and as lastingly established as is their own personal identity, can they be rightly said to have found God.

79

They turn to New Thought as they turn to fortune telling—in the hope that it will promise them that their life will not always be as frustrated or as miserable as it is now.

80

"New Thought" is not philosophical thought. The difference between the "Dollars want me" attitude and the "My future is with the Overself" attitude is the difference between the retention and the surrender of the ego.

81

Joel Goldsmith's assertion that "God is supply" is true enough, but to leave it stated as simply as that is likely to mislead its believers. For "God is also lack." He takes away as well as gives, according to each person's particular karma and higher needs.

82

It is quite likely that satisfying results were gained directly or through the services of a professional practitioner. But it is just as likely that a day will come when these results cease to appear, when improvement in health or worldly conditions will obstinately elude him. This very failure is a sign of help given, albeit it is help up to a higher level of understanding and a purer concept of truth.

83

It is materialism wearing the cloak of spirituality, worldly desire pretending to be ethereal aspiration. But whether it is open or hidden, we need not wonder that it attracts many followers.

84

(a) Those who want to "demonstrate" material well-being by following the methods taught in such cults, under the belief that they are demonstrating, at the same time, a godly power, need to correct their notions and re-study their religious history.

(b) They will then learn that the men and women whose attainment of true spirituality is unquestionable seldom paraded much wealth and often lived in humble circumstances. It does not need more than a cursory study of the world around to show that the temptations of prosperity have obstructed the way to inner freedom much more than have the tribulations of poverty.

(c) It is not the demonstration of material gain but the demonstration of spiritual detachment from such gain that is true progress. Yet to avoid misunderstanding, it must be firmly stated that the Quest asks no one to embrace either poverty or prosperity but only truth.

85

"Seek ye first the Kingdom of Heaven and all these things shall be added unto you," was the uncompromising injunction of Christ. Whoever has the courage to test the soundness of this counsel will discover its truth. But many people, like the Christian Scientists, make the mistake of trying to exploit the Kingdom for the sole purpose of financial rewards and physical health. In other words, they do not seek first things first, and therefore do not attain them. They may reach an intellectual understanding of spiritual purpose, but this is in no way the same as living realization. Yet, this said, it is good to remember also that the distortions and perversions and confusions which have accreted around this great teaching cannot engulf its pristine spiritual greatness.

86

Krishna in the *Bhagavad Gita* says: "He who is happy in poverty and free from things of earthly desire—him I call a rishee, an illuminated one." Contrast this to the rejection of poverty by American mysticism, whose "illuminates" would be unhappy in it and who regard it as a sign of not yet having reached illumination.

87

Dr. Walter Siegmeister: "I worked for twenty-six years to establish nonprofit, humanitarian, idealistic colonies in Central and South America for U.S.A. vegetarians and spiritual seekers. In Panama I found that at a co-operative undertaking there was a general grab for money and land, or fighting about how the money was to be used. I found that humanity today is unfit psychologically for any co-operative undertaking. Consequently today I consistently refuse such involvements, which lead only to trouble, or to form any form of organization."

88

They are merely materialists, these New Thought demonstrators, who have penetrated into the camp of the idealists and stolen some of their baggage and then quickly retreated to a safer spot. They want material things first and divine life last. God is merely a convenience for them to use in order to get the former.

89

On the religious and religio-mystical levels it is necessary to keep in the foreground the Prophet's name and to demand unlimited faith in what he says. Theosophy started with a universal outlook but degenerated with time into a sect, because Theosophists made the mistake of basing their doctrines on the say-so of certain persons.

90

These Yankee cultists fondly believe that they have but to "switch on" the divine wireless and they will immediately hear that mental voice of God which has eluded the cleverest philosophers down through the centuries. Their teachers are worse, for they spend so much of their time teaching others how to become perfect that they fail to find time to perform this admirable operation for themselves. As a rule God's voice usually flatters their personal importance and puffs up their vanity, if he does not straightaway charge them with the mission of saving all mankind.

91

This, incidentally, is not the same thing as the "demonstration" claimed by Christian Science and kindred cults. The latter make the mistake of attempting to measure inward spiritual attainment by outward material gain, an absurd and materialistic notion and one which could never have taken hold had these cults truly understood the message of Jesus. They claim that fortune can be amply supplied through the services of the Divine Mind, as though Providence took a special interest in our private purse. They wish to effect an unholy conjuncture of God and Mammon, wish to widen the narrow way. It cannot be done. They are really worshipping money, not spirit and truth. They are entitled to do this but they ought not to deceive themselves in the matter.

92

Christian Science offers material benefits as a bait to induce men to seek for the Kingdom of Heaven. But Jesus himself is authority for the statement that the Kingdom must be sought for its own sake, or it will not be found. And all history shows that those who have succeeded in finding it were individuals who had, through wide experience or deep insight, abandoned earthly desires. For them the Christian Science bait would have been the very opposite—a bar!

93

It is hard to give up the attractive theory of abounding health and abundant wealth coming to him in reward for his belief in it. But if he is to grow spiritually he will have to take this difficult step, however slowly and reluctantly. There is no escape from it.

94

Buddha was a mendicant. Jesus was penniless. But Mrs. Eddy was a millionaire. The early Christians renounced the world and embraced asceticism, but the Christian Scientists seek prosperity and comfort. They are entitled to do this. But are they entitled to assert that their system is primitive Christianity restored?

9

INSPIRATION AND CONFUSION

Conflicting tenets, contradictory "revelations"

Why are there so many different revelations, so many rival sects? There are at least two main causes of this situation. The first, that the divine care blesses all people and not only a single one, flatters the revelator. The second, that the general terms of the message may be true but its particular terms may be false, discredits him.

2

Mystical doctrines have taken different forms with the consequence that some mystical writings may criticize or even contradict others. This situation is familiar enough in purely intellectual circles and to some extent in religious circles, but is less to be expected where direct communion and even union with the Supreme Truth and Reality are claimed. Access to a sufficient number of sources in five continents and a sufficient number of historical periods will uncover that this is an existent situation. One is not writing here of the charlatans, the self-aggrandizers, the mentally disturbed, and others whose claims are false, but of those who are sincere and mostly well regarded.

3

Whether the mystical experience represents a revival of ideas previously acquired or a genuine penetration into a spiritual world is not to be answered by a brief yes or no, for it does in fact involve both these elements. This is of course why so many mystics' reports frequently contradict each other. The visions they see and the intuitions they acquire contain forms or thoughts which have previously been put into their minds by teachers, traditions, environment, or reading. The intellect contributes a personal element whereas the deeper level of mind contributes that which is common to all these experiences. If it were possible for a mystic to free himself of all pre-possessions, both conscious and subconscious, he might gain the pure experience of this deeper level wherein neither intellect nor emotion would interfere. The philosophic discipline seeks to achieve this.

4

All the conflicting tenets of religion, all the contradictory revelations of mysticism point plainly to the fact that delusion must somewhere have got mixed up with inspiration, that the ego has sometimes simulated the voice of the Overself.

5

If the different revelations made by mystics do not agree on several points, here is a warning that first, although a mystic may honestly describe what is revealed to him, this is no guarantee of its perfect truth, no safeguard against its being partly mistaken or even wholly biased, and second, the spiritual authority of no man should be so exaggerated as to deify his statements.

6

Does this mystical phenomenon really defy rational analysis? This is what most mystics assert, but we do not agree.

7

It is quite commonly assumed that the mystic's experience, the prophet's revelation, must be accepted altogether or not at all, since they transcend the need of interpretation.

8

There is no unanimity among the leading mystics on all points. Their revelations should be received with sympathetic yet critical judgement.

9

India's sacred scripture, the *Bhagavad Gita*, sets the scene of its teaching on the battlefield of Kurukshetra. India's two most renowned modern yogis differ completely in their understanding of the scene. Sri Aurobindo took it literally and historically; Mahatma Gandhi took it allegorically and spiritually. The question arises: why do such opposing interpretations exist for two minds which have touched the same high level of illumination? Philosophy alone supplies a fully rational and satisfactory answer.

10

No informed student of comparative mysticism dare deny that mystics contradict each other. Swami Ramdas, in India, makes joy both an evidence of spiritual fulfilment and an ingredient of spiritual practice. Simone Weil, in Europe, takes an exactly opposite stand and substitutes unhappiness and suffering for joy. What has happened here is that each has laid down a merely personal experience for a broadly universal truth. This is an error into which teachers and followers have fallen.

11

The need of unwrapping particular theological clothes from mystical experience becomes clear when we note that Saint Teresa, brought up in the Roman Church, fit her trance revelations neatly into the Catholic dogmas, whereas a modern Christian mystic, Holden Edward Sampson, brought up in the Protestant Evangelical Church, was led by similar trance experience to regard those dogmas as false.

12

In historical religion and mystical revelation there is often a mingling of truth and myth. A frank admission of this fact can save us from pondering uselessly and deceptively over problems of interpretation.

13

Test all principles and doctrines by nothing lower than universal standards.

14

If he is a genuine see-er and know-er, and something in me or in him testifies to the fact, some inner voice or supernatural faculty, then I gladly welcome and acknowledge his superior status. But here is where the inexperienced or naïve, the fanatic or youthful follower, joiner, or partisan mixes his planes of reference and gets sidetracked. He forgets that the Great Soul is encased in a human mind and an animal body, that the way he lives, speaks, eats, dresses, and conducts himself belongs to this persona he has inherited or formed or received from outside, from others, from family and society, from the geographical, historical, and genetic circumstances of his birth.

15

When will the Christian saint, the Muhammedan Sufi, and the Hindu yogi comprehend that if and when they reach a height of inspiration, what comes through is not different in any of the three experiences? Difference begins with their own personal interpretation or interference.

16

Why is it that there are such differences in the teachings of the seers and mystics? The answer is partly—and only partly—that in each case the human response to the superhuman visitation forms, shapes, or colours the communication or the interpretation of it.

17

Because a man has had some kind of inner revelation it does not follow that everything in life and the universe has become plain to him and that he has become a kind of human encyclopaedia.

18

When men claim to be God's mouthpiece they claim nonsense. If they rise to their best level they see more clearly and sharply than their fellows in the dazzling Light of that level. But they still see as *human* beings and, in the moment that they try to formulate in thoughts for themselves or in speech for others what they now understand, they are subject to human colouring or error.

19

Visions and messages that confirm or mirror the beliefs of a particular sect may have little value. Suggestion, working on the imagination, may help to produce them, or the disciple may unconsciously wish to oblige his guru, his co-disciples, or his own expectations. They are always to be regarded with caution. In the atmosphere of their own circles, sectarian bias may prevent proper understanding of the need to discriminate between the real and the imaginary in them.

20

What men communicate to others is not the Real which they actually touch, however authentically, but their human reaction to it. This is one reason why the religious world is divided, why religious and mystic revelations are contradictory, why truth-seekers get confused and bewildered, why they move on from one sect to another.

21

It is a pity that the Hindu holy men I met did not know that the Mormons reserve their highest post-mortem heaven for the white race, else their merry laughter would have rung out so loud and so long that its echoes would have reached and mocked the fortunate inhabitants of the heaven itself. The fact that this revelation was based on mystic revelation might, however, have instructed some of them. And the Mormons themselves might find it instructive to note that in a two-thousand-year-old Jewish revelation, the angels in the same heaven are circumcised!

22

Saint Bernard's mystical advancement and enlightenment did not stop him preaching the Crusades or denouncing Islam, although the latter faith has its mystical core, too—in Sufism—with as much holiness and spirituality as Saint Bernard ever found.

23

That these differences of view exist even among illumined mystics is a striking but rarely studied fact. Why did Ramana Maharshi poke gentle fun at Aurobindo's doctrine of spiritual planes? Why did Simone Weil uphold the lofty spirituality of Greek culture whereas René Guénon deprecated and even denied it?

24

His interpretation of the experience cannot help but be personal, cannot help but express the sort of man he is. This is how misunderstandings and contradictions arise in the world of mystical teachings.

25

When we are warned not to inquire into the how and why of a revelation, not to question its intellectual and psychological basis, it is time to look elsewhere.

26

Rudolf Steiner asserted that H.P. Blavatsky was "unable to arrive at fair conclusions because of a certain antipathy to Christ." Annie Besant said that Steiner was similarly prejudiced because of his bias in favour of Christ! All this should act as a red warning signal to the followers of both Steiner and Blavatsky to do some independent thinking, if they can.

27

The truth found by transcendental revelation is not different in America from what it is in India; it is the same in both countries, and in England too. What is different is men's capacity to receive it and their tendency to falsify it.

28

It is something to be noted by the student of comparative religion and comparative mysticism that each faith and each minor sectarian movement sets up its own leader as the supreme personality among holy men, the universal teacher of all mankind. Consequently, he is most often put forward as the last World Teacher, for after him there will come no more—unless, of course, he himself returns as a Messiah. Such claims should be instructive to the student as displaying the egotistic psychological attitude of the claimants and betraying their spiritual limitation. Thus it is a mistake to believe that because the prophet-founders of religion were divinely inspired, they were therefore equally inspired. The divine reality expresses itself through various channels. The prophet who regards himself as the only one to whom divine revelation has come has already lost it. The sect which believes that only to itself has God spoken has never really heard Him. All these inexplicable miracle stories which gather around the life of every renowned saint must not be swallowed uncritically. In the Orient, the simple common people, the devout and the mystical, have usually failed to distinguish legend from history, observation from imagination. Let us not believe that by encouraging superstition we encourage spirituality. We must discard the one in order to find the other. We must differentiate between the noble disinterested efforts of the prophet and the ecclesiastical systems men set up in his name after he has passed away.

29

The belief that a mystic can manage certain kinds of affairs with faultless wisdom, solely by the light of his mystical intuition, depends for its truth upon the purity and quality of his intuition. But it does not mean that he can manage *all* kinds—engineering and technical affairs, for instance.

30

It is pathetic for the philosophically minded, and especially for the inheritors of the formerly close-guarded hidden teaching, to observe how followers of a mystical or religious guide take all his words without exception quite literally and all his revelations as incontestable truth. When Sri Ramakrishna said that a man must die within twenty-one days of achieving illumination, he said what other mystics are likely to contradict rather than confirm. And when he asserted that hardly one man in a century attains the goal through following the philosophic path, there is no support from the traditions of the hidden teaching for his assertion. All this is written despite my most respectful admiration and warm reverence for Ramakrishna and despite my unhesitating belief that he was a man of genuine spiritual self-realization. I do not select his statements for criticism deliberately but only because they are the first ones which happen to come to mind. There are several other mystics, whom I and most of us honour, whose sayings could equally have been drawn upon as containing examples of this kind of contestable teaching.

31

The longer I live the more I see that there is so much contradiction in the findings of great seers, mystics, occultists, saints, and prophets, that a substantial part of their higher revelations must ultimately consist solely of their merely human opinions. The corollary of this is that the only true opinion is to hold no opinion!

32

There are striking resemblances in the writings of mystics scattered through the different nations but there are also striking divergences. A just appraisal notes both facts. The reason is simple. Divine inspiration explains the first, human opinion the second.

33

Because a mystic is sincere and good, the deliverances of his meditation or trance are not, therefore, guaranteed infallible.

34

In one and the same day I was asked to comment upon two utterly opposed doctrines by two truth-seekers unknown to each other. Yet both doctrines were put forward as tested truths by mystical teachers with considerable public followings. One asserted that the closer a disciple came to spiritual self-realization the more was he provided by the Spirit with material satisfactions. The other claimed that the advancing disciple was provided with so many sufferings as to be utterly crucified. The earnest student whose reading brings him up against them is bewildered by such contradictions. He may end his bewilderment if he will accept the assurance of philosophy that neither assertion is accurate.

Interpreting mystical experience

35

The Overself provides the light but the man provides the thought-form through which it shines. The deficiencies or distortions in this form affect the result.

36

It is one thing to have an authentic mystical experience, another thing to have an authentic explanation of it.

37

They are imperfect earthen vessels for perfect divine offerings.

38

Although he has become the recipient of God's infallible truth he has not ceased to be fallible man. Consequently when the two mingle, each is coloured by the other.

39

The truth comes to every man alike because the presence of his higher self makes every man its recipient. But the conditions within him are so bad, his receptivity is on so low a level, the interference of his ego so strong, the distortion by his emotions so marked, that what he calls truth is really the ugly caricature of it.

40

I honour and revere these saints. It is good for us that such men have been on earth. Nevertheless man cannot perfect himself *in* this world although he must do so *through* this world. Hence we must grant the fact that the greatest teachers of the race were human, after all, and therefore subject to human limitations. They did not cease to be human beings merely because they became spiritual geniuses. If their declarations reveal the heights above, they also reflect the plains below. Respectful courteous criticism in my own private notebooks, to clarify my ideas of their theoretical standpoint and practical attitude for the purposes of elucidating the truth, is allowable. This is different from public denunciation in print. Where is the alleged resemblance of doctrine and unity of spirit among the different mystical schools really to be found? The contradictions and even oppositions are as numerous as the similarities and harmonies. If this means anything, it means that mystics do colour their perception with their individual characteristics, however much they may claim to be above the ego. It means, too, that such colouration is most often effected quite unconsciously. The white light of the pure experience is always coloured by prepossessions or emotions, and always suffers from the change.

41

How much has the mystic himself contributed towards this experience? Unless he can answer this question correctly, his understanding of it may be partially unreliable, his expression unsatisfactory. When he tries to reveal his experience or express his perception to others, the personality's interference may begin again. Where the intellectual world-view is primitive and undeveloped, the illumination will be understood in a primitive way. Three men at three different levels of development will express their experience or perception in three different ways. Therefore two different recipients may produce two different "revelations" derived from identically the same level of mystical experience. But, of course, the differences will not be total, as there will be a clearly recognizable common factor running through both interpretations. This situation introduces a varying amount of unreliability in all their interpretations. Only when the aspirant has passed through and finished this philosophic discipline has he provided the requisite conditions for receiving and perceiving truth. It will then be truth in all its purity and finality. If he attempts to make a record of it or to tell others about it, the result will be unaffected by his personal ego.

42

Just as convex and concave mirrors variously distort the images reflected in them, just as dirty, spotted, scratched, or cracked mirrors show a mixed, altered, or imperfect image of the object placed before them, so human minds variously distort or sully the spiritual truth revealed to them by the Overself. Rare is that one which lets the light shine forth unhindered, unchanged, and uncoloured. This is why the philosophic discipline, which exists for precisely such an objective, is so needed by every seeker after truth.

43

The teachings given out by the higher spiritualism are not received by the low-grade séance method, but by what can be described as "inspiration." This is a phenomenon which is found among the mystics, too. But investigation of mysticism shows that although the experience itself was genuine enough, its fruits in revelation and communication were usually coloured by the medium (in the higher and not in the spiritualistic sense) through which it had to manifest on our plane. That is, the personality of the man through whom the teaching was given, the complexes which governed his attitude, often unconsciously, the degree of inner development, and the width of outer experience which he possessed—all these contributed to shaping the message.

44

Whereas Saint Thomas Aquinas stopped writing his books when the inner experience came to him, Shankaracharya started writing his own. Thus one and the same kind of spiritual consciousness illuminating two different kinds of mind brought about two different and opposite decisions! What does this show? That the human mind *does* colour the revelation's reception or its communication.

45

Some power higher than oneself, over and above the ordinary self, then takes control of the thoughts and actions and expels their baser element.

46

The gems of truth lie buried underneath the earth of personal opinion.

47

It is sometimes quite hard to excavate the foundation of true insight which lies beneath this tall structure built from opinion alone.

48

The influence of the ego upon his reception of the truth is as inevitable as the day after night.

49

It is a fact that most men give the truth, deliberately or unwittingly, a personal colouration, just as when trying to understand it with the intellect or to convey it to others they interpret it.

50

The mystic who is filled with emotions too deep for words has still to bring about a balance whereby he can understand them for himself and explain them for others.

51

His capacity to receive the soul's enlightenment may be quite large but his capacity to formulate it correctly in his own thinking—and consequently for other people's thinking—may be quite small.

52

Many a mystic has been carried by his ego beyond the actual frontier of the illumination granted him, and so led into making statements which embody both error and truth, both opinion and fact.

53

He may only expect to receive such enlightenment as he is inwardly prepared to receive, not what is likely to be above his level of comprehension.

54

No matter how he try, the mystic will not be able to express his inspiration on a higher intellectual level than the one on which he habitually finds himself. This has been plain enough in the past when over-ambitious attempts have brought ridicule to an otherwise inspired message. This is why the best prophet to reach the educated classes is an educated man who possesses the proper mental equipment to do it, and why uneducated masses are best reached by one of themselves. What is communicated— and even the very language in which this is done—always indicates on what levels of human intellect, character, and experience the mystic dwells, as it also indicates what level of mystical consciousness he has succeeded in touching.(P)

55

What so few understand is that a mystical experience may be quite overwhelming and quite genuine in character and yet leave a large number of the mystic's inherited beliefs quite untouched.

56

It needs again and again to be explained that after the Overself takes possession of a man's consciousness and begins to rule his will, it can take possession only of what it finds in his whole personality. If, for example, it finds an undeveloped reasoning power it cannot and does not suddenly develop it for him. Its communications to and through him will be perfect but their interpretation in his own mind and expression to others may, because of this imperfect reasoning capacity, be partly right and partly wrong.

57

What he sees, and is, in that deeply withdrawn state, is not the same as what he experiences later when he is back in the outer world again. The transformation is not steadfast and abiding. There, he was superhuman; here, he is all too human. Even his remembrance of it will necessarily be in terms of what he himself once again is.

58

The mystical experience is at the mercy of his meagre development when it comes to being intellectually interpreted or communicated, or when his feelings about it are to be transmitted or conveyed.

59

How much truth or falsity there is in his interpretation, how much of his own human devising there is in his revelation can be ascertained only by a judge who is ruthlessly impartial and one who is possessed of the keenest philosophic insight. He himself is safe, however, in making universality a fair test of validity.

60

When the psychological derivation of a mystical pronouncement is thus known, it is easy to grasp why such pronouncements are seldom much higher than the intellectual reach and moral capacity of the mystic himself.

61

It takes all of a man to find all of the truth: part of a man will find only part of the truth.

62

Most mystics who claim to know God really know a mixture of their own reactions to the divine experience together with the experience itself, a blend of their own opinions and beliefs with what they have learned from the experience. This is because they are conditioned by their past history and present social surroundings as well as several other factors, and this conditioning shapes the understanding of the experience. Each person brings his individuality into it more or less according to the person. All religious mysticism of a sectarian kind, all sectarian revelations which have not been preceded by thorough discipline and training in philosophy belong to this order of experience.

63

Without sufficient skill in the technique of presenting his message, the prophet or mystic may be unable to present it clearly. His inspiration is not miraculously able to overcome this deficiency, although it will certainly help.

64

The experience enlightens him only to the extent that he lets it do so. For if the trend of his belief and thought is based on a wide knowledge of comparative religion and philosophy, thus opening his outlook and explaining the experience, he will meet it with acceptance and without fear. Otherwise his dominant belief, expectancy, and bias get entangled with the experience—either at its onset or later—and are confirmed in part or wholly.

65

The pure truth becomes too easily mixed with caricatures of it brought in by the ego's ignorance. Too often the man cannot keep them separate, too often he possesses neither the training nor the humility to know what is happening, which spoils this beautiful experience.

66

He may or may not understand the mystical experience which has come to him. If he does not, the chances are that some misinterpretation will creep in and distort its meaning or message. Such chances are greatly reduced if he is able to turn to a master for correction or to a teaching for knowledge.

67

Every logical chain of thoughts, every group of imaginations, every set of remembered opinions, beliefs, and teachings acts upon the pure truth to bring about an interpretation of it. Its purity is thereby lost. What the man receives from his contact and what he gives out is then a mixture of divine communication and human formulation.

68

It is inevitable that the man's interpretation of this inner event should be limited to the arc of his own knowledge and experience.

69

When he enters into this tremendous experience with only a part of his psyche—with the emotional feeling, for instance, but not with the practical will—he emerges with only that same part cultivated and stimulated by the divine inspiration. But the parts which did not enter remain untouched and uninspired. Nor is this all. The unbalance of the psyche will necessarily affect harmfully the character of the realization, or rather the way in which it is received and experienced. Thus it is plain that only an integral approach will yield both a full and perfect result. Whether the light enters his intellect or heart or will or all three, depends on whether a part only or every corner of the whole man has engaged in the quest.

70

If even mystics and seers disagree about certain truths, this is because their natures are not equally purified and their intelligence not equally developed.

71

A muddled understanding based on a fleeting glimpse by an unpurified character, a biased, disturbed, prejudiced, and ill-informed mind, can produce only a vague, unclear, and partly mistaken communication.

72

Stupidity can and quite often does coexist in another area with fully rational behaviour.

73

So long as the human will, ego, imagination, or belief plays a part in the experience, so long will the possibility of error be present.

74

The truth or falsity of the mental concepts which get involved in the intuitional processes or mixed in with the mystical communions will affect the results.

75

To touch the truth is one thing; to be able to accept it in all its purity is another. For the sympathies or antipathies, wishes or dislikes, preferences or repulsions may easily enter into a man's relation with the truth.

Admixture of ego

76
It is not the original revelation of the Overself which they communicate or transmit but the impact of the revelation upon their own mentality. A prism does not transmit the pure white light which strikes against it but only the several colours of the spectrum into which it breaks that light. The mystic's mentality is like a prism and breaks the pure being of the Overself into the egoistic colours of ideas and beliefs.

77
The original revelation itself may be truly cosmic, but the finished product will be so only in patches.

78
The ego personalizes all its experiences, even those concerning the truth. But it does so only partially, so the resultant is a blend of its opinion, wish, vanity, or ignorance with the pure verity.

79
To the degree that his own opinion is contributed unconsciously by his own ego, to that degree he fails to communicate the message. Or, put in another way, to that degree he obstructs the influx of truth's light.

80
Just as a stained-glass window colours every ray of light which enters a church through it, so an egoistic mentality imposes its own conceptions on the spiritual truths which enter a man through it.

81
His ego builds an entire intellectual and emotional superstructure on the original foundational mystic experience.

82
We must separate the universally true message from its locally made wrapping, discriminate authentic divine insight from its fallible human counterpart.

83
So long as he lacks philosophic training, the interests and desires of his ego shape the pattern of his experience of his spiritual experience. Religious fervour is admirable but it is not impersonal enough to let the pattern shape itself.

84
While his mind is closed behind the doors of ideas and beliefs previously put into it and then held there firmly, he may shape his interpretations of experience accordingly. The result may be self-deception.

85

It is quite possible for personal opinions to mix with, or even masquerade as, universal.

86

If a man has not sufficiently purified his nature and correctly prepared his faculties, all his mystical experiences of God or the Soul will not be truly mystical at all but emotional counterfeits or psychical self-deceptions. That is to say, he will have them within the circle of his personal ego, however thrilling or delightful or revelatory they may be. He will merely escape from one kind of illusion (the world's materiality) into another kind (his own spirituality).

87

The mystic whose revelations can fit only into the framework of a narrow sect, whose inspirations are hostile to all other religions except the one in which he was born, may be getting a genuine inspiration, but he is also drawing on his own ego for the unconscious interpretation of what is being revealed to him. Consequently, he does not give us the pure truth, but rather the distorted truth. If he brings light into the world, he also brings back some of the old darkness in another guise; thus the result is a mixed one—partly good, but partly bad.

88

During his mystical childhood and adolescence he is to some extent an easy victim for perversions, deviations, and deformations of truth. The suggestions which he receives from his environment may be false; the impressions which he receives from his emotions may be wrong. It is needful to bring in reason and intuition, impartial authority and factual results to check him.

89

The intrusion of the thinking intellect or the egoistic emotion into the intuitive experience presents a danger for all mystics. And it is a danger that constantly remains for the more advanced as for the mere neophyte, although in a different way. It is the source of flattering illusions which offer themselves as authentic infallible intuitions. It crowns commonplace ideas which happen to enter the mind with a regality that does not belong to them. The prudent mystic must be on his guard against and watch out for this peril. He must resist its appeals to vanity, its destruction of truth.(P)

90

Consider the fact that few even have the wish to evaluate objectively the truth of their revelation or message. Few ask themselves whether they were merely reflecting human opinion or really getting a divine illumination. Most are too swept away by the emotional impact or vanity-flattering thought of the event to make such enquiry. This is why personal fancies, hopes, or fears are perpetuated as sacred truths.

91

The revelation gets entangled with the contributions of desires and fears, race and religion, yearnings and hates, community and heredity—that is, the ego. If the soul's voice is brought through faintly but the ego's echoes strongly, the revealed message will be poor in quality. Seldom does the developing mystic align his consciousness with his essence and bring back the result unaffected by his individuality. Seldom is the revelation faithfully, completely, and perfectly brought down intact in every particular. On the contrary, it is usually and unconsciously adjusted to the human channel through which it passes.

92

It is easy to be carried away by both the dramatic and the ego-flattering associations of this experience into an exaggerated falsified interpretation of it.

93

Into the revelation goes not only the mystic's inner experience itself, but also the suggestions of his upbringing, his surroundings, his wishes and fears, his tendencies and illusions; more, his ego inserts new meanings into it or changes those that belong to it. In short, part of or even the whole revelation is made to serve the ego, or fit its limitations.

94

We must go through the revelation with a farm-rake and remove the prejudices, the preconceptions, the whims, and the self-interest which have been inserted by the revealer's personality rather than by his soul.

95

Even where sensitivity of telepathic reception has been developed, the ego still cunningly interferes with accurate reception. It will take the current of inspiration from the master and, by adding what was never contained in it, give a highly personal, vanity-flattering colour to it. It will take the message of guidance from the higher self and, by twisting it to conform to the shape of personal desire, render it misleading. It will take a psychical or intuitive reading of a situation and, in its eager seeking of wish-fulfilment, confuse the reading and delude itself. It may even, by introducing very strong emotional complexes, create absolutely false suggestions and suppose them to be emanating from the master or the higher self.(P)

96

When a man puts forward his own scriptural interpretation as true and all others as false, he puts forward the claim that spiritual insight belongs to him alone and no one else. This is a vast claim and all history contradicts it.

97

If the intellect tries to make the experience conform to its preconceived ideas, as it will, the mystic's deliverance may no longer represent the truth but partially misrepresent it.

98

The mystic's account of his inner experience contains an interpretation and communication of his own beliefs, opinions, and expectations. He is entitled to them, but he is not entitled to use them in order to alter, distort, exaggerate, minimize, or otherwise change the basic facts of the experience itself.

99

These mental aberrations are purely personal and have nothing to do with the truth. It is really the particular person, and not truth, which is thus exposed to ridicule or criticism. But this is not sufficiently understood. There is much confusion here.

100

How much of this intuition comes from the Overself and how much from inferior, from mistaken, or even from evil sources is something he does not usually seek to know.

101

Evil and absurd notions may mingle with the good and wise ones that come from a genuinely intuitive source. Fanatical and foolish messages may find expression among exalted and luminous ones.

102

Intuition itself is always infallible, but the man receiving or expressing it is often inferior in receptive quality or poor in expressiveness or egocentric in handling it or obstructive in understanding it.

103

Those who doubt that mystics can be so blind or so narrow need to read their Dante and note that he allotted hell to Muhammed.

104

The extravagance and distortion, the fantasy and bias of these revelations unfortunately destroys the credibility of what is truly authentic and definitely factual in them.

105

Men bring their little bigotries into this limitless illumination, mix the two together, and present the adulterated product as the latest revelation from God.

10

THE IS IS NOT AN ISM

Limitations of dogma

The whole sphere of occultism and mysticism is a sphere of illusion. All the experiences obtained therein are illusory ones. All leaders who profess to teach are misleaders in consequence. There is no escape from this position, no cessation of the waste of precious years through worshipping illusion save by rising to the higher level of philosophy, which alone is concerned with the truth and the reality of what is experienced, believed, and thought.

2

The ideology which prevails in so many of such circles—if I may use such a pretentious but popular word with reference to those whose noteworthy characteristic is not seldom the absence of intellectual culture—is diametrically opposite to that for which we strive to stand. For they represent the world's vanishing age of intellectual imposture and superstitious credulity, and this teaching is for the nascent age of verification and profound enquiry.

3

Only a very small percentage of these cults which feature the study of Truth and the life of its quest, ever actually realize the pure truth or stay on the right path. Most are wandering astray, with leaders and led losing themselves in a mixture of truth and error, and functioning on a level of fantasy and opinion, illumined with shafts of inspiration and revelation. Quite a number are unconsciously tinted with hidden black magic and harmful evil. No man can arrive at the quest's goal through their agency; he must leave them first.

4

Such an imaginary picture of the world either hides or distorts its realities. One consequence is that it attracts failures and misfits who are thenceforward prevented from searching within themselves for the true causes of their misadjustments.

5

If a spiritual teaching is maintained in an unspiritual way, it is no longer what it purports to be.

6

Superstitions which afford innocent satisfaction to those who believe in them are pardonable, but superstitions which commend cruelty to other persons are unpardonable.

7

Despite the idealistic talk and tall claims, he who follows these cults gradually destroys his intuition of truth, stops his *real* progress, and endangers his psyche.

8

If a superior cult takes away some of the truth-seekers' old illusions and errors, it too often puts back new ones.

9

If he has received instruction which was stippled with errors, not only was that a partial waste of time but also he will have to spend further time in unlearning it.

10

Each person has his own peculiarities and idiosyncrasies of temperament, his own asymmetries and disproportions of mentality. Some of these may be very pronounced. Yet he is expected to follow the same system, in the same way, and to the same extent, as every other person! How can such a dictatorial imposition from outside—so unrelated in part to his actual and unique psychological constitution—truly serve his real needs?

11

Once he joins an organization of this kind his capacity to think and judge for himself will be slowly and insidiously destroyed, for he will be expected to imitate the thinking and judgement of the mass of other members.

12

Those who tether themselves to an organization or to a set of dogmas, lose the capacity to seek for truth outside these cramped limits. Henceforth they must think and behave with sectarian narrowness.

13

As soon as he comes under the sway of a master or, worse, of an organization, his mentality, outlook, beliefs, and attitudes come under sectarian conditioning, implanted suggestion, and stiffened indoctrination. The result is that he becomes incapable of learning truth because he is no longer open to it (he believes he already possesses it).

14

Do not get locked up in a particular sect and exclude all others from it in your mind. This too is a form of attachment and life today is teaching most people the futility of such attachments. Look what is happening to the Roman Catholic and to other churches! See how the idea of ecumenism among them has taken on. See what happened to the Theosophical Society, which started out to find the truth in all religions by being unsectarian, but has ended up becoming another sect itself by establishing centres, lodges, branches, headquarters.

15

Those who join a cult get the benefit of its gregarious comfort but must suffer the disadvantage of its self-centered limitations and prejudices.

16

The danger of embracing these false teachings is that the more ardently they are embraced, the more effectually do they prevent misguided followers from coming to the true teachings.

17

Only when he is away from the cult's hypnosis and adjusts himself to the fact as it *is*, not as it has been suggested to him, can he hope to find truth!

18

Now, doctrines of the early sages have been obstructed, Truth destroyed; evil theories and depraved doctrines expand and spread, men give rein to passions and indulge desires—all are drowned. If one does not cleave to his teachers, he will be submerged in the prevailing customs and will not know how to escape. Is it not pitiful?

19

If the inmates of so many ashrams could be aroused from the apathy in which they are sunk to engage in an enquiry as to the purposes of ashrams, it might end in new ideas and nobler feelings.

20

The self-indulgence which characterizes some of these modern groups is in some cases a misconception and in others a perversion of the authentic earlier movements and traditions.

21

Foolish beliefs and ungrounded faiths can weaken not only a man's intelligence but also his conscience.

22

There will be far more truth and wisdom in studying the words of Socrates for half an hour than when attempting to understand the empty jargon of occultists for half a week.

23

They will find that the occult and, to a lesser extent, the mystical litera-
tures are tangled jungles, hard to get into but harder still to get out of with
sanity unimpaired. It is questionable whether the good or the true that is
in them is sufficient to render worthwhile a struggle with the massive
spurious spirituality which enshrouds them.

24

These romantic doctrines offer consolation to the unhappy and com-
pensation to the unfortunate at the price of being deceived. For they issue
from dreamland and need not be taken seriously. They cannot fulfil their
promises.

25

One may have a profound faith in the possibilities of unfoldment, a faith
based on the actuality of one's own experience and the observation of
many other persons' experience. Therefore one writes with hesitation anything which, because it may be easily misunderstood, can dim that faith.
But some warning is certainly needed here. It is needed by those who let
themselves be led astray by the glowing assertions or the marvel-sprinkled
claims of teachings whose real ground is part-truth and part-untruth. Not
only is the proof still wanting for some of their most important statements, but lives have been thrown into chaos by accepting their actuality
too literally.

26

This is no matter for tea-table cults; we have to devote our whole lives
to it.

27

"Before we attain to the Truth we are subject to a thousand fancies,
fictions, and apprehensions, which we falsely suppose and many times
publicly propose for the truth itself. This fantastic region is the true original seminary of all sects and their dissensions."—Thomas Vaughan, an
advanced mystic of the seventeenth century.

28

We may witness the amusing scene of our own occult, mystical, psychological, and religious demigods slipping and sliding all over the ice of
Uncertainty.

29

There are eccentric individuals and peculiar cults which have fastened
their attention and belief exclusively on some chosen part and excitedly
proclaimed it to be the whole. They fail to see how disproportionate is the
place they have given it, or how unfair they are to all the other parts of
truth.

30

He will find such a diversity of opinions among these cults and creeds that he may emerge from their study with some confusion. For there is too often less interest in finding facts accurately and interpreting them rightly, than in speculating and imagining theories.

31

These occult systems and cosmologies have a deceptive clear-cut outline, a fallacious finality, and a pseudo-scientific factuality.

32

To declare that we are all metaphysically one and the same, that a common essence makes us spiritually brothers, is an assertion which needs careful scrutiny before acceptance for there are both true and false elements in it.

33

They talk themselves into the clouds, deserting the solid ground beneath their feet and deriding interest in the body's hygiene, but all the while they are living in a fleshly body in a physical world.

34

When the student gets tired of these vague platitudes and this windy emotionalism, he will long for something hard, precise, and tough into which to put his teeth.

35

Such absurd propositions can only be maintained by those who confound Superstition with Spirituality, never by those who refuse to desert reason in order to find Truth.

36

Superstitious belief keeps a man out of the kingdom of heaven just as much as sceptical disbelief does. For being false, it has no place in, and no title to, the truth.

37

The truth should generously enlarge a man's perceptions and sympathies, but those who can receive only a single aspect of it imprison their perceptions and narrow their sympathies.

38

When a single aspect of truth is mistaken for the whole truth it holds no place for equally important facts which balance or compensate it, and then the fanatic and the sectarian are born.

39

There are perhaps more misconceptions, unscientific exaggerations, factual contortions, half-truths, and total errors in the statements publicly or privately made by the leaders or by the followers of some cults than are found even in political statements.

40

Too much self-satisfaction, too little acquaintance with the world's great thinkers, seers, and sages—this ignorance enables too many cults and sects to thrive.

41

Paradox is the very nature of our existence; it transcends logic and reason: but when unbalanced minds use this mystery of truth to put forward their personal insanities, it is outrageous.

42

Religion has elaborated a series of worldly stunts and salesmanship campaigns which Jesus would have been the first to reject, because they arise out of a mental confusion about religion's true mission to humanity. Mysticism has deftly produced, on the one hand, pseudo-psychologies and half-mysticisms which are unhappy compounds of smart salesmanship and aspiring idealism and, on the other, an eccentric medley of queerly varied cults which link a little borrowed wisdom to the crankiest notions and the most astonishing claims ever born out of half-baked minds or distorted balance. When Fergus Hume, the Australian novelist, wrote in one of his stories, "Start anything, however silly, and you will find followers!" he may have been thinking of California where religion pullulates into dozens of different sects. I found twenty-seven churches of different denominations in one town of 7,000 population!

43

The aberrations of those who mix some of the Quest's ideas and practices with their own, or with some imposed on them by their cult-leader, stretch back historically to long before Christ's time, geographically as far as the distant limits of Asia.

44

When the saturation of superstition in a religion or in a mystic cult is so heavy that it renders more disservice than service, it is time for thoughtful followers to get out of it.

45

So long as men persist in organizing themselves into religious groups, so long will they run the real risk of failing to get into the real spirit of truth, getting only its letter at best.

46

The comedies which are unconsciously and solemnly played out in some of these ashrams in all seriousness, the characters who congregate there, the ideas which are entertained when reason, fact, practicality, and common sense are abandoned—all these factors make it unlikely that truth will be found by the inmates, or the awareness of Reality obtained.

47

There is here a confusion of planes, a mixing up of levels of reference, an unlawful crossing of frontiers.

48

A movement which denies the very life-force which is the source of man's existence can never lastingly shape the way he carries on that existence, nor give it inner sustenance. But since there are those who want it like that, they must get the result of their desiring and creative activity for a limited time, until its negation of the higher laws brings it to disintegration and collapse.

49

In the Appendix to *The Hidden Teaching Beyond Yoga*, I protested against the setting up of mystic *experience* as the goal of this quest, placing my emphasis upon the word "experience." That Appendix was written in 1940. Since then we have witnessed the deplorable consequences of methods which ignore such a protest. Especially is this true in the case of "mind expansion" through drugs. But cults have sprung up which, although catering to thirst for "experiences" through a kind of meditation, use very elementary and mechanical means that alone cannot lead to genuine insight but only to a mesmeric lulling of the thoughts. This may have a temporary value and be a pleasant experience, hence the wide spread of these cults. But the belief that initiation into them opens the door to the divine is gross self-deception. It opens a door to self-hypnotism, while the guru gives the apparently mystical experience at the time by his own personal hypnotic power.

50

Trying to strike a cosmical attitude, they succeed only in striking a comical one!

51

When people who have either voluntarily surrendered the right to independent thought or lack all capacity for it proclaim such doctrines, nobody need be fluttered about it. But when people who are put both by their own claims and by general reputation on the loftiest pinnacle of spiritual insight proclaim such doctrines, it is time to utter a protest.

52

Too often these cults are merely foolish systems of self-deception or clever devices to avoid the gruff confrontations of reality.

53

The attempt to harmonize the violently differing teachings of all these cults would not only leave him not far from where he started but would also risk his sanity.

54

The fantastic beliefs and gross superstitions which get a following in mystical circles thrive better in California than in rational England, better in India than in sceptical France.

55

They hold such beliefs either because of self-deception or because of stupidity. In the first case they are the victims of external suggestion, in the second case of personal immaturity. In neither case, therefore, can we really blame them. We can only be sorry for them.

56

These cults exaggerate some one aspect of truth, ignore the compensating aspects, and end by partially misleading themselves.

57

It is no less a mistake to ascribe profound meanings where only surface ones exist as it is to do the very opposite.

58

Silly fantastic teachings which cannot stand the test of a real confrontation with contemporary life—ever waiting outside—may be found in this domain. They have nothing to do with philosophy even if sometimes they appropriate the name.

59

This concept of salvation by easy cheap methods or short tricky ones is false.

60

The tragedy is that the world needs spiritual bread but it is deceived into accepting, and often deceives itself into accepting, spiritual stones.

61

They want the Truth to come down from its lofty plane and accommodate itself to their false ideas, their limited views, their personal pettiness. But of course it never does. So they unconsciously inject these things into the Truth and produce a deceptive mixture.

Misuse of mystery

62

That these masters imparted certain knowledge or transmitted certain experiences only to their more confidential disciples but hid them from the others, is a fact whose simple and natural purpose has been distorted in the advantage taken of it by promoters of secret or semi-secret societies and propagandists for occult fantasies.

63

Secrecy attracts a certain kind of person. The secret may be valuable or it may be worthless: it may provide the imposter with favourable conditions for his fraudulent activities and it may allow the genuine hierophant a chance to teach what the populace is not ready for.

64

It is certainly a fact that charlatans usually prefer to keep their alleged knowledge and pseudo-technique secret. But it is equally a fact that they use this secrecy as a bait to lure their victims into their trap.

65

Mystification was unknown to the great Teachers of Religion whom the modern occultists seek to enclose within their dubious societies.

66

Unnecessary secrecy is a warning sign that something is wrong: that mental balance is disturbed, or that ulterior motives are present.

67

They put mystery into the most ordinary persons and events; they pump an atmosphere of revelation into rehashed tenets and teachings.

68

They may even tell you that truth is too high to be testable.

69

It is a common trick for these men, whether outright imposters or unfinished mystics drunk with pride, to give mysterious hints about their marvellous occult powers and miraculous occult feats. But the hints remain as hints only.

70

Mystery exists where the facts are plain and simple. The naïve inexperienced student is kept back by imbalance in teachings, over-weighty emphases wrongly applied, and confusion between what is only a means with what is properly its end and goal. The results are unnecessary complication and avoidable obfuscation. The beginner himself helps the incompetent teacher by his own tendency to refuse to believe that the truth is so utterly simple.

71

The occultists who claim to give initiations and the mystics who talk of communicating Spirit by silent thought were both rebuked hundreds of years ago by Chuang Tzu, when he wrote: "It cannot be conveyed either by words or by silence."

72

They use the excuse of secrecy to gain power over others, to exploit and use them for selfish personal advantage.

73

The need of prudently avoiding conflict with conventional religions is an ancient one, and has helped, along with other causes, to keep the higher truths generally uncommunicated and unknown. But this quite legitimate need has been taken advantage of by unscrupulous mystery-mongers to make claims of concealed, privileged, hierarchical, traditional knowledge and to offer initiation into their occult secrets to gullible seekers, who will be well exploited financially or otherwise.

74

What such men fail to say about their methods and results is often more important than what they do say.

75

Beware of cults and their exaggerated claims. The IS is not an ISM.(P)

76

The first fallacy in all the thinking of these cults is the ascription to the ego of qualities which properly belong to the Overself. To take a single instance: deathlessness is claimed as a possible achievement for the physical body, which is a formed and compounded thing, when it can only belong by nature to the Overself, which is simple and unitary. The second fallacy is the belief of the ego that it can issue orders to the Overself and actually get them obeyed—orders, of course, which confer riches, position, and other satisfactions upon itself.

77

We could not fail to behold that the abysmal depth of these cult-leaders' failure is in direct ratio to the preposterous height of their extravagant claims to wisdom and power. Of what outstanding value have they been to their fellow men and women? We are entitled to ask for the visible fruits of all this verbal commotion and general mystery-mongering. What proof have they given that there is anything substantial behind their claims? They can show no practical achievement or productive effort that has made a deep mark in any sphere of contemporary history or even revealed that they possess any capacity to make it. They have not brought to the concrete problems which confront mankind any better counsel than the non-illuminati have brought—unless the utterance of abstract nouns be such. The final demonstration of their futility is given by the personal failures of their followers in consequence of such unprofitable influence and hollow teaching. Hardly any have developed and balanced the trinity of head, heart, and hand, the harmony of brain, feeling, and will. Few possess the ambition which works hard for what it wants, but almost all dream of great good fortune coming effortlessly to them through some divine Grace, auspicious planet, invisible adept's working, or other miraculous means. In short, the personal lives of a large proportion of these believers are stamped with frustration and failure, as the public lives of their leaders are stamped with utter inability to accomplish any marked positive benefit for mankind. It is as comical as it is tragical to contemplate how ineffectively they drift through the years as mere dreamers lacking power but ever talking of it. Even when their miseries and sufferings impel them eventually to some reflection, they apportion the blame everywhere except in the right place. It is God's will, or adverse stars, or evil spirits, or unavoidable karma, or a spiritual test, but it is never the harvest of the gullibility which they have sown, of the intellectual exaggerations to which they have yielded, of the one-sided, unbalanced, and negligent view of life which they have been taught, nor of the self-deception which permits them to take so many illusions for realities.

78

Under the self-praised exterior of the absurdly exaggerated claims, hidden dark maggots are busy creating ethical rot within its core and substance. Its short but shady history is already stippled with unsavoury incidents, demoniac intercourse, and financial exploitation of the crudest kind.

79

The question therefore arises: To what cause is such a situation to be attributed? For if the professions of esoteric wisdom and claims to extraordinary power made by the cults are true, then both their leaders and their followers have failed miserably in implementing such declarations, while if they are untrue then many seekers after truth are being misled.

80

What strikes the observer first about these cults is their spiritual futility and ridiculous vanity. They create their own fantastic legend about their past and live in an equally fantastic dream about their future.

81

Once a sect starts, it is only a matter of time until it begins to believe itself to be the "Chosen People."

82

When he gives utterance to exaggerated claims and extravagant doctrines, he leads himself, as well as others, astray.

83

He usually claims surrender to supernatural guidance, to superpersonal inspiration. Indeed, anyone listening to his speeches for the first time, with their exaggerated claims and confident declamation, might be forgiven for deriving the impression that his opinions are shared by God!

84

The first mistake of an organized religio-mystic group is to behave as if it were here among men for its own sake, to make its own cause higher than the cause of truth or compassion.

85

They will not grant that theirs is only one of the ways to Reality and not the sole way. Or, admitting this obvious fact, they claim that theirs is by far the best way!

86

They overstate the case; their assertions need some discounting. The pity is that such exaggeration is quite unnecessary. The inner life offers benefits which are real enough and valuable enough, but to raise expectations which go far beyond them is unfair, undesirable, and even misleading.

87

Each cult claims theirs is the true and only teaching from God.

88

Do not accept the exaggerated claims made by any teacher that salvation or illumination can come only through him or through his religion. This is a form of intimidation, which frightens weak souls into acceptance and belief.

89

These petty sects take on majestic airs, make claims, and announce staggering revelations as if they were of cosmic importance and as if their sect alone held the impenetrable cosmic secret.

90

All these cults cunningly appeal to the ego in man, however much or often they cull New Testament texts or quote Christ or affirm lofty metaphysical truths of being.

91

These "demonstration" cults have carried the orthodox idea of God intervening in worldly situations for the benefit of particular persons, into a new garb which disguises but does not alter the idea itself. The life of man is then no longer ruled by causality but by a mixture of causality and caprice—that is to say, no longer ruled by God, but by a being who is part God, part man, who is liable to disturb the highly complicated world-order to please one human being with effects that might displease other human beings.

92

The dangers of membership in an occult group or society are several. One is spiritual pride, a swelling of the ego arising out of the belief that the group is intimately and importantly associated with the higher powers.

93

Those groups are so stubbornly convinced that they are right that they become aggressive at the slightest show of defense against their voiced opinions, or on hearing statements of differing opinions.

94

H.P. Blavatsky said in her second message of 1889 to the American Theosophical Convention: "There are dozens of small occult societies which talk very glibly of Magic, Occultism, Rosicrucians, Adepts, etc. These profess much, even to giving the key to the Universe, but end by leading men to a blank wall."

95

One turns with relief from this unreal atmosphere of a tiny sect engaged in colossal self-aggrandizement in its own eyes to the wider, saner world outside, even if that world be less talkative about its so-called spirituality.

96

This eagerness of ignorance to explain the universe would be ironical, if the results were not so pathetic.

97

The religious exhibitionism of ritualistic cults finds its parallel in the psychic exhibitionism of mystic cults.

98

The minds formed by these cults quickly fossilized, congealed rapidly around their own dogmas, and narrowed into attachment to an orthodoxy hardly less rigid than the ones they denounced so vehemently and so vociferously.

99

The spread of mystical movements may be achieved by putting forward exaggerated and indefensible claims.

100

Even prosaic everyday happenings are clothed by their arrogant imagination with delusional meanings and given divine significance. In their own estimate they and their cult occupy tremendous importance in the world's spiritual history. They feel that God has entrusted them with the task of redeeming mankind and placed them at the very centre of the cosmic scheme for this purpose. So the intuitive voice is perverted into a self-aggrandizing attention-getting instrument.

101

What effectual difference can a few hundred obscure and scattered persons make in a population of many millions? The disproportion is so enormous and the influence of this tiny group is so slight and unnoticeable that there is something pathetic about its belief in its own importance, something hallucinatory about its pompous self-regard.

102

The true mystery of life is serene and grand whereas the artificial mystery of these occult sects is disturbing and denigrating.

103

The God whom most men worship has been built up out of their own imagination or out of the imagination of other men whom they follow. The consequences of this false worship are to be seen in the superstitions and disillusionments and exploitations which mar human history.

104

Against a background of little thought and less study, these optimistic dabblers imagine that they can explain—as they generally do in glib meaningless phrases—what acute-minded thinkers have failed to explain despite the efforts of thousands of years.

105

When we begin to remember how inexhaustibly varied the different levels of World-Mind's space-timed universe must be, how infinitely long-drawn its own time-life must be beyond our farthest possible conceptions, we begin to realize how absurd are those claims made by occultists and clairvoyants to the knowledge of all the universe's secrets in their infinitude or of all God's life in its fullness.

106

If we follow them too closely, leaving behind our critical faculties and penetrative powers, in too many cases we meet eventually with disillusionment and sometimes disgust. "Things are not so easy of comprehension or explanation as people would have us believe," wrote the German poet Rilke. Beware of those who tell you that they can see the secret works of the universe as easily as one can see through a glass window. If they are sincere, the likelihood is that their knowledge is hastily or prematurely promulgated; if they are deluding themselves or deceiving others, they are worse guides than none at all. Creation still remains a great riddle.

107

We may laugh at those who imply they have private information about the mental habits of the Deity.

108

Occult systems, which claim to offer a complete chart of the universe, do not live up to their claims for the reason that they cannot. They are communicated through and to limited minds, dwelling on a single level. How could they absorb that which only the unlimited mind of God, dwelling on and transcending all possible levels, could absorb? No human can map out the sum of all existences, for no human has the needed resources to do so.

11

FANATICISM, MONEY, POWERS, DRUGS

Fanaticism

Beware of the fanaticism shown by certain gurus and their followers. Intolerance of other teachings or of other interpretations of their own teachings, harshly denouncing every deviation, implies a narrow sectarianism.

2

The bands, small or large, which gather around a guru, or attach themselves to the latest movements, or join the organized groups, need to exercise much care if they are to escape from the zealotry and bigotry, the little-mindedness and carping criticism into which most of the members too often fall.

3

The fanaticism of these foolish followers is proof against all evidence and all argument. Faith kicks Reason out of the room, and then proceeds to lock the door against the discomforting intruder. Texts will be tortured in order to tamper with truths; history will be distorted; facts will be conveniently forgotten and even the clearest utterances will be mauled and misrepresented to suit their jaundiced minds. To make matters worse, the enthusiast is never satisfied with deluding himself but deludes others also.

4

They are less interested in arriving at the truth than in disseminating fiercely partisan propaganda for their beliefs.

5

They defend this vast credulity—this instant acceptance of commingled fantasy with fact—by ascribing absence of spiritual intuitiveness to the sceptics. But if doubters are really impervious to intuition, the believers are equally impervious to reason.

6

Mystical societies should in theory be the most co-operative of all groups. Yet in practice we find them quite often the least! They should be the most disciplined emotionally yet they are often the least! Quarrelling, jealous, back-biting, eccentric, and cranky members make them what they are.

7

The greater their enthusiasm for an anti-materialistic view of life, the blinder their narrow fanaticism in following some queer sect. This is a sad consequence.

8

Such frenzied fanaticism is remote from philosophy and impervious to truth: that is why it is so utterly humourless, too.

9

There is peril in joining the parties which tend to group themselves around strong personalities or particular ideas.

10

When we see these cults shaken by internal dissensions and their followers shocked by internal scandals, we see that they are unable to practise what they preach.

11

Reason cannot argue with such silly fanaticism, so utterly and so blindly sure that its apocalyptic predictions must come into being visibly in due course.

12

These devout converts pursue these illusory goals with fanatic intensity.

13

The fence which encloses his own group excludes all other groups. How much larger is the philosopher's outlook which encloses everyone, shuts out no one.

14

The hysterical fanaticism and misplaced loyalty of these unsophisticated followers are pathetic. Their foolish conduct quite rightly makes critics doubt whether they are ahead of the mass-level in evolution as they assert, or whether they are behind it.

15

To reach truth naked and unadorned, we must perforce thrust our way through the ranks of occult fakers and sectarian faddists who throng the path. Their circumlocuting minds are not satisfied with the straight and narrow way, but they would have all other seekers follow them in devious and weary wanderings. The time has come to lash out with stinging whips and cutting flail at all those whose stupid pretensions masquerade as profound wisdom.

16

Those very features of the sect and characteristics of its leader which create doubt and scepticism in rational minds, only increase the enthusiasm and fanaticism of credulous ones.

17

Some affiliations and organizations are actually hostile to the purpose, the spirit, the teaching of their founders.

18

In the mystical cults of our time, of which there is an abundant variety, the followers generally take an extremely hostile attitude towards the teacher, writer, or prophet who is *not* the one favoured with their personal allegiance. He is a devil in disguise, an arch-sinner, a black magician, and so on. The attitude taken toward their own guide is equally exaggerated. He is God on earth, an angel in the flesh, omniscience personified, and so on. A more moderate, more reasonable attitude rarely enters their heads. This is possibly one reason why these cults are hotbeds of gossip, criticism, envy, and bickering.

19

Too often sects breed tyranny, uncharitableness, and fanaticism. They shut out the freedom which permits spiritual adventure and hence true spiritual seeking.

20

When they push their sectarianism to extremes, as they often do, they become exclusive, blind to truth anywhere else except their own beliefs. Even where they accept in theory that truth has more than a single spokesman, they desert this liberalism in practice. The sectarians shut out the spirit bequeathed by the great enlightenments, and let in what suits them of the letter. As for sectarian public propagandists, it is from their ranks that, given the chance and the power, the great fanatics and even the great persecutors emerge.

21

Why should anyone denigrate the character of another man out of envy of his attainment or detract from his reputation out of scepticism concerning the attainment itself? To hear such news is good news indeed, and such confirmation ought to bring joy to the heart.

22

The number of followers of any established cult—short or long-lived— is neither a sign of its truth nor one of its closeness to God. Discords will come sounding through. The harmonies will be there but only to a measurable degree and for measurable times.

23
The automatic obedience which these credulous followers give their psychotically fanatical leader follows naturally from the unreason in their minds.

24
The imbalanced followers, the fanatical adherents, will usually ignore the most temperate criticism of their cult or, if aroused, meet it with abuse.

25
The wild abandon, the careless spilling of slogans which show up the user's ignorance, fanaticism, and deficiencies, may be left to the intellectually adolescent. There is nothing to interest the truth-seeker here.

26
The feminine disciples often begin to compete with one another for the attention and love of the master. This leads to jealousy, intrigue, and backbiting—to an unwholesome and undesirable atmosphere.

27
Sometimes it is hard to know where their high-mindedness ends and hysteria begins.

28
I have taken a view which conflicts with the conventional assumptions of the X-ists that all Y-ists are fools, and of the Y-ists that all X-ists are knaves. I believe that some X-ists are likewise fools and some Y-ists are also knaves.

29
Within these groups, schisms and rivalries, sectarianism, jealousies, controversies over the interpretation of the Leader's words appear just as they do in worldly organizations.

30
These small religio-mystical or occultist sects are as notorious as the large and old religions for splitting into opposing factions and suffering internal feuds. The troubles are sometimes personal, sometimes ideological, more often the two together.

Deluded guides, gullible followers

31
Mystical movements are often infested with half-crazy fanaticism and astonishing delusion. The earnest enquirer ought to be warned, even

though in many cases the warning might as well be given to the waves. The subject is unpleasant, yet it must be addressed. Too many mystic paths have their beginning in mental aberration. Those who follow them with misguided enthusiasm bring harm to themselves and may bring suffering to others. Such paths are dangerous to their followers in particular and to society in general.

32

Those who follow one of these insane guides will in the end be led close to insanity themselves. But, with the cunning which so often is allied to madness, the guide may present them with great revelations and grand visions of the past, present, and future evolution of mankind, all of which may seem in accord with the teachings of the seers whose reputations time has established. From this impersonal level, there will then be an abrupt descent into tremendous personal aggrandizement on the part of the guide and magnificent promises of mystical experiences to the disciple. Both are nothing more than wild vagaries of a disordered brain.

33

An incompetent spiritual guide may cause mental, moral, or nervous injury to his followers as much as an unqualified physician may cause physical injury to his patients. He may bring about a serious nervous breakdown, a dangerous mediumistic loss of self-control, or a condition of hopeless impracticality.

34

The blunderer who meddles with an already half-unbalanced mind may bring his victim to a wholly unbalanced state.

35

During a long life I have observed many gurus and their followers in both East and West, many teachings and movements in religious, occult, mystical, metaphysical, spiritistic, and allied areas. And though there certainly are pearls of truth, there is also more lunacy than is recognized. In literary, poetic, and art circles the situation is the same. Several figures hailed as brilliant geniuses in the spiritual and cultural areas are in fact brilliant semi-lunatics. Their followers who are attracted to or try to copy them lose more and more sanity. This is why I have put forward so prominently the quality of balance, its importance to all alike, both teachers and taught. Give all things their just weight; put them in their proper place. In the figure of Libra, the scales are very evenly held so that justice may be done—that is, the truth may be found.

36

In Subud it seemed that the weekly meeting called Latihan had much of the flavour, or rather the atmosphere, of a spiritualist séance. The believers would sit in a group waiting for something to happen to them, some psychic experience. They were told by their guides, technically called Helpers, that the force at work would be God, whereas the spiritualists were told that it would be the spirit of a departed person. In both cases they were told to remain entirely passive and to yield themselves to whatever urge was felt. The results were certainly curious, sometimes alarming.

37

There is a sect of hippies in California who call themselves the Crackpots of Christ. The leader is a young man who travels throughout the country on a motorcycle and his name is Arthur Blessit, obviously an assumed name. They publish a journal called the "free journal of Hollywood."

What is interesting about them, apart from the fact that most of them were formerly drug-takers and have been freed from this habit by Blessit, is their communal prayer. This is done by raising their arms towards the sky out in the open, closing their eyes, and then beginning to hum all together. This hum gets slightly stronger and stronger until in the end it becomes a thundering cry. No word is actually uttered. How shall we interpret this prayer? Is it the anguished cry of the soul towards God?

38

The maniacal occurrences at these Subud meetings do not indicate the presence of God but rather the reverse. Such manifestations are not new in religious history. Christian, Hebrew, Hindu, and Muhammedan sects have displayed them, shrieking, shouting, singing, crying, yelling like animals, swaying, leaping, crawling, dancing. The delirium of madness is not spirituality.

39

Some of these gurus and more of their followers are to be considered as not quite sane. It is true that total sanity seems hard to find in the modern world anywhere, which is due to the lack of balanced development. But the oddities in occult circles show not only this lack but also other odd qualities.

40

There are insane leaders who form insane cults and gather unbalanced fanatics around them. The heads of the followers are constantly filled with mad dreams until there is little room left for the real facts of this world and less for those of the authentic spiritual world. The cheating, the betrayal, and the disappointment of these foolish people is inexorable but they may refuse to acknowledge the futility of their dreams and may resist disillusionment to the end.

41

They get swept into the current of imagination which flows through the master's mind, and are thus led to share his hallucinations.

42

The insane man's mind tells him that he is Napoleon. The deluded mystic's mind tells him that he is a master. The initial lie, once accepted, leads logically to the final delusion. This is why they are wrong who assert that one mystical school, belief, practice, or teacher is as good as any other for the beginner, so long as he gets started. It is a fact that men who live in mad fantasy or wild imagination, and whose teaching emanates from the same disordered source, can soon collect a following if they mutter the magic words "Indian yoga" or "Tibetan masters."

43

It is an unpleasant fact, yet one too serious to ignore, that quite a number of cults and teachers lead their naïve followers, not gloriously to spiritual reality, but unfortunately to spiritual lunacy. By the initial act of adherence to the cult or pupilship with the teacher, these followers make their own subsequent karma and fall more and more from the path of sanity each year. In their defense let it be said that their intentions were mostly good, but good intention is not always a sufficient virtue in life, especially in connection with spiritual seeking.

44

A certain proportion of what passes for occult doctrine and religio-mystic prophecy is sheer insanity. Its effect upon those who believe it is to render them still more unfit for philosophic truth than they already are, for it weakens their faculty of discrimination.

45

Subud's is a mediumistic method; the risks involved make it difficult to trust any such method.

46

There is too much sick apocalyptic neurosis in the new mystical cults, too much pessimistic assertion about the bankruptcy of the race and its leaders, to bespeak their mental health.

47

What I have seen in these circles convinces me that a mild insanity pervades many of them, from much reputed gurus to just beginning disciples. It was a man of the sharpest intelligence, of the acutest psychological insight, who first pointed out this fact to me. V. Subramanya Iyer illustrated his thesis again and again during our textual explorations and personal excursions in India itself, but it was found still valid when I continued the investigation in Europe and America.

48

If we turn away from philosophical circles to religio-mystical ones, we find less rational and more emotional practices. One of the eighteenth-century Hebrew Hassidic groups practised the turning of somersaults during their prayers. In defense they claimed that this turning over of the body helped to turn down their pride.

49

Those who found their manna in a robot-like personal relationship with Gurdjieff, so that they never awoke to the facts, got what they deserved. But they were to be pitied for grovelling at the feet of a somewhat boorish half-lunatic, a heartless exploiter of trusting women and men, a man who thrived on mystery-mongering.

50

Gurdjieff's training of disciples showed in their control. At his command they suddenly froze their position as if caught by a camera, in arrested motion. A theory of Gurdjieff's was that when one is so tired that collapse is imminent, strength will come from an inner source of reserve power, a second wind. A cardinal point in Gurdjieff's teaching was the breaking of all habits, to free life from slavery to them. Another was exercise to make physical nature obedient and responsive to the will.

51

There is one important quality that seems to be missing from the Gurdjieff-Ouspensky training, and that is the heart element of love.

52

Rosicrucians seemed to have taken the greatest pains to keep their teachings secret, and themselves in the background, but these American Rosicrucians offer to send you their sublime philosophy through the posts, while they take care to keep themselves in the foreground by plentiful use of the arts of publicity.

53

Gurdjieff, like Meher Baba, often made abrupt changes of policy at his Fountainbleau Institute in its early and floundering years. This confirms his lack of balance. Gurdjieff also made some of his male disciples drink vodka and himself slept with some of his female disciples. This need not necessarily mean he was evil, it may mean that he was practising Tantra; but it was morally wrong and inexcusable.

54

These articles should be critically judged by students of the esoteric. Therefore, the idea of the King of the World and of his Subterranean City does not correspond with the physical facts. Similar statements about related ideas belong to fantasy.

55

In religio-mystical circles one meets from time to time those who believe they have a mission either to establish some utopian colony, community, or settlement, or to bring about a certain transition to peace on earth and goodwill unto all. Such visionaries usually fail to produce much practical consequence of their visions. No great change can be brought about in human history without first bringing about a great change in human nature: but lesser changes can be achieved.

56

Those who look eagerly forward to a time when all troubles have disappeared, all wars have been dismissed, and all society turned into a Utopia are merely fooling themselves.

57

If a crazy person declares that he is Napoleon, it may not be long before he finds himself in the confinement of a lunatic asylum; but if someone equally crazy declares that he is God, it will not be long before a worshipful following collects around him.

58

The claims of these cults are sometimes so plainly absurd that their followers must be too stupid to deserve anything better.

59

Some cults are merely foolish, others are quite mischievous. Some set up colonies intended to become utopias but never even approach the ideal.

60

Their published writings fail to show any logical basis; but they do succeed in showing a semi-pathological condition in the writers.

61

Some of the qualities, attributes, and practices demanded of spiritual aspirants are so queer, exaggerated, or unbalanced that the ultimate result will be not a human being, but a strange, half-insane creature.

62

A psychiatric study of the contents of these writings would show that they are the productions of a half-insane person, a psychopathic case, yet the followers read them with awe reverence and credulity.

Money

63

Cults whose leaders mix the motive of extracting money from the wallets of their followers with the motive of helping them are immensely better than those which seek money alone. But they are still far from the pure spirit of service which is the mark of true attainment.

64

The wide sale of books which promise to bring the help of God for the furtherance of personal fortunes, or to increase the power of man over others or over circumstances without requiring the discipline of man, shows how confused is the public's understanding of their authors. The offer of quick returns for little or no moral investment, of cheap easy ways to get something for nothing, belongs really to the witch-doctor, the primitive magician, and the necromantic sorcerer.

65

Those who seek for gain financially and notoriety personally are one kind, those who seek to hide their unethical acts behind occult secrecy are another kind. But all the different kinds share one thing in common—they are animated by, serve, and worship their own ego.

66

In the hands of cheap imitators exploiting the grand tradition of Asiatic wisdom, truth has become a cover for personal ambition and financial exploitation. They are as much under the influence of worldly motives as those whom they denounce. They proffer sanctimonious precepts to living worldlings, for the benefit of others, drawn from the code of defunct saints.

67

The peril which, as history attests, plagues all organized movements is that the maintenance and power and wealth of the organization become the chief motives of those who control it, while the free spiritual growth of the individuals who compose it tends to be hindered and sometimes even smothered.

68

An amusing variant of this cult will, for instance, enjoin hydrocephalic followers to spend spare time thinking, "Money is coming to me!" This magical phrase is concentrated on, chanted aloud, repeated vocally or mentally *ad infinitum* and *ad nauseam*. Even when money is quite evidently not coming in sight, and poverty is becoming a more intimate companion, the hypnotic glamour of this startlingly simple method persists in lulling its practitioners into great expectancy. Its practitioners ultimately receive what they deserve. They receive nothing. A saner system would teach its disciples the straightforward truth: "If you want money you must work, beg, borrow, speculate, or even steal it from somebody else!" But wishful thinking is an ancient habit. Weak persons lose their heads when they find an extravagant teaching.

69

The cults which hold out a bait of teaching followers how to achieve prosperity in their financial affairs and how to bring therapy to their bodily ailments need careful scrutiny.

70

The divine self does not necessarily demonstrate "supply" as money; it may demonstrate it by reducing one's bank account still further. True supply is entirely spiritual, the bringing up of a set of circumstances to the personal self which will afford it the spiritual lesson, expression, or opportunity necessary at the time. Those circumstances may be either prosperous or poverty stricken, as the wisdom of the Overself determines. Destiny, too, has something to say in the matter, but it is best left in the background of our reckonings; for, needless to say, destiny always works hand in hand with the Overself because both arise out of the same great Source—God. Poverty for some has been a gateway to higher things, for in times of prosperity the necessity of obtaining some understanding of the deeper side of life is not so strongly felt.

71

Every cult that cleverly tries to turn the inner life into an instrument for acquiring health and wealth puts its followers in danger. They are either flirting with black magic or falling into self-deception.

72

There are religious adventurers just as there are financial ones. They start new sects, seek to acquire followers, play the minor king, and are too often sustained in idleness.

73

In the United States there are many who use these silly incantations. Those who use "Dollars Want Me" are perhaps the most credulous of all.

74

Every attempt to commercialize this knowledge betrays its own source— the grasping greedy ego. Consequently it cannot give what it claims—truth from the Overself—but only the deceptive imitation of such truth. No matter what claims are made by these commercializers, reject them.

75

When the relation between a spiritual guide and an aspiring seeker is one of greed, no truth can pass from one to the other, only the illusion of it.

76

The practitioner who "demonstrates" more money for his clients and better health for their bodies is using an occult power and not a spiritual one. By this I mean that it is a power of the ego, not of the Overself. He serves his clients at a great cost to himself, which the fees they pay will never balance. They may congratulate him on his successful demonstrations, but these succeed only in keeping him imprisoned within his ego and out of his Overself.

77

Those who would turn the kingdom of heaven into a convenience and replace its blessings by affluence, worship their own ego and violate the first commandment.

78

Father Divine does not allow his followers to accept gifts. That privilege is reserved for himself. That is the source of his Cadillacs, his elegant home, and his large luxurious wardrobe. He claims to be Christ, yet not a week passes without his putting an un-Christlike satanic curse upon some hapless person who has dared to criticize him or to express disbelief in his divinity.

79

When their personal career is involved in their movement or they have a financial relationship with their cult, the very Quest which might have advanced them spiritually now hinders them spiritually.

80

The wide gulf which separates these pseudo-mystical, prosperity-seeking, modern sects like New Thought and "Science of Mind" from true mysticism is lit up by the emanation from a single Arabic word *fakir*, which has spread its usage throughout the Orient from Morocco to India. The word literally means "one who is poor" but usually means a holy man, while the condition of poverty has come to be associated with the Sufis, the most important order of Muhammedan mystics.

81

To be poor in spirit, in Christ's sense, is exactly the same as to die to self. More plainly, it is to achieve a total detachment from all things. How remote from truth, then, are all those who seek to turn the kingdom of heaven into a convenience for acquiring worldly goods!

82

These cults fall into the mistake of making worldly success and triumphant ambition synonymous with divine response to their prayer or divine reward for their meditation.

83

In his early days, Rasputin was sponsored by such men as Father John of Kronstadt, the Christlike healer, who declared that he was inspired by the Holy Ghost! Yet even then Rasputin refused to be parted from what he called his "spiritual sisters" with whom his relations were sensual as well as spiritual.

84

Instead of teaching people how to pray aright by praying for more strength, more wisdom, and more peace, they taught them to look for dramatic happenings following a useless practice like praying for national material benefits, when not one percent of such prayers were ever answered nor could ever be answered by the deaf, dumb, and paralytic Pantheon.

85

It is a foolish cult which makes worldly prosperity a measuring standard of spiritual effectiveness.

86

Their primary desire is a materialistic one, but it is mixed with such a thick serving of spiritual principles and quotations from Jesus that the cult is able to deceive itself into saying that it is a religion!

87

These cults never suspect their own motives, never see that they want to bring heaven into their little egos instead of bringing their egos into the kingdom of heaven. But then, they dare not desire the latter, for it would mean the vaporizing and vanishing of all their materialism, their attachment and acquisitiveness.

The abuse of power

88

When spirituality turns professional, when it begins to wear special clothes, possess particular titles, advertise its presence in certain men, it begins to become an artificial pretentious thing. It is no longer its pure self but an adulteration of itself, no longer spontaneous and natural but forced and self-conscious.

89

Before they can make fools of their followers, they have first to be foolish themselves. This is obvious enough in the case of those whose disordered brains breed wild fancies, but not in the case of those whose crafty self-seeking shows active intellect. Here the foolishness is moral, for the practice of such evil breeds a dark karma.

90

This is not difficult because his most devout followers are composed of the most impressionable, the most suggestible and easily deceived elements of society. They are the younger generation on one side and hysterically emotional women on the other, who readily come to believe what is constantly said, not what is rightly or rationally said. Their minds are too untrained to detect in his language that over-emphasis which conceals doubt. He resorts to the methods of a mountebank in order to impress such people. When persons become so mesmerized that the actual state of affairs no longer matters to them while the supposed state of affairs alone matters to them, when crazy rationalizations of wrong-doing enable them to justify it as right-doing, and when the will to believe wrongly has eliminated the need to reason logically, their doom is certain. The harm their teacher does to their possessions may be terrible but the harm which he does to their minds and hearts is worse. He turns morality upside down and they eventually accept the upset.

91
These evil teachers question the moral values offered by religious prophets and mystical seers. They proclaim the bad man to be better than the good one, the egoist superior to the altruist, and the bully a more evolved type than the meek.

92
All men who develop these mystic powers do not use them in a benign manner. Some use them malignantly.

93
Rom Landau writes in *Sex Life and Faith*: "Over and over again in the course of the last fifteen or so years I have been approached by men and women who had thrown themselves whole-heartedly into movements that practised public confessions, sharing, surrender, and all the rest. As a result of their conversion they imagined that they have solved all their spiritual, mental, and material problems, but after a short time they found themselves more entangled in their own complexes, phobias, and vices than before their 'change.' Often their married lives had been shipwrecked; their business affairs, conducted in response to 'guidance' and not to reason and professional knowledge, had become chaotic; and their sexual lives were either repressed, warped, and full of psychological ill-effects, or indiscriminately promiscuous. It seemed as if whatever moral stamina they had once possessed had deserted them; and they were left without self-reliance or the ability to discriminate between right and wrong. Believing that God had 'let them down,' they substituted for their former religious faith an embittered cynicism, and, as a result, were lacking in most of these elements out of which they might have built a new philosophy of life. This was inevitable."

94
Any man who uses mental power to prey upon innocent victims is practising black magic. Any man who uses his occult knowledge to obtain his desires at the expense of other persons is practising black magic too.

95

He is one of those who failed in his own quest through a strong egoism and vanity, and in consequence became the instrument of evil powers. He is doomed to spend his years in the evil task of striving to drag earnest seekers down to the same miserable failure that he has achieved.

96

If the guru is only half-purified of egoism, he may transmit to the disciple something of his own darker quality.

97

Their followers are not fundamentally bad, as are the leaders whose evil spell is thrown over them. But they waste valuable years, or even whole lifetimes, struggling in the marshy pit wherein they have fallen.

98

If spiritual institutions and organizations had really spiritual persons at their head, and not merely power or funds-seeking administrators, they would be much more worthy.

99

The organized group too often falls into the hands of one man, or a few men, whose personal ambitions make them sooner or later oppressors and tyrants, imposing *their* will, ideas, demands upon the others.

100

The yogi who sits so solemnly or squats so obediently may think himself more spiritual than the artist who does neither. But this sort of profes-sional spirituality can easily become artificial and self-deceptive.

101

They have lost control of their animal self and indulge in sordid amours and squalid dissipations miscalled "adventures," "being oneself," or "living one's own life."

102

Some find it a means of making a career for themselves. If they are also inwardly dedicated, their sincerity will not thereby suffer; but if they are not, then it will.

103

The outcome of all black magic is an unhappy one for the magician, the witch, or the sorcerer. Study the closing years of the professional practi-tioners of these cults and you will find that by dabbling in grey magic they have prepared a somewhat similar end for themselves.

104

The danger of these cults which stimulate desire and profess to reveal techniques for gratifying it is that they may easily lead their followers to slip by degrees into paths of grey magic and spiritual ruin.

105

Those who want to play with the sex practices of Tantrik yoga may do so at the twenty-to-one risk of becoming nymphomaniacs and satyrs.

106

Rasputin is reputed to have belonged to a religious society which believed that sin was the path to repentance and this in turn to salvation: and so to sin greatly was to be saved more quickly.

107

So powerful an urge as sex assumes, in the eyes and minds of young men, so dominant a place that it is often futile to advise all of them to renounce it entirely in favour of lifelong chastity. Most of them will be both unwilling and unable to follow such lofty counsel. They have little power to control what is happening to them here, for a universal force is behind it. Is it not more prudent to suggest a graduated discipline to them? Most people can move only from one level of thought and character to a higher one by slow degrees; very few by sudden jumps which miss those degrees. The case of a non-sectarian American monastery founded by a well-known religio-mystical writer and lecturer only a few years ago proves this point. He gathered more than a score of young men and put them under his direct personal supervision in this monastery. All practised meditation and asceticism strenuously. Within a comparatively short time, some of them took to homosexuality, others went mad, still others had nervous breakdowns, and a couple gave up mysticism altogether. The founder had to close down the monastery and he himself became a physically sick person. I do not assert that it was only his harsh unbending attitude toward sex which was responsible for all this. I say that it certainly was a powerful contributing cause, along with other causes, especially his anti-philosophical stand. "I will let no student of Brunton's teachings come here," he informed one candidate for monastic virtue. He also naïvely believed—and told the world in his books—that humanity could be saved by organizing similar groups. This is in direct disregard of Emerson's warning that "souls are not saved in bundles." Only an inspired master has ever saved anyone else in past history. The mere pooling of ignorance or multiplication of helplessness cannot save anyone.

Drugs

108

The drugged mystic finds a counterfeit god, however exact the imitation may seem to be. The true mystic will know and show the differences in the after-effects of the experience.

109

Whatever "divine" experience the taking of a drug yields, however high seems the enlightenment it enables the man to attain, the God, Reality, or Truth thus known is *at best a reflection as in a mirror, at worst a product of the liberated but wandering imagination.*

110

Despite the pleas and assertions of the drug-takers, the two worlds are emphatically *not* the same. What the truly enlightened man experiences is the reality; what the drug-taker experiences is, in part or very largely, a plausible copy with dangerously misleading insinuations.

111

This higher condition cannot be attained by the use of drugs, but it can be copied, which is a great self-deception.

112

What they feel and find is not the genuine historic and traditional mystic experience but the mere semblance of it, a drugged mockery which delights but deceives its victims and actually blocks the way to the authentic real experience.

113

The heavenly conditions given by drugs are hallucinatory ones. They soon pass and have to be sought again until addiction to the drug is established, and with it all its harms and dangers to one's character and fortune. There is however another way, a natural way, to find this heavenly condition and not an artificial one like the drug way. That other way can be found through philosophy.

114

The glimpse brings him to himself, but no drug can do that. The drug brings him before a vivid mental picture which he lives; it is still only a picture—sometimes horrible like a nightmare, sometimes sublime like a mystical ecstasy. But never in these experiences does he enter his true self. Always he is looking at and living with a picture.

115

Although the mystic experience got through drugs is only a copy, not the genuine thing, it has been useful to some persons because it is both suggestive of new concepts and confirmative of old ones. In the first category is the possibility of higher realms; in the second is the factuality of religious beliefs.

116

The real fact is that they are not the same, that many drug-induced experiences only *look* the same, if they are uplifting—and belong to the nether astral world if degrading, frightening, or fantastically absurd.

117

Success in meditation is most often hard and slow to achieve; patience, and more patience, is needed. So the drug offer of instant escape from this world of time, care, toil, problem, and suffering makes a better appeal to the ill-informed.

118

These drugs—the bhang of India, the hashish of the Near East, the LSD of America—make it more difficult to find truth, not easier as addicts claim.

119

Those who use hashish (Indian hemp) as a means of obtaining temporary mystical glimpses really get hallucinatory experiences whose bringing on is helped by the temporary loss of memory. But these may be followed by a fall into sexual fantasies, since there is no real control of what is happening. It may be that clear inner experiences seem to present themselves, but this still does not do more than offer duplicates. Unless the danger is seen and the drug addiction abandoned, the man simply decreases the ability to open himself to genuine mystical experience.

120

The drug-born God-experience is only a mirror image, though it may still seem quite lifelike; such images are lifelike, as forged copies of Old Master paintings are. But it remains an imitation, not the real thing.

121

A drug which blows up the mind, explodes it into another dimension, substitutes a false reality for the real one when it seems to give the God-experience. What the taker does not know is that he has entered a region of consciousness affiliated with the image-making faculty, with imagination. This is a difference which is tremendously important.

122

Drugs yield no true enlightenment but only a parody of it. The experience passes, craving for it returns, so the dose or injection is constantly repeated. With time the dose gets larger, the injection more frequent, the addiction more dangerous to sanity or disastrous to health. The counterfeit Nirvana may turn into a frightening hell with dreadful nightmares.

123

Young persons are easily deceived by the sham uplift which drugs may confer. It is an astral plane experience, not a Buddhic plane one, as it seems to be.

124

Mind-tearing by drugs is not the same as mind-stretching by philosophy.

125

A famous contemporary member of the intelligentsia, who is also an adherent of Vedanta and Buddhism, has advocated the taking of a certain drug which, on the basis of an eighteen-month acquaintance, he declares harmless. My own acquaintance with natives of the country where it is produced shows it to be harmful. This writer thinks its use a shortcut to gaining both psychic and spiritual enlargement of consciousness. Let us be generous and believe that such advocacy must have been a temporary mental aberration on his part. All narcotic drugs make slaves of those who fall into the habit of taking them. The habit itself often begins with such seemingly harmless and apparently casual indulgence as this gentleman proposes. The end result of the addiction is to create physical moral and mental sickness and to produce individuals who injure themselves and become a menace to others.

126

The drug route to metaphysical enlightenment and spiritual liberation is too often taken to be the cheapest route, but in the end it becomes, again too often, one of the dearest.

127

Those who use intoxicants, drugs, or narcotics to escape from the common normal human condition will find that they have put obstacles in their own path when the time comes later to abandon these artificial methods for the natural ones which alone can give a permanent result.

128

What the drug-taker gets is *imagined* reality, not real reality. Consciousness *assumes* the experience of knowing Truth, gives him the most vivid idea that this is IT. The end effect is not to bring him nearer to the goal, as he wrongly believes, but farther from it. Such are the tricks that mind can play on self.

129

It is possible these persons puff their pipes of hashish because it quietens doubts and gives a benign feeling of personal welfare. Yet it could be illusory.

130

The drug experience, however exalted it is, never really gets beyond being an astral plane copy, a pseudo-contact with a pseudo-god. It is illegitimate for modern man to break Nature's safety barrier in this way. He may pay a penalty with health, sanity, or self-deception.

131

A happy feeling of freedom from care may be got from drugs, but the happiness is illusory and brief while the side effects or long-range effects of the drug may be harmful.

132

There is quite a detectable difference between serene profound withdrawnness in meditation and drugged immobility in addiction.

133

Each has his own personal reasons for using drugs; they can be widely different.

134

They experiment with drugs in hope of getting a personal experience of the Transcendence. But even if they get it, will it be real, authentic, safe, and not a personal phantasy? Is there any assurance that the earlier period of rapture, ecstasy, revelation, and mind-expansion will not turn into a later one of nightmare, terror, deception, and mind-destruction—as in quite a number of cases it does?

135

Because certain drugs seem to duplicate the psychic or mystic experiences in their effects, superficial minds have leapt to the conclusion that it is unnecessary to put in the hard unremitting labour which inner practices require.

136

Those who find the work of meditation too arduous, its diurnal regularity too tiresome, either abandon it or take to a substitute. This may be ceremonial magic or narcotic drug.

137

Drugs: (a) People take to these drugs like LSD and heroin for different reasons. One of the reasons is that they feel so full of tension that the need to relax becomes imperative. But this they are unable to bring about by themselves; so the easy artificial way is used. That a habit may be formed, that one day they may break up their consciousness through it, losing reason and control for short periods while hallucinatory heavens or monsters surround them, is something they need to be warned against.

(b) If you study the eyes of a *fakir* long addicted to smoking the Asiatic narcotics—hashish and bhang—you will observe that the irises often tend to become bloodshot. If, however, he is addicted to smoking opium the effect appears in the pupils, which tend at times to narrow down into pinpoints.

(c) All these narcotic drugs like opium, belladonna, and LSD which alter consciousness are poisons and, if taken in sufficiently large quantity, could kill a man, or at least bring about a state of stupor or complete unconsciousness. The habit of taking them is hard to break, and itself breaks the taker—morally and mentally and to some extent even physically by inducing convulsions.

138

Nirvana is not reached by LSD trips: the old way is still the only way. But just as you can get substitute paper suits that look like real wool or cotton cloth suits, so you can reach imitation nirvanas by travelling on certain chemical or plant drugs.

139

The danger is not in the marijuana itself: it may be comparatively harmless to many people, although positively harmful to others. The real danger is that, finding it so satisfying, there are those who will be allured to the more powerful drugs in search of more powerful satisfactions. Thus they graduate until they drive through red traffic signals or jump from windows or stare at the sun until they go blind.

140

LSD intensifies perceptions, vivifies colours, re-animates long-forgotten memories. A common experience with it duplicates one that comes to mystics. It is as if one part of the man is entirely outside the other part, as if he were two persons. As mind, pure "I"-consciousness, he is invisible. As physical body, he is the object looked at a short distance in front of the "I." Some subjects found the experience horrible and would have no more of it. But others found it delightful and could not get too much.

The normal safe dose of LSD is 100 micrograms, hardly a pinhead. The tremendous power of this chemical drug far exceeds all the old natural drugs hitherto known.

In *The Island*, his last novel, Aldous Huxley seemed to recommend drug-taking as a means of procuring spiritual glimpses, and to assert that there is no difference in result between them and orthodox ones. This is no more correct than the assertion that there is no difference between a real object and its duplicate in a glass mirror.

Drugs destroy character, weaken the will, and sabotage the memory. They pervert the reasoning faculty. Drugs taken long enough turn the taker into an addict. In the end, when dependence is complete, he will be a nervous, moral, or physical wreck, depending on the kind of person he is.

141

The conclusion of this matter on the moral level is that Buddha was wise to ban drugs. The dangers and delusions inherent in their use are too serious to permit it.

142

A drug like LSD is favoured by the young on the claim that it opens the mind up to truth and love. That may be, but at the same time it opens the mind up to illusions and self-deceptions. These could be dangerously harmful.

143

Hashish, bhang, ganja, and charas—to name the four principal drugs—have been used in India since the early historic days, but those who used them were the lower, less cultured yogis.

144

In the secret Mysteries of the ancient Egyptians and ancient Greeks the accepted candidates were put in the trance state. This was done in some cases by mesmerism, in other cases by the use of certain herbs such as the now well-known sacred mushroom. They did not have chemical drugs in those days and the knowledge was carefully controlled so that there was no risk in the use of mesmerism or danger in the herbs.

145

Instead of arriving in the future at a consciousness altered into a higher one, they arrive in the present at a rotting one. Such is the danger of these chemical hallucinogenic drugs.

146

The drug way of coming into this consciousness belongs originally to a distant era, when spiritism, of which ancestor worship was then also a part, was the most widespread religion on both sides of the Pacific Ocean. For primitive people, descendants of Lemurian and later Atlantean races, it was as far as they could develop at the time. A minority of the higher evolved followed, drew beyond the herd and prepared the way for higher teachings yet to come. The astral, or psychic, centres were sufficiently alive to need only a little prompting by the tribal leaders or priests—usually a group affair at certain festivals. It was then that their drugs obtained from Nature were used or, in the case of followers of her darker side, misused, even abused, resulting in sorcery, sex orgies, and black magic. In the more moral use of drugs, although the higher kinds of religious and mystical experience were not attained, the idea of survival was firmly implanted, along with respect for traditional codes teachings and ways. The development of intellect dimmed the astral centres. The use of drugs is an attempt to revive what is no longer proper for modern man.

147

The dangers of seeking an experience *alone* as the highest in life is shown by the drug-takers, the LSD addicts, the hippies and yippies, and, on a different level, the alcoholics.

148

The stronger drugs may turn their user into a robot, a victim of seemingly outside forces which compel him to do what he normally dare not or would not do.

149

The Greek guardians of the Mystery Temples put drugs in the bread and wine of accepted candidates and thus gave them visions.

150

It is a fact that many practitioners of the black magical systems have taken drugs, that teachers of such methods put many pupils upon the way of drug addiction.

151

Even the so-called harmless drugs, hashish and marijuana, cause a lack of energy and an aura of lassitude, which is not the effect of the tobacco smoking they are supposed to resemble.

152

During my researches in Egypt many years ago, I noted that men who were excessively devoted to the use of hashish formed the largest group in Cairo's insane population, and that another, smaller group suffered from religious mania, believing they had divine missions to fulfil or messages to deliver. It was interesting that autopsy revealed that in those of the first group who died, the brain had dried, shrunk, and become smaller.

153

When I lived in Mexico, the natives who had used mescaline told me also about marijuana which, in those days, was almost unheard of by young American students. The point is that the Mexicans who smoked marijuana cigarettes did not do so to expand their minds or to alter their consciousnesses—the common phrases today. They did so simply because these cigarettes were regarded as aphrodisiacs.

154

It is not surprising that in the past history of India, drug addiction among occult sects and yogic groups was not uncommonly associated with such activities as sex perversion, drunkenness, sorcery, and witchcraft.

155

Although the consequences of taking LSD vary so much and may be quite pleasant and, in a single dose never repeated, may in some cases be even harmless, its use is quite a gamble. Homicide, suicide, or insanity are always a possible result. In England there was a recent case of a nineteen-year-old student who tried to cheer himself by twice taking it; he jumped through a closed window, fell sixteen feet, broke a collarbone, and collapsed a lung. He had used the commoner, more available, less harmful, weaker, nonchemical drugs for five years without serious injury, but LSD was enough to make him demented!

156

The drug *nepenthe*, which leads to "neutral emotions," is mentioned by Homer in the *Odyssey* as a drink which confers "freedom from chagrin" and "complete emotional indifference," so that even if members of one's family, including one's own son, are killed in front of one's eyes, one can bear to see it calmly.

157

The real danger is when the man begins to externalize some of these fantasies, to express physically in murder or suicide, or some other desperate act, the pictures and ideas which roam or rave within him yet outside his control.

158

In 1877 an Indian Government report stated that 30.6 percent of Bengal's lunatics were insane because of taking excessive quantities of ganja, a decoction of hemp, which is also a pernicious poison.

159

Those of us who know from personal observation of many cases that the harmfulness of taking drugs is a real possibility cannot be misled by those cases which seem to have escaped it.

12

THE INTERMEDIATE ZONE

The pathway of the mystical goal is strewn with human wreckage. Why? Several reasons would be needed to give a complete answer but one of the most important is this: Between the state of ordinary man and the state of the matured mystic there lies a perilous and deceptive psychological region which has been given various names in mystical literature. It has been called the astral plane, the intermediate zone, the hall of illusion, and so on. The early efforts of all aspirants in concentration, meditation, self-conquest, and study, bring them into this region. But once here their egoism becomes stimulated by the subtle forces they have evoked, their emotional nature becomes more sensitive and more fluid, their imaginative power becomes more active and is less restrained. The consequence of failure to negotiate these changes properly is swollen vanity, superstitious credulity, emotions run riot, and imagination gone wild. The safeguards against all this are first, submission to the philosophic discipline and second, submission to competent guidance.

2

During the early stages of the meditator's career, ecstasies, visions, and messages may manifest themselves. He may accept the encouragement they bring to his feelings, but he should not accept the communications they make to his mind without screening them severely. It is easy for the ego to fall into self-flattering moods as a consequence of such experiences, and to pass from them into spiritual pride and vanity. But even if he succeeds in critically judging them, he must still remember and keep in mind that they, and even the emotional raptures, pertain only to these early stages and that he must become indifferent to and detached from them in the later ones. Otherwise, they will hinder his further development and cause him to stagnate.

3

These powers are latent in all men but active in few. To seek them before we have sought the divine Soul itself is a premature, unwise, and often dangerous enterprise.

4

All occult experiences and spirit visions are mental, and not spiritual, in the sense that the mind has various latent powers which pertain to the ego, not the Overself. The question of which is real can be answered differently according to standpoint. He need not trouble about the occult side, which would be a degeneration for him. His chief aim must be to realize pure B-e-i-n-g, not to see or experience anything outside it. Only after this has been done is it safe or wise to concern himself with anything occult.(P)

5

While the aspirant is still unbalanced in personality, undeveloped in capacity, and uninformed in attitude, his psychical "experiences" are not likely to be of much real value or importance. Yet, precisely because of this immaturity of his, he will exaggerate their value and magnify their importance. One consequence of this is that they may not only obstruct but even harm his progress if he dwells on them. Hence a competent teacher will discourage most talk about them. He wants to hear that the aspirant has begun to overcome an unworthy impulse, not that he has "seen" some mystical vision.

6

It is natural for beginners to become excited or enthusiastic about the psychic phenomena but to let them be overvalued or misunderstood is dangerous to further progress.

7

He must not misdirect his intelligence at the bidding of his thirst for occult powers, nor his devotion at the bidding of his yearning for a teacher. He must not befog his outlook by acquired antipathies and picked-up prejudices. He must beware of the neuroticism which often passes for mysticism.

8

The beginner should not seek communications, messages, oracles, predictions, or impressions from the divine. He inevitably lacks the capacity and knowledge to discriminate between those that come from the true divine and those that come from the pseudo-divine. Because the first class is rare but the second common, he is more likely to be deceived than inspired. This kind of effort may lead to dangerous results.

9

What novices regard as psychic gifts are more often psychic ills. What they regard as spiritual development is more often spiritual affliction. They are the victims of their visions. Farther from God and nearer to madness leads the path of their heard voices and automatic writings.

10

Temptation begins when he becomes aware, through phenomena occurring in his presence or by his thought, that occult powers are developing within him. He may then come to regard himself as an extraordinary superman—which is nonsense—or as a somewhat imperfect channel.

11

It is just as possible to use these occult powers evilly as it is to use them beneficently. Indeed it is more possible. Therefore the way to them is guarded vigilantly, both by Nature and by those who hold the necessary knowledge.

12

Emotional vapourings may, at this early stage, be mistaken for authentic inspirations; even neurotic ravings may be welcomed as sacred revelations. Their content may even be partially or totally false.

13

He who would avoid unknown terrors should reject the pursuit of occult powers and the courting of invisible spirits, until he understands what he is doing. Let him learn before he moves, know light and shadow.

14

All occult development should be shunned until the character has been thoroughly changed, the emotions purified, the will hardened, and superstitions removed by knowledge. It may then come by itself as a resultant by-product of advanced mystical practices in meditation. In this way it will come safely and prove useful. In any other way, moral and mental deterioration may ensue, personal dangers may be incurred, while general futility may be the end of all.

15

The practices of psychism and occultism, with their pursuit of psychical and occult powers, have this peril: that unless the seeker is quite well informed he may be led astray from the correct path if he is at a lower stage, or be kept too preoccupied with his own ego (or extensions of it) if at a higher one. What might be useful adjuncts to a sage could become snares to a seeker.

16

The reason why the Yogi is called upon to reject the miracle-making powers which he earns is that unless he does so he is stopped in his onward progress to the Highest. He must go on and on until he gains the latter; "*Neti, neti*"—"Not this, not that"—must be his constant exclamation when new privileges of a superhuman kind are presented to him. In brief, he is not to be satisfied nor to stand still until he reaches his Goal. But once he has won his way to the truly spiritual plane of being, he can then safely turn around and pick up and use every occult power by which he has hitherto refused to become ensnared.

17

These mysterious unrealized powers in man can only be safely developed by an adept in philosophy, by a man who has already the knowledge to understand what he is really doing and the character to do it without danger to himself or others.

18

The *siddhis* represent the occult powers. They have no spiritual function, as they are on a lower level, although men who have attained spiritual realization may find themselves in possession of such powers. But also men who are not so interested in spiritual realization as in realizing their personal ambitions may deliberately seek and develop such powers.

19

He must understand that if he is clairvoyant and easily has visions, he is actually hindered in his progress at a certain stage, whereas this will become a great and helpful asset when he is more advanced. To get through to the higher consciousness these powers of clairvoyant vision must die down in him for a period and he must therefore co-operate and try to assist this process by the effort of deliberately willed self-repression.

20

A time may come when he may seek to get rid of those occult powers which, formerly, he sought so eagerly.

21

It is necessary to remember that a power which has been given may later be withdrawn.

22

If a student is devoted to the lofty ideal of finding what is finest in life, Nature mercifully withdraws possession of these supernormal powers from him after he has become, through his own short but startling personal experiences, both conscious and convinced of the wonderful power of Mind.

23

Then, of their own accord, they are mysteriously if slowly restored to him. During all this time they have preserved matured and perfected themselves through the unconscious workings of mind. Consequently he gains a superior form of them, as it were. Whereas before they were fragmentary fitful and sporadic, now they are ripe and forever to hand; whereas before they were vague and dreamlike, now they are precise and sharp. Nevertheless, the more authentic his possession of them is, the less will he speak of their existence. For several reasons—practical, prudential, and mystical—it is an unwritten law that they shall be owned and used in silence. Another reason for this silence is, however, almost ethical. These perfected powers arise when the ego is sunk, because they are powers belonging to the universal Mind, not to the ego. Hence to the degree that he identifies himself with the universal Mind he begins to manifest these miraculous powers. Because they are pertaining to universal Mind he cannot honestly say they are his. But neither can he honestly deny their presence in him. It is better, therefore, to keep silent about them.

In other cases, where the initial motive is low and unscrupulous but the patience to prolong meditation is high and determined, the loss of these powers comes much later. The man who is interested in merely gaining these powers for his own personal and selfish aggrandizement is entitled to receive what he has worked for. But his motive may not only cause him to injure others and thus bring down the eventual retribution of karma upon him, but also cause him to fall afoul of malignant invisible forces. A Mongolian philosopher with whom I once discussed the topic of developing occult powers dryly remarked that a man who tried deliberately to do so before being prepared by moral, mystical, and metaphysical disciplines was to be compared to an infant lying helplessly on its back liable to all kinds of dangers against which it had no shield.

24

That is not to say, however, that there are not strange faculties lying latent in the human mind. On the contrary, because mentalism is a fact in Nature, most *successful* yogis discover that some extraordinary faculties automatically arise in them. They offer a fascinating field of exploration to a properly trained competent investigator who has not only mastered the subject in a rational manner, and knows enough of the dangers and risks attending it, not only disciplined his mind and desires through the scientific, metaphysical, and yogic courses, but also consciously brought his ego within the framework of universal being. But amateurs who invade this field through motives of mere curiosity or immoral exploitation sooner or later discover that it becomes a region either of sheer time-wasting or else of grave danger. Even the best of men will find his way through this field with the utmost difficulty, while for most dilettanti it is an undertaking which is usually foredoomed to failure. In any case these powers not only are hard to get but may prove dangerous when gotten.

25

Psychic powers may develop of themselves as a consequence of mystical self-culture but should not be sought as its end. The first way is safe, the second is dangerous.

Tests, ordeals, temptations

26

The psychic experiences that may come to him on the Quest may be important preliminary phases in which some truths are passed on from the Overself in the form of mental pictures. Such a probationary period is usually filled with tests and ordeals, temptations and tribulations. In this connection, the events themselves are important to his personal life; but his *reactions* to them are what is important to his spiritual life.

27

Mysticism and meditation are but stages on the way up; their value lies in forming the fineness of mind, concentration of thought, and abstractedness of mood which are required to reach the higher stage. Of themselves they cannot bring us into truth or realization. If correctly practised they shape the mental instrument, or if incorrectly done they damage it. Hence all visions, psychic experiences, and occult initiations experienced in this stage are not only transient but of no real worth in themselves, while many are quite imaginary or the result of suggestion, however real to the experience for the moment.

28

Before we can reach the reality we have to cross a world of fanciful imagination and time-wasting delusions.

29

It is an unfortunate fact that some pilgrims become afflicted, either for a while or for a whole lifetime, with a mild madness. Their insanity is too mild to stop them from carrying on with their ordinary business of living, but it is sufficiently developed to make them waste time and energy in the pursuit of vain phantoms and absurd fantasies. If it takes the form of a hunger for occult phenomena or a desire to get spiritually transformed without working for it, they usually fall victim to some charlatan or imposter who aggravates their sickness and spoils their chances of recovery. If it takes some other form it is because they do not bring to the Quest sufficient practical judgement, emotional stability, and logical capacity. Such persons should abstain from meditation and limit their devotional exercises to prayer. They should greatly curb their mystical studies and give themselves up to the duller work of improving themselves. This work is absolutely necessary as a prerequisite to entering the real Quest; otherwise they will merely follow a hallucinatory one.

30

Another danger on the quest is a kind of mild madness during the long phase when occult phenomena are sought everywhere, esoteric interpretations are read into everything, and entry into the Overself is expected every day. No natural cause, no physical explanation will be accepted for any event if a supernatural one can be found. The worldly career may be marked by foolish acts which not only harm the actor, but, unwittingly, sometimes others too. Possessions may be squandered, opportunities thrown away, and false friends cultivated.

31

They begin to see their persecution by evil spirits and to feel the opposition by adverse forces, at every turn. But, in fact, the only enmity they have to endure is that which they fearfully imagine into existence.

32

It is by trying, aspiring, daring, that the latent creative forces in us are called into activity. Occultism teaches that all kinds of hindering and hostile forces surround us to drag us down. But if a man believes an influence or person or thing or environment to be hostile, if he thinks it will make it impossible for him to progress, then it may well be so; he will not progress. What occultism teaches is true, but it is not necessary to burden oneself with doubt and pessimism. There is also a higher truth.

33

There exist murky regions, lower worlds, which are best left alone, uninvaded, and not made visible by misguided efforts to become "clairvoyant."

34

If his feet remain solidly planted on earth, if his emotion does not outrun reason, if respect for fact is not failing, and if balance is kept always, he is in no danger of verging on that mild insanity or of entering that cloudy cuckoo-land which afflicts too many mystics.

35

Between his present stage and the ultimate goal, there lies a misty world of fantasies, illusions, snares, absurdities, and dangers. Here he may become as utterly confused about truth as beyond it he will become utterly convinced.

36

For some persons these are perilous studies: incipient madness finds in them its sun and water.

Danger signals, protective measures

37

Between the clear-cut solidity of the outer life in the sense-world and the impalpable delicacy of the inner life in the divine spirit, there is a region which many aspirants have to cross, but which a few succeed in avoiding. This is a region of illusion, fantasy, and psychism, where the ego uses its most cunning devices to entrap his emotions and entangle his passions, weaves its most specious flattery to seduce his intellect and imagination. On this part of his journey sensuality assumes the subtlest forms, fancy weaves the strangest occult experiences. Vanity receives the greatest encouragement through oracular or mission-bestowing messages, and unbalance is heightened to the pitch of neuroticism, hysteria, or even insanity. In this psychical stage of his development where error masquerades as truth, he will unconsciously impose upon the world of reality forms which properly belong to the world of sense. Here visions and messages, experiences and phenomena, things seen, heard, or touched by the imagination will constitute a subtle materialism designed to lead him astray. He must protect himself by drawing upon a strong, impartial self-criticism and self-denial, a strong, impersonal intelligence, and by seeking the counsel of a competent guide.

38

One's personal mystic experience is an important, perhaps the most important, test of the truth; but it should not stand alone. It needs to be checked by other standards. And it should be kept in the direction of the true and highest goal—discovery of the Soul. It should be kept away from the direction of occult phenomena. Psychic experience is something heard or felt or seen or touched—it is a sense-contact and belongs to the body's realm. The senses may deceive a man—or be used to deceive him! For such experiences involve the same five senses, albeit in another dimension, and need even more checking than physical ones. They belong to a road that is beset with temptations illusions and deceptions but in any case it is not "the straight and narrow path" to the kingdom of heaven. Psychism easily leads to a feeding and fattening of the ego, whose vanity glories in "powers" which it can show off to impress other people or even use to exploit them for its own benefit.

39

The dangers of letting his attention and energy be drawn aside from the main quest into psychic, occult, and mediumistic activities must be looked for in their early beginnings. It is then that they are easier to deal with. It is then that he must be vigilant and hard with himself, for the cost of going astray into these temptations is heavy.

40

It is true that to analyse with scientific detachment these most intimate and precious experiences, visions, and messages could, if imprudently done, easily destroy their value or prevent their recurrence. Yet this is precisely what he has to do if he is to protect himself against illusions.(P)

41

He must learn to discriminate between what is genuine and what is false, what is good and what is evil, if he is to pick his way through this deceitful region.

42

If he can catch any of these psychic manifestations at the very moment when they begin, that is the best time to prevent their arisal altogether, for then they are at their weakest. That is the proper time to nip them in the bud.(P)

43

The region of prophetic visions, clairaudient voices, and predictive messages opens up a veritable pit of possible illusions to the mystic. He must beware of the sights and scenes, the self-glorifying revelations which may present themselves to the mind during meditation. He would be better employed chasing such phantasmagorias from the mind rather than seeking to attract them! The mystic must put a stern check upon his imagination if he wishes to pass safely through his apprenticeship. The last word is that the course of meditation may or may not be accompanied by these occult phenomena. Neither does their addition improve the value of the mystic experience nor does their non-existence lessen it. Where they are genuine and authentic communications from the Overself, their value lies rather in personal but transient satisfaction or in immediate but momentary help.

44

A sincere motive is praiseworthy but not enough to give complete protection for untried, untempted, inexperienced innocence against these psychic and other dangers. It cannot be a substitute for cautious prudence, critical judgement, and psychical knowledge.

45

The intellectual weakness which permits such credulity must be removed if truth is ever to be found.

46

Humility is willing to question the reality of the figures it thinks it is seeing, but conceit is not.

47

Open-eyed observation and clear-headed enquiry will supply the true facts where fantastic imagination and psychic tendencies will largely misrepresent them.

48

We must make no pretensions to secrets which we do not possess. Since what we do not know is so much more than what we do know, it is better to be humble and straightforwardly to say, "I do not know." It is then possible to learn, to amend our ignorance; but once we pose as holding a knowledge which in fact we do not hold, we put up the shutters of the mind and doom ourselves to continued darkness.

49

He must endeavour to understand what has occurred, seeking to substantiate his understanding by scientific methods. Not that there are no genuine manifestations of this order; there are. Telepathy and telementation, clairvoyance and clairaudience, revelation and inspiration are actual facts *in* Nature, which means that they are not really supernatural but are spontaneous workings of little-known powers of the human mind. But they happen much less frequently than occultists believe, and what mostly passes for them are the workings of disordered impressions and philosophically untrained thoughts.

50

The man who exhibits repeated credulity thereby shows his unfitness for the highest truth. The seeker must not only not practise self-deception but must not let others practise deception on him.

51

All that is recondite, unusual, occult, and strange may attract a man but it may not serve him unless he finds a compensating attraction in what is holy, aspirational, divine, exalting, sublime, and wide. Without that it may disserve him.

52

Those who have to deal with physical things whose manufacture depends on precise measurements or practical skills cannot afford to work carelessly, think nebulously, or lose themselves in false or misty imaginings out of relation with the crude realities—certainly. no carpenter and no engineer dare do so. Yet so-called religious mystics, occultists, and psychics do, for there is no way to show up their errors.

53

Those who give themselves to these studies do not necessarily suffer a diminution of their intellectual integrity or emotional balance, although a proportion do. This is because they are already neurotic, hysteric, or irrational types. Such a person should first attend, or get a psychologist to attend, to the restoration of mind or character, and leave mysticism alone until this is done.

54

A student should try to use his will to stop any psychic development. He should change his posture the instant he is aware of it: not remain lying down, but either prop himself up in bed or get up and walk around.

55

If he seeks power at all, he does so not to establish it over others but over himself.

56

These experiences and revelations are to be received humbly, or they will become a source of harm rather than benefit, of swollen rather than attenuated ego.

57

"You are seeking," Cleon said, "for what is not of the world you live in, and you do not know how to judge soundly of what is under your eyes."— Thucydides

58

One danger of occult experience, if outside the philosophical training, is its inflation of the ego, causing the man to regard himself too highly and to appraise his spiritual position beyond its real one.

59

By this rigid discipline, the seeker is safeguarded from the danger of walking into his own mental creations under the belief that he is walking into spiritual reality. But those who have not undergone this discipline quickly fall into self-deception and stop there. They do not know that they have to pass through and beyond these mental creations if they would reach the reality behind them.

THE OCCULT

A choice of directions

The first reason for the warning not to pursue occult powers is that pursuing them is a sure way to prevent the soul's self-revelation. For the soul cannot be found unless its Grace has been granted. And it will not grant its Grace unless sought in all purity for its own sake. Hence the aspirant has to choose between it and occultism.

2

The way of the occult is one of blurred vision and mistaken choice. For those involved walk a way beset with inevitable dangers; and it is in every manner more difficult. It is not even more rapid to compensate for its danger, since it is less direct. It is a way strewn with camouflaged pitfalls. You can be safe—or sorry; choose which path you will follow: safe in the serene quest of the God within—or sorry after long years of dubious and dangerous occultism. The first is divine, the second dark. The first can result only in greater eventual happiness; the second often produces moral deterioration and mental derangement. The seeker after self-wisdom is not concerned with exploring the dormitories of the dead with the spiritist; neither does he seek, with the magician, to evoke those strange and terrible creatures which infest their entrances. The student who confuses Divine Truth with occultism or magic, with spiritualism or psychism, makes a great error.

3

If anyone comes to this Quest in order to obtain more power for his ego, even if it be occult, magical, or psychical power, he is wasting his time and had better leave it alone. There are ways to such powers but they lead off from the Quest, not to it. For they may all-too-easily, as observation often shows, inflate a man's vanity and increase his desires, thus thickening the illusions which befog him. Moreover, some of them expose him to grave perils: he may end by becoming possessed or going mad, by falling into the quagmires of necromancy, sorcery, or black magic. Seeking to glorify his own ego or to bend others to his will, he will be cast ingloriously to the ground and crushed by the very forces he has evoked.

4

He needs to beware of wandering into pseudo-occultism, spiritism, magic, and kindred undesirable subjects, as then adverse destructive forces would degrade his effort in time. Nothing of this kind should be dabbled in; otherwise he might become a conscious or unconscious medium. Only the pure and unmixed godly life should be sought, not the satisfaction of occult curiosity.

5

The attainment of psychic or occult powers by anyone who has not also attained freedom from his own emotional imbalances and intellectual inadequacies, and especially from his own basic egotism, is likely to prove dangerous to himself and others and to do more harm than good.

6

Just as only good can come from the realization of the Overself, so only evil can come from following the false paths that pretend to, but never can, lead to this realization.

7

The spiritual seeker who is under the impression that he must enter upon a course of occult experiences is utterly mistaken. Instead of being beneficial, such practices can, and often do, lead to serious unbalance, insanity, and dangerous and frightening occurrences.

8

Those who seek occult powers, superhuman capacities, have entered the wrong door. They should look elsewhere, not to philosophy, whose secrets concern primarily the kingdom of heaven. For the paths to hell are strewn with the wrecks of would-be witch doctors, sorcerers' apprentices, and magicians' disciples. For all this leads in the end to ego-omnipotence, not to ego-surrender.

9

The misuse of any occult power will effectively seal him in the ego and prevent union with the Overself.

10

No authentic spiritual growth can be made by means of the practices of either spiritism or hypnotism. They are unhealthy and unnatural, even though they do serve some value for scientific investigators. Above all, they cannot lead man to transcend his ego, without which the Overself remains inaccessible.

11

When this love of the marvellous becomes excessive, it prevents the man from finding truth, for his perceptions and sensations, his thinking and feeling, his judgements and observations are no longer reliable. Everything is thrown out of balance by his eager anticipation of miracles.

12

All attempts of the ego to wrest powers from the Overself and use them for its own independent purposes may succeed only for a time; in the end those who try are stricken by dismal failure, while in the beginning and the middle they are punished by being forbidden entry into the territory of the Overself.

13

The pure waters of spiritual life are not to be drawn from the dubious well of ghosts and goblins.

14

Those who seek in psychic realms find only reality's ghost. The peril here is that a reality may be turned into a delusion, and what is authentic may be turned into a sham.

15

The temptation may come from time to time, but a prudent seeker will refuse to let himself be corrupted by traffic with necromancy or by dabbling in magic or by pursuit of occult powers.

16

Only an illusory or transient progress can be made by these psychic and occult methods.

17

The foolishness of following wrong leads or trying wrong paths has to be paid for.

18

These gropings in the shadows of the twilit worlds that surround us are of little use. Such experiences can stretch out *ad infinitum*. It is in their very endlessness that the temptation lies which has lured so many seekers from the duty that lies to their hand.

19

Whoever lets himself become bemused by the occult into gullible acceptance of every wild fancy bearing its label, departs from the true quest and gets lost for his pains. He misplaces faith, an error whose penalty is painful disillusionment, and becomes an eccentric crank.

20

The seeker should pay no attention to the siren calls of so-called spirits of the departed, the promptings of megalomaniacal assumptions of messiahship, or the witchery of occult powers.

21

The time will come when he will throw tears on those years when he let the occultists hook him and thus turned the "simple way" into a steep impassable ascent.

22

Those who really seek thrills rather than truth may get them. All kinds of experiences await them. A lifetime could be spent having them. Truth is missed on the way.

23

Curiosity and inquisitiveness, but more especially the thirst to possess magical powers, lead him onto this way. Progress here fattens the ego, whereas progress on the true path thins it.

24

The genuine truth-seeker tries to keep out self-delusion in all its forms. He knows that the road is beset with it, that he must be watchful, and that the warning counsel of those who are farther on the way must be heeded.

25

My lamented friend, the Irish poet A.E., wrote with his celestial pen, "We are in our distant hope,/ One with all the great and wise,/ Comrade, do not turn and grope/ For a lesser light that dies."

26

If he is not careful, critical, balanced, sensible, and self-disciplined, the eager seeker may find after many years that he has simply been moving around the labyrinth of occultism to his own confusion in the end.

27

Those who meander in profitless occultism but call it divine science delude themselves. They tread a treadmill but imagine it is a path.

28

How many aspirants have travelled in circles, arriving, like Omar Khayyam, in the end at the same door by which they entered in!

The seductive shadow-world

29

Because it deals with matters not readily discernible, occultism's door is wide open to the bogus.

30

This seductive shadow-world of psychism lures many persons into its jungle-like depths, but it lures them only into the *shadows* of Reality, not into the Reality itself. Those who posture before the public as Hierophants of the Occult are unable to initiate their followers into that serene state wherein turbulent discontents and worldly desires wither away. They can, however, provide air-pies for those ready to swallow the solemn mysteries of occult lore; they can fool around in a fog of words and draw their followers likewise into it.

31

The occultist who sits like a mandarin before his devout but bewildered disciples and spins out whole systems of planes and spheres showing that he knows everything and more, has his pupils entirely at his mercy. They cannot answer back to him, for he is in the privileged and exclusive position of being able to "see" these planes and thus they must accept his reports.

32

The average occultist and psychic *knows* much less of his subject than he would have us believe. He may have lifted a corner of the veil but it is only a corner.

33

Just as acetate of lead is pleasant to the taste but deadly to life, so are the claims of these false occultists.

34

The idealized occultist of the author's imagination is not the mercenary occultist we find in reality.

35

The occultist takes pleasure in complicating simple truths or in concealing important ones.

36

Those who know the mind's capacity to indulge in fantasies and how quickly it submits to wishful thoughts, know also why these revived superstitions raised to the rank of revelatory theories have held so much fascination for so many students of the occult.

37

The gropings of medieval alchemists can hardly help him, and are better left alone. Whatever of truth he finds in them must already be known to him, and more clearly.

38

If educated people have been suspicious of occult societies in the past, they have had reason to be.

39

Grandiloquent revelations are preached by freaks to circles of oddities. They amount to nothing in the end, being the vaporous products of eccentric imagination collected around some psychic experience.

40

Here are problems which call for tremendous specialized erudition and for a high standard of scholarly exactitude and prolonged investigation before they can be adequately treated. Yet these impertinently amateurish occultists with little history and no archaeology or anthropology, without a scientifically trained judgement, and with credulous biased mentalities, sail swiftly and easily through the task!

41

The seemingly solid earth of kabbalistic magic and demoniac supernaturalism gradually becomes a marsh into which the unfortunate benighted wanderer sinks deeper and deeper.

42

Pious fancy sometimes pushes beyond actual fact.

43

How much farther can foolishness go towards insanity when the claim of revelation is naïvely used to make the most absurd beliefs appear as reasonable?

Occultists and psychics

44

Beware of pseudo-spiritual people. They are pests. Avoid meeting them; avoid talking to them. It would be far better for them to become out-and-out materialists than to go on deceiving either themselves or others with their wordy but fake spirituality. Under this heading I include also the spiritualists, the occultists, the psychics, and the "mental science" demonstrators. These people move through a fog of fake uplift. It is useless to try to give these people that which they are neither seeking nor asking for. They are not interested in finding REALITY but only its reflections and shadows. Hence, they have to be shown cosmologies, planes, occult powers, and miracles of magic. To teach Truth to such people when one is not asked for it is to commit an error with results that will act as a scourge to oneself. They themselves are always ready to teach anybody at any moment. We must be far wiser. We shall teach only when asked, only when we understand that it will do some real good, and even then only so much will be revealed as the querent is fit to take in. These pseudo-spiritual people are like living corpses, bodies which have taken on the appearance of life but are really dead.

45

The occultist who seeks to expand his life by enlarging his personal powers is often less near the Source than the artist who surrenders himself wholly to grace-given moments of felt beauty. The one is fastened more securely to the ego, the other released from it.

46

Edgar Cayce was not a mystic, he was a psychic. Although he brought much knowledge of a curious or interesting kind from his psychic experiences, it would be an error to regard them all as reliable, for most psychics can be misled.(P)

47

It is a fact, although not a commonly known one, that the Führer Hitler for years secretly cultivated the habit of going quite frequently into a passive semi-trance condition. Occasionally he used an enormously large crystal to induce such a condition. In this state he believed himself to be in communion with occult forces, with spirit "controls," from whom he got both guidance and inspiration. To take counsel of the forces that possessed him and to promote his inner communion through such trances with them, he built the glass-walled private retreat six thousand feet high on the snowy precipitous summit of Mount Kehlstein where, unlike his famous mountain resting-place at Berchtesgaden, visitors were hardly ever permitted to enter. Thus he could remain in the virtual solitude which this communion required. To find the time for these solitary meditations, he left the largest possible amount of State work and Party direction to his collaborators. Even as late as the last years of the war, when the pressures of military necessity upon his time became more tremendous than ever before, Hitler insisted upon being alone for at least an hour each day. And it was known to a number of his close associates that this solitude was used to satisfy his occult interests and to carry on his magical practices.

48

However essentially honest and serious the researcher may be, he will have to suffer for the near-criminal misdeeds, the aberrations or credulous silliness of those irresponsible fanatics or unscrupulous exploiters who have alienated educated opinion.

49

It is dangerous to have any dealings or enter into any communications with such obsessed persons. For their conduct is entirely unguided by conscience or reason or consistency, their words entirely unguided by truth or self-control. Instead, evil passions and insane emotions are at the helm; hysteria, hatred, anger, fear, jealousy, greed, vanity, lying, and so on may take it in turn.

50

The possession of any supernormal power endangers an aspirant with vanity or conceit, even though he protests that his desire is to be just an instrument in God's hands. This danger particularly refers to healers.

51

Occultists writing on Tibetan masters have written too many erroneous or unverifiable statements to have their work accepted uncritically.

52

All forms of fortune-telling ask to be used with caution; all messages from psychics must be treated in the same way.

53

Max Freedom Long's book is not reliable. He took what is known of kahuna culture and twisted it into the shape of pre-existing occult ideas, and added much which is not in the original.

54

The attempt to use the Spirit's power to satisfy personal desires may fail simply because it fails to make contact with the Spirit. But it may also fail because even when contact is established, those desires may be negated or transformed as a result.

55

Joel Goldsmith gave great truths to mankind but also made some errors. He lived in an unreal fantasy world. Gigantic miracles became obtainable in this world at a low price. It is the old witch-doctor magic presented in a twentieth-century guise. It is the kind of world in which only dreamers can live, and from which only dreams can issue.

56

An American, Baird T. Spalding, wrote three volumes on his visits to Tibet and about the lives and teachings of the "Masters of the Far East" before he had ever left the American continent. (He added two further volumes after he had gone to India and returned.) He attached himself, with a party of fourteen disciples, to me for a couple of weeks when he discovered that I was in India at the time. I pointed out to him that his descriptions of the Masters did not tally with the facts as some of us knew them. He finally admitted that the books dealt with visits made in his astral body, not in his physical body as readers were led to believe. A similar situation arose more recently over the book *The Third Eye*, written by "Lobsang Rampa," an alleged Tibetan who turned out to be an Irish plumber writing under the dictation of an alleged Tibetan "astral body"!

57

There are dangers in the theatrical exhibitionism to which neurotical excess and unbalanced posturing may lead. Self-deception, fanaticism, irresponsibility, and misleading of the young are some of them.

58

He must beware of those who mistake the sub-normal for the super-normal, sub-conscious throw-ups for divine messages, and emotional titillation for spiritual rebirth.

59

A spiritism which reveres the messages of ghosts as though they were the messages of gods has strayed far.

60

"I am beginning to wonder whether such immortals ever existed. Is it not possible that the stories in the ancient books about Taoists who never died are exaggerated by the writers?"—Su Tung-po (who searched all his own life for the alchemical philosopher's stone to prolong life)

61

That spiritistic messages are mischievous or lying is a common experience.

62

Aleister Crowley died cursing and snarling.

63

The danger is that morally unevolved persons may misuse this knowledge selfishly to get what they want from others against their welfare. This is black magic. It is needful to put in strict warnings to such persons.

64

They calculate this world-event to take place in a particular year. When the year arrives and nothing happens, they adjourn the date to a later one. When that year passes with the prophecy again unfulfilled, they fix upon a further time. On each failure a plausible excuse is offered.

65

To try to use any of the powers gained through concentration to harm others or to subjugate them to one's own will is to practise black magic. It may succeed in its object but it will not succeed in evading eventual relentless punishment.

66

It is in bringing home the pitfalls of psychism, the dangers of mysticism, the perils of untrained intuition that a study of his inner life will be fruitful. Hitler, a distorted mystic, a perversely inspired man, claimed that his intuition informed him that he was carrying out God's will. It is in the critical examination and testing of such a claim that the value of metaphysical training proves itself. The fact is that neither Hitler nor anyone else can correctly make such a claim before two efforts have been successfully made: first, to ascertain what God is, and second, to ascertain how His will expresses itself. Gandhi too claimed that the inner voice of God gave him guidance in affairs of State. But he was always honest enough and great enough to admit later, as Hitler in his arrogance never did, that he had several times made what he himself called "Himalayan blunders." Let us admit that Hitler was the most astonishing man in Europe and that Gandhi was the most powerful force in political India. But this said, let us not deceive ourselves about nonpolitical matters in the essential need of discriminating between pseudo-intuition and genuine intuition.

Occult practices

67

Occultism is but a blind alley whose entrance is wide and inviting, whose promise is radiant and entrancing, but whose ending narrows into deception and danger.

68

It is generally quite undesirable to indulge in any occult activity, such as automatic writing, in order to produce psychic phenomena; indeed, it is often dangerous to do so. The mediumistic conditions thus aroused expose one to influences—even possession—by unknown and possibly evil spirits. The true mystical experience has nothing whatsoever to do with such proceedings and seeks to be influenced and possessed by the divine Overself alone.

69

What the evil-doer forgets is that no crystal exists anywhere which could show him a future free from retribution for his crimes. What he does not know is that black magic always contains within itself the terrible recoil of its own monstrous power. What he does not realize is that no astrologer ever lived who could write a horoscope which would let him escape the doom of retributive ruin that he earned.

70

Tantrika Yoga: Its methods are physical, ceremonial, sensual, and dangerous; its aims are the arousal of sleeping occult strength. In its highest phase, where the motive is pure and egoless, it is an attempt to take the kingdom of heaven by violence. But few men have such an exalted motive, as few are pure enough to dabble in such dangerous practices. Consequently, it need hardly be said that in most cases this road easily leads straight down to the abyss of black magic. This indeed is what has happened in its own history in Bengal and Tibet.(P)

71

In the Malay Peninsula, North Africa, Indonesia, and India, as well as elsewhere, there are individual persons and whole groups who exhibit, for religious or financial reasons, unpleasant or even bestial practices which seem magical. Through drum-beatings, frenzied dances, whirlings on their own axis, convulsive floor-rollings, and half-trances, they enter a condition of bodily immunity. This includes holding red-hot coals, cutting their arms and slashing their chests with knives. It is evil.

72

David Devant, *Secrets of Magic*: An amusing account is given of Sir Oliver Lodge's superstitious awe in face of the performance known as "Translucidation." Members of the audience were asked to write on small cards, which were placed in envelopes, sealed, marked, and placed in a bag held by Miss Devant, who was seated on the platform: "My sister would simply take an envelope out and put it on her forehead and then read the contents. This was duly carried out with the six envelopes. Each one, after it had been read, was handed over the footlights immediately, and passed on to the person who claimed it. It seemed impossible and inexplicable; so much so that one day Sir Oliver Lodge came to the performance armed with a specially-sealed envelope, which he challenged my sister to read. She read it with the rest, and he was so surprised that he got up from his seat in the stalls and made a short speech to the audience. He said he could not understand by what means this marvel had been accomplished, as he knew nothing in science could account for it." The book itself explains how the trick was worked; it involved a trap-door, two accomplices, and a powerful electric lamp—a simple mechanism but not so simple as the mentality of this great man of science, the High Priest of Spiritualism.

73

It would be an error to attribute all these queer phenomena to mere trickery, sleight-of-hand, imposture, or chicanery. If there is a natural explanation of most of them, there can only be a supernatural explanation of the remainder of them.

74

The court magicians were employed by King Montezuma of Mexico to lift supernatural barriers against the Spanish army Cortes advanced from the coast to his inland capital city, but they failed to stop him. Is this not stuff of identically the same piece of superstition as that encountered in Tibet four hundred years later by the army of Sir Francis Younghusband, and described in *A Hermit in the Himalayas*?

75

Those who know it from inside know the reality of the dangers to which a man exposes himself when he ignorantly sets up necromancy as a revealed religion and when he sets ajar promiscuously the psychic door which Nature's wisdom has kept closed.

76

Nowhere in history have sorcery and magic demonstrated that they are utterly and always reliable means of dealing with distressful personal conditions. We feel the need of tested procedures which have yielded more satisfactory results, which means that we feel the need of rational understanding and rational techniques of dealing with those problems.

77

The drum-tattoos to drive away evil spirits I heard in primitive Africa, and the charcoal-blackened faces to achieve the same purpose which I saw in primitive Malaya, did not depend on either sounds or sights for their main effect. They depended on the concentrated thought behind them.

78

Northwest Shamanism (Shaman means medicine-man): During initiation or becoming possessed by, or for communication with, mystic power, the devotee not only fasts but also abstains from drinking water. The most common way of acquiring or deliberately seeking Shamanistic power is by individuals entering the state of dreaming, of waking vision, and of trance while physically conscious, wherein a spirit-being visits the candidate; communion and the connection thus established between them is the source and basis of the medicine-man's power. This spirit becomes his guardian spirit, from whom he receives the mantram, the understanding, and the capacity which enable him to cause or remove disease, to do and endure what other men cannot, and to practise psychic powers. At first he may become demented but after a time he becomes normal and has control of this supernatural "influence."

79

The American Indian "medicine-man" (priest) forbade a photograph being made of him because he believed it drained away his forces.

80

Beware of those gatherings where blind movements of head, limbs, and trunk sway the crowd, where strange voices are heard and uncontrolled feelings are let loose. There is nothing holy there; on the contrary, evil forces should be suspected.

81

The concept of the male-female soul is another item which belongs to the higher spiritualism. There was a somewhat similar concept propagated by Laurence Oliphant. However, it is not acceptable because in the loftiest mystical experience the body is lost and forgotten. With it the thought of sex must inevitably go too. There is no room for it, in however refined, disguised, romanticized, or intellectualized form it may be, in the utter purity of the timeless, spaceless, supersensual form—Spirit.

82

The practices of witchcraft, black magic, or sorcery necessarily expose the practiser to serious dangers. The chief of these is madness.

83

If he is not able to detach himself sufficiently from them, he will be the victim of the various forces acting upon him. This is why sensitive persons are advised not to meddle with necromancy, magic, or the like.

84

The line which separates the use of meditation for worldly purposes, and especially to influence other people, from black magic is sometimes a thin one.

85

The drums which beat insistently and monotonously throughout the full-moon nights in many an Oriental community have the ultimate object of putting the thoughts to rest and lulling the senses.

86

Yet there are dangers to those who dabble in these psychic and spiritistic practices, these mystic and metaphysical workings arising out of their ignorance of the forces they are evoking and playing with.

87

Automatic writing and other such psychic phenomena are ordinarily to be avoided because they develop mediumistic tendencies. However, there are rare exceptions where an individual may safely practise such activities—providing he keeps in personal touch with someone highly advanced who considers the writings worthwhile. In mystical circles such a person is regarded as having found what is called "the interior word."

88

The so-called astral travels and mental-plane journeys of the occultists are very far from being what they are popularly taken for. They are nothing but a series of subjective visions, dreams woven by the mind under various influences.

89

Most of the experiences of occult "initiates," all their travels on "the seven inner planes," are nothing but a series of subjective visions. The occult worlds are mirages born from the imagination.

90

Those who hear voices and see visions had better be careful. They are touching dubious ground and sometimes dangerous ground. Before proceeding further on this path they should consult someone of mature experience in these matters, someone well-informed and balanced in judgement. The danger here is of getting lost in a condition for which they are unprepared and which they are unable to cope with. They may even embrace delusions under the belief that they are realities.

91

Anyone who hears voices that have no physical origin should immediately stop whatever practice—occult, psychic, meditational, necromantic, or religious—he or she has been following, should take a holiday from all such interests for a time and get back to the normal, the outgoing, and the ordinary. Otherwise there is the peril of madness or obsession.

92

Automatic writing is not an activity to be encouraged. Some form of psychic manifestation may appear until one has reached a certain level of discipline and understanding, but it is quite transient with sensible persons. It does no particular good and usually no particular harm either. It is better not to be sidetracked into these things, because we must see where we are going and keep a firm hold upon ourselves at all times. The only genuine automatism which is permissible, acceptable, and even to be sought after is that in which the personal self allows itself to be played upon as though it were a musical instrument by the Overself. This should be the goal of all our endeavours, this surrendering of the little self to the larger one. But when this happens it seems perfectly natural, there is nothing magical or mysterious about it, and there is the utter certitude of rightness and safety.

93

Although automatic writing has sometimes yielded accurate or admirable statements of the truth, more often it has merely reflected the beliefs and opinions, the limitations and ignorance of its practiser. But the dangers which accompany this phenomena are frightening: possession by an earthbound spirit is the worst.

94

Most of these presumed "messages" from dead or distant masters or from God are really formulated by the mind along the lines of its habitual tendencies and within the frame of its limitations. This clarification will, however, not be acceptable to those who can take truth only when it pleases and who always reject it when it hurts.

95

The experience of leaving the body very often accompanies or leads to poor health, and it originates from a psychical and not a spiritual cause. It is, therefore, not desirable ordinarily to encourage its continuance. The way of inward relaxation is much superior and more to be recommended.

Hypnotism

96

The power of suggestion is not properly acknowledged, but only partially. If it can put one person into a trance, if it make another temporarily change his identity, surely this indicates that here is one of the greatest of psychological powers?

97

We habitually underestimate the power of suggestion, whether it be derived from within self or from outside it. A human personality, an environmental setting, a tone of voice, or an inherited tradition often make us think, believe, or do what otherwise might not have occurred to us.

98

Why is it that the person who enters the deeper stage of hypnotic sleep hears and obeys the hypnotist alone and nothing and nobody else in the world outside? Why is it that on awakening he even does not then remember what he said or did? The answer to both questions is the same. It is not his own but the hypnotist's mind which operates during his sleep. It is not the subject who is doing this or saying that during the sleep, but the hypnotist himself who is doing or saying it, unconsciously using the subject's vocal organs and bodily limbs for the purpose. Those who cannot concede this should try, if they can, to find an explanation of the following further problem: if a person during ordinary sleep cannot hear spoken words or obey spoken commands, why can he do so during a sleep induced hypnotically? The fact is he does not really do so but merely yields the illusion of it to outside observers. What happens is that the hypnotizer superimposes his own mind on the sleeper's and unconsciously utilizes his body. He who hears the hypnotizer speak is his own self. He who obeys his commands is likewise himself. But the process of using the medium's senses and obsessing his mind, being an unconscious one, hides these facts. The value of this instance for our present purpose is that it helps to throw light on the inner mechanism of certain mystical phenomena which accompany advanced meditation.

99

Just before I went on my first journey to the Orient, my friend Professor Chellew, who was a professor of psychology at the University of London, warned me that there were gurus who used hypnotism. He instructed me how to defend myself against such a man. "If a guru," he said, "is looking straight into your eyes, then do not return the gaze fully but rather only into his left eye. This is because the positive currents which he is trying to direct towards you flow through his right eye. His left eye is passive. Or, instead of looking in the guru's eye, stare over the shoulders and thus avoid direct confrontation. Or, if a direct return gaze cannot be avoided, then use it for only a couple of seconds and turn away again: but the gaze should really be a mere pretense, for it should be directed at nothing in particular. It should be blank, expressionless, as if looking far into space. In this way you protect yourself and yet do not disturb the other person. If, however, the guru is one who can be fully trusted, who is a pure channel for the divine power, well then you may gaze at his right eye and so receive the inspiration he may be giving you."

100

Most writers on hypnotism have defended it by putting forward the notion that the victim will not accept a suggestion which is contrary to his moral code. This is simply not true. For hypnotic power reaches into the subconscious mind; here decisions are really made and actions impelled.

101

Where hypnotism is used to overcome another person's will, it is used wrongly and immorally. Where it is used to overcome the weaknesses in oneself by planting opposing suggestions, it is used rightly.

102

Why does the hypnotist so often ask his subject to look into his eyes when making the suggestions or giving the commands? Is it not because the mental interaction between them finds its easiest to-and-fro passage through the most sensitive points on the outer surface of the body—the eyes?

103

The limitations of egoic life can be pushed aside for a brief period by hypnosis in some cases, or by drugs in other cases.

104

Hypnotism may be employed with evil intentions for evil ends. In that case it comes very close to black magic, witchcraft, and sorcery and must be prohibited. But it may be employed also with good intentions for beneficent ends. In that case, and if the hypnotizer is of honourable character, and provided the welfare, rights, or interests of the hypnotized subject are fully respected, it is allowable, especially in the domain of the healing and surgical arts. If hypnotism is used by a person of dishonourable character or even by a person of average character flawed by some particular weakness, there is always the possibility that it may be used immorally. A crime may then be committed against the person submitting to it, or else he himself may be influenced to commit a crime against somebody to suit the hypnotizer's purpose, covering up the real criminal. These dangers are real and are dreadful enough to require that society be protected by limiting hypnotic practice to special trustworthy persons, and hypnotic objectives to allaying bodily pain and to inducing artificial unconsciousness, or sleep. Otherwise hypnotic passivity is undesirable for the same reason that mediumistic passivity is undesirable: *both surrender the use of the subject's free will.* In the one case it becomes enslaved to a living operator, in the other to a supposedly disincarnate one. Whoever gives it up to the control of another entity renders himself helpless and powerless against, and utterly at the mercy of, that entity. This is a dereliction of personal responsibility, sinful despite any benefits which may be sought and obtained.

105

H.P. Blavatsky: "Hypnotism and suggestion are dangerous powers. The victim's will is stolen from him. These things may be begun with good motives, and for right purposes. But I am an old woman, and have seen much of human life in many countries. I wish I could believe that these powers would be used only for good. Whoever lets himself be hypnotized by anyone, good or bad, is opening the door which he will be powerless to shut; and he cannot tell who will be the next to enter."

Mediumship, channeling

106

What is spiritualistic mediumship? The answer may be found by relating it with hypnotic mediumship. The principle at work in both cases is identical. Give a hypnotic medium in trance or semi-trance a suitable suggestion and it will be taken up and fully obeyed. If you tell him he is Napoleon he will believe, act, and speak as though he were. Tell a spiritualistic medium that you wish to communicate with the spirits of the departed and you have already given her a suggestion which she will take up and obey. She will provide all kinds of details about the spirit she supposes she evokes, details which are worked out either consciously or unconsciously by her imagination. We must remember that the residue of accurate facts which such mediums communicate may arise from the fact that reverie or full trance are states of mental concentration and, as such, telepathy may come into play and the sitter's mind be tapped.

107

The claim by both hypnotism and spiritualism that one human mind is capable, under certain conditions, of entering another human mind is true enough. It is also capable of dominating the other one. These two possibilities exist mostly in those situations where a person has willingly thrown himself open to another person's influence, has sat in the hypnotist's chair or at the spiritist's table. They also exist outside of these situations, particularly if someone sits for meditation by trying to make his mind a blank, without previously trying also over a sufficient period to purify his character, uplift his motives, and achieve some balance between his emotions and reason.

108

Quite a number of those who try the adventure into practical mysticism, as apart from its theoretical study, fall into the practice of mediumship instead. What is equally regrettable is that they remain captive to the delusion that they are still mystics.

109

He can have no higher aim than to be possessed by the divine Overself. This is the only kind of mediumship which can safely be practised and the only kind which ought to be practised.

110

Spiritual development is one thing; spiritual domination by other is its opposite. The first is mysticism, the second mediumship. The first leads to the taking possession of oneself, the second to losing one's most valuable attributes: will and reason, self-control and, in certain cases, even consciousness.

111

There are fourteen signs of the mediumistic condition. The medium suffers from: (1) loss of memory, (2) inability to keep mind on conversation, (3) frequent mental introversion, (4) decreasing power of prolonged concentration, study, thought, analysis, and intellectual work, (5) increasing emotionality, (6) weakened willpower, (7) greater sensitivity to trifles, with nervous irritability and silly vanity resulting therefrom, (8) more suspicions of others in his environment, (9) more self-centered and egotistic, (10) frequent glassy stare of the eyes, (11) increased sexual passion, (12) appearance of hysteria or uncontrollable temper where previously absent, (13) disappearance of moral courage, (14) the feeling at times that some unseen entity takes possession of him.(P)

112

When the individual is entirely introspective, when he no longer knows or wants to know his physical environment, he may become wrapped up in ideas or images which thereby assume vivid reality or he may fall into a state of utter blankness. If his preparation and training have been correct, he may be touched by the higher consciousness. But if he is spiritually unprepared and philosophically untrained, he may become the victim of an unseen disincarnate mind; in short, he may become a medium.

113

The student who wishes to keep away from unnecessary moral and psychical danger should keep away from dabbling in hypnotism or playing with mediumship.

114

What happens during mediumship is that the mind, will, and body of a living person are surrendered in part or as a whole to a disincarnate one. Such a process may be imitated by frauds or fanatics, but it is also genuinely possible.

115

The mediumistic condition is not one to be admired and valued, as so many spiritists believe. On the contrary, it is one to be avoided by every seeker after the higher life. It will bar his way to that life or it will drag him away from it. For it allows the will to be paralysed, the capacity for self-control to be lost, the mind to be surrendered to someone else's domination, and the eyes to be shut to where one is going. Such a condition is the very opposite of that sought by philosophical mysticism. It is as degrading as it is dangerous.

116

If you consider the silly, irrational, and crazy actions which hypnotized persons are easily led to do, you will understand why a hypnotized spiritist medium—for that is his condition—is easily led into obsessions.

117

Someone once told me an amusing story which well illustrates the necessity of never abandoning common sense and the critical faculty when one treads this mysterious ground. She was dining with a certain Russian Grand Duke who was a complete believer in spiritualistic and psychic theories. A medium regularly visited his mansion and gave him messages from a certain spirit. He pointed to a small black metal figure of Osiris and said that he treasured it exceedingly. The spirit had told him that this figure of Osiris should be kept with care as he, the Grand Duke, had been a Pharaoh in a previous incarnation and at that time he possessed this very figure of Osiris which was now with him again; it was a link for him with that incarnation. The visitor listened and later, idly picking up the figure, discovered that a small label on its underside said: "Price 2 fr. 50, Galleries Lafayette, Paris."

118

The continued practice of mediumship may lead to deplorable results, especially to nervous breakdown, insanity, immorality, or suicide. It cannot help anyone to attain a higher life but may help him to lose it. Consequently philosophy earnestly asks its students to refrain from being led down its tempting side-paths to their own destruction.

119

To permit himself to be possessed by an unseen entity whose true identity he does not know, is clearly foolish. To do so unwittingly is bad enough but to do so deliberately is unpardonably insane.

120

No student should make the mistake of accepting spiritism as a part of mysticism or of attending séances as a practice in meditation. Mediumship is both mentally and morally harmful. In the end it does not yield what it promises but deceives those who trust it. The student who dabbles in it will actually retrogress under the delusion that he is progressing. He may lose in a few months what it has taken him years to gain.

121

The difficulty with such a person is that after having fabricated these scandalous but unreal episodes, she soon and obsessively believes them to be actual happenings. That she is a little mad through the excessive practice of spiritualistic mediumship does not make her less dangerous to the gullible victims who listen open-mouthed to her and exclaim, "You don't say!"

122

What is believed to be a communicating unseen entity, the spirit of a deceased person, is, in so many cases, only a split-off of the medium's own subconscious mind.

123

The deceptive messages which so often lead a medium astray begin by flattering him or her with the notion that he or she is destined to become the leader of a great spiritual revival at least, or the long-awaited Messiah at most. But they end by destroying the medium's sanity, morals, happiness, or health.

124

Even if mediumship did not yield harmful results because of its evil origin, it would still be a thing to be avoided because it falls into the class of psychic powers, which, as Patanjali, the great master of Yoga in ancient India, says in his classic manual on the subject, "are injurious to that mental stillness which it is the ultimate object of meditation to attain."

125

It is morally wrong and psychologically risky to surrender the mind, the will, and the body to an unseen entity, whether this be done in unconscious trance or in partially aware mediumship. The *inner* history of spiritism is full of instances of the heavy price paid by those who embarked on such a foolish course.

126

The spiritualists use the term "trance condition" in a special sense. They think of it as a complete loss of consciousness, wherein a disembodied personal entity takes over and uses the entranced person's vocal organs to speak, or his hands to write. The medium's identity completely changes and becomes that of the purported spirit. Philosophy rejects such a condition from its desired goals and warns students against such dangerous states. What it seeks is not this negative passivity but a positive state wherein the meditator does not lose his consciousness but only deepens and widens it. It is true that the mediumistic condition resembles the meditative one in some respects, but not in the fundamental ones.

127

Any medium who lets himself be possessed at times by lying and malignant spirits in his séances would be fortunate to escape with his sanity and peace of mind. He should first learn how to protect himself before he opens himself up to outside and unseen powers. But such protection can be gained only by developing his own strength, character, knowledge, and aspiration. Indeed his personal spiritual growth calls for this passage to a higher stage. But this can be reached only by abandoning mediumship, at least for a time. At some future date, he might be able to resume it, but it would then be so vastly superior and so fully within his control that it would really be mysticism. For the controlling entity would be either his own higher self or a genuine living master.

128

The man who practises mediumship gains nothing spiritually by it, since even his noblest utterances do not become part of him but merely flow as water through a pipe. Even after fifty years of such practice he gains only a means of earning a livelihood.

129

There is a lower form of Spiritism, expressed through cheap paid mediums, as well as a higher form, expressed through non-professional persons who mix the mystical with the mediumistic. The student of philosophy must scrupulously avoid both these forms, must reject their so-called revelations and faithfully stay on the superior level which he is so fortunate to have attained.

130

Professor Ernest Wood told me the story of his father's visit to an exhibition which marked the opening of the Manchester Ship Canal in

England. A few weeks after the visit his father was given a message from a supposed spirit whose description exactly tallied with that of a waxworks figure of a man which he had seen at the exhibition. What happened in this case was that the medium had picked up correctly the picture of this figure, but had let his imagination incorrectly construct a message because of his own personal belief in, and bias towards, spiritualism. Thus what began in psychic vision as a truth became adulterated as a mixture of truth and error. The case cited here illustrates the possibility and actuality of mistakes not only on the lower levels of occultism, but also on the higher levels of religious mysticism. Here inspired revelations are sometimes mixed up with personal belief or even interpolated unwittingly with priestly imagination.

131

That mediumship and hypnotism are undesirable, that they can lead to mental disturbance, was an opinion held by both Helena Blavatsky and Mabel Collins. It must be noted that even though they were right in several cases, they were wrong in others.

132

The mind becomes more and more sensitive and receptive, rejecting nothing presented to it. This unselectivity becomes a danger if it is constant, for the mind would be flooded not only with unhelpful useless material, but also with negative, unhealthy, morally low and unhappy material. The defense and protection against this invasion is to be true to the Overself and thus to be open only to the Good, the True—a two-way awareness.

133

He can be sure that he has fallen into a mediumistic or a psychic phase if the phenomenon of receiving messages shows itself and if, after the first period of exciting discovery, the messages become more and more unreliable.

134

Just as it is possible for the dream-mind to assume different personalities, each speaking and behaving according to type, so it is possible for other hidden layers of the mind to dramatize themselves and speak as they might be expected to in their respective capacities. We are only on the fringe of discovering what latent powers the human mind possesses. The entity which controls can quite well be himself in another guise, not only because of the foregoing but also because of characteristics developed in former births and still lying beneath the surface of this birth. On the other hand, there is a less likely possibility of genuine spirit-control. This is true even if, during the delivery of trance addresses, the medium himself is quite unconscious of them and of everything that is happening at the time.

135

The medium yields up her mentality before she has developed it, hence prematurely and against the tide of evolution. Hence most mediums are usually illiterate or half-educated types.

136

This feeling of being directed by some other power, of being under compulsion to think and act in a certain way, is good if the reference is to the Higher Power, but dangerous if not. For obedience may then be mediumship not mysticism, or drug hallucination not inspiration.

137

The medium is either deceived by, or confused about, the very nature of the phenomena he encounters. The aspirant should not dally in them but should pass beyond as quickly and as far as he can.

138

The medium is in the end brought to a point where she has no will, no power to choose, no free life of her own. She obeys the enslaving entity's suggestions and orders in everything. If this entity feeds its passions and satisfies its instincts through her, she is lost indeed.

139

Where a spiritualistic medium has escaped harm despite the practice of mediumship during the earthly life, the escape is only an illusory one. As soon as she passes out of the body at death, an unseen entity will fasten upon her and gain further control over her in such a way as to cause serious harm and bring much suffering during the post-mortem existence. And when the next birth in this world is taken, moral retrogression and spiritual retardation will be the final price to pay for this dubious practice. If its victim succeeds in escaping from mediumship and takes to a higher life, even then the unseen creature becomes her evil tempter, her hidden tormenter. Such are the creatures whom Jesus called devils, but whom our modern mediums in their pitiful ignorance invite into their very being and life. How many cases of madness, of immorality, of crime, of drunkenness, suicide, and even murder may be traced to these malevolent demons, through their suggestion, influence, or obsession?

140

It may interest you to know that probably half the cases of patients in lunatic asylums are possessed by evil spirits. Many of them could be cured if the spirit could be exorcised and driven out.

141

Many of the spirits who influence mediums are evil, diabolic, or malevolent. Others are only mischievous, deceptive, and lying. Some are harmless and a few may even be good. But the risks from the first two types are so large and so dangerous that the practice of mediumship is banned to its students by philosophy.

142

By giving up his personal responsibility to the unseen entity, which in most cases is never what it pretends to be, the medium takes an easy road to moral disaster. By failing to exercise this responsibility he does not free himself from the painful effects of such a disaster.

143

When these evil spirits have led him up to the peak of trust in them, so that he is ready to do their slightest bidding, they have led him also to a hidden chasm of deception yawning at his feet. Unless he withdraws in time, he will fall into it and be destroyed.

144

The evil spirits which attend such séances can cleverly imitate higher beings, claim lofty famous names, and even create an aura of light in the darkened room under the pretense that it is the authentic holy Divine Light.

145

Rasputin and spiritualist mediums were at the last Czar's court. Spiritualist mediums attended Napoleon III's court. What misguidance did evil or lying spirits give?

146

Even a harmless control may open the way for a harmful one later. There is the added danger that a lying spirit may give uplifting messages and wise guidance until confidence is established. Then, when the censorship of reason and experience are overcome, the victim is lured to folly or sin or disaster.

147

The woman who cultivates mere passivity rather than purity, who seeks contact with "the other world" rather than truer knowledge of this one, lays herself open to mediumship. In this deplorable condition, lying spirits may enter her mind and misguide her, evil spirits may enter her body and degrade her.

148

The medium can do nothing beyond receiving weakly what is implanted in him, for he is no longer in a positive purposeful state of activity. He has lost his own individual selfhood, and especially his power of logical rational thinking. Thus he lies at the mercy of whatever entity or whatever subconscious image overshadows him. The danger is that malevolent forces may take hold of him and make him their captive.

149

Whoever takes on the travail of mediumship, surrendering his body at times to disincarnate spirits, takes the risk of being controlled not only at undesired times but also in undesired ways; and, worse, by undesirable beings; still worse, without the medium's own awareness. It then becomes treachery to his own individuality.

150

If the would-be mystic is to keep out of these pitfalls he should keep out of spiritualism. He should refuse to engage in any practices which lead directly to mediumistic subjection. If, however, he has already engaged in them, he should renounce them at once and try to bring his mind back to an alert, wakeful, and active condition. He should seek with the true mystic the highest degree of self-control rather than with the spiritistic medium the lowest degree of self-submission.

14

THE SENSITIVE MIND

The psychic experience and mystical phenomena are certainly very interesting and reveal the unsuspected powers which lie latent within the human soul. He should not, however, preoccupy himself too much with them, as they are only the by-products of the spiritual path. Much more important is the experience of a mental stillness and emotional purification and superphysical consciousness. The ennoblement of character and the discipline of thought are really more valuable in the end than psychic phenomena.

2

The so-called supernatural or miraculous incidents which may happen are exceptions and should not receive undue attention. He ought to be reticent about relating them to others, and even when he does so he ought to be restrained in his description of them. This does not mean that they need be undervalued or ignored but that they should not be regarded as foundational. They do have a value and they do require attention, provided they are authentic and not hallucinatory, for they come in fulfilment of a need. But there is danger in speaking of them, the danger of encouraging superstition in others and conceit in himself.

3

Beware of attaching too much importance to the appearances and disappearances of visions and spirit "callers." These are but by-products and should be noted and dismissed. We have to BE and not to see. Even visions are as objective from the higher standpoint as material things. What you really ARE can be discovered only by going deeper still and becoming it.

4

When he comprehends that such psychic manifestations are either preliminaries or by-products of genuine spiritual operations, he will be able to avoid pitfalls into which so many aspirants often fall.

5

The visions may help him and are to that extent acceptable. But they should be accepted with a clear knowledge of the limits upon their usefulness and of the risks inherent in their guidance. They are not to be made the supreme goal, but to be regarded as what they are—transient phenomena, obliquely mediated from the soul, perhaps, but still not the soul in its pure super-sensuousness.

6

He may perceive authentic visions concerning former incarnations, but he ought to keep them to himself. They are beyond the understanding of others, and discussion of them would often arouse antagonistic mental reactions.

7

He could keep on collecting inner, mystical, or psychical experiences for years, for undoubtedly they are fascinating. But to whom? To the ego: but that is not the point of this quest. Ramana Maharshi told me that he had had thousands of such experiences. The essential point is to treat them as incidental and to rise into Overself awareness and stay there.

8

Visions are compounded of the workings of dream-mind and what may or may not be authentic fact. Ordinarily, they are fleeting phenomena whose importance lies mostly in their indication of growing sensitivity, although occasionally they are significant.

9

Saint Paul speaks of the gift of tongues. This phrase has puzzled many of his readers. The Church, not knowing its meaning, usually considers it to mean speaking in languages unknown on earth. The Spiritualists, possessed by their own theories of spirit-possession, usually consider it to mean speaking in languages unknown to the speaker but used in other countries. Mystics who develop this gift find that it means either the ability to speak in symbolic metaphoric enigmatic or allegoric language or the ability to interpret such language when heard or to translate it when read. On this definition, Saint John's Book of Revelation is a striking example of the working of the gift of tongues.

10

However different a transcendental experience may seem from a worldly one, both are usually bound together by an egocentric tie.

11

He should not reject these visions but neither should he dwell overlong in them. He must receive them but also learn to pass into the pure presence beyond them.

Psychic sensitivity, personal sensitivity

12

As a student progresses on the path he arrives at a highly sensitized condition when dealing with the world, and this becomes painful at times. The problems which thus arise cannot be eliminated, for increasing sensitivity is a natural result of finer mental and emotional development. However, the reaction to difficulties caused by this can be controlled. This is done by immediately switching attention to something else, preferably to the thought of the Overself, or to some purely physical activity. When in the presence of anyone who unduly affects or disturbs him, he may also strengthen himself to magnetic self-protection by not letting himself glance in the direction of this person and by clenching the palms of both hands with the thumbs inside the fingers.

13

This mass of emotional-mental-auric influences deposited all around him may not—often does not—accord well with his sensitivity. It is not necessarily evil but it is discordant, uncomfortable, a polar opposite, and he may need to shield himself against it. The methods vary; they include both psychic and physical kinds, from imagining a mental wall to constructing a brick one; from performing religious rites of purification or exorcism to moving beds, burning incense, taking herbal baths, and avoiding crowds.

14

The space that lies between two persons is filled with their two auras, with the vibrations from the electromagnetic, if invisible, extensions of their physical bodies, and with the mental-emotional atmospheres surrounding them. In that narrow space lies paradoxically all their inner being, their mutual attractions and personal repulsions, the inscribed status of what they really are.

15

Through the solar plexus and the cerebrospinal and sympathetic nerve systems we pick up from others the influences surrounding them and radiate to others the influences surrounding us. The thought-atmosphere of other persons affects us and the result of this impingement should tell us something about them. If we feel out of harmony with them, if we are uneasy in their presence, if we get depressed, distressed, or disturbed through being with them, then we had better protect ourselves by avoiding such persons and not exposing ourselves to their contact. But if we are to protect ourselves against the destructive and dark mental atmospheres of the persons we are forced to meet through the exigencies of our circumstances, it is needful to build up a strong and superior mental fort within ourselves by daily and repeatedly concentrating on self-improvement through right thinking.

16

The only elementals are vivified thought-forms. If they are evil and attack you, oppose them with thoughts of an opposite character. If your thoughts are strong enough and sustained enough, the elementals will eventually vanish.(P)

17

It is unpleasant to be forced to sit in other people's auras so closely as in the library. But where there is any choice, it is a lesser of two evils to sit in a female aura than a male one: the magnetic blending is more harmonious and less disturbing, the ego less aggressive and more passive.

18

Psychic sensitivity and excessive passivity which render the close presence of certain persons almost intolerable must be resisted. Helps in this matter are (a) draw deep breath, hold it, centre mind on inner strength and positivity; (b) hold spine erect, breath withheld, hands clenched, feet firmly planted.

19

For the troublesome spirit, if it is possible and not against his beliefs, he should try to find a good priest and ask to have the rite of exorcism performed. Since the spirit comes at night he should sleep with a small light burning. Also, when the annoyance begins he may make the sign of the cross over himself, take a deep breath at the same time, and with great conviction pronounce these words: "In the name, presence, and power of Jesus Christ, I drive you out of this body."

20

C.D. Paxton, in practising meditation, fell into semi-mediumship and got possessed frequently, always at night during sleep. Finally he was in a suicidal despair and decided to make a final effort to rid himself of it. He stayed awake all night for two nights. During that time he tried to keep all thoughts out, leaving his mind blank, so that any suggestion by the spirit was also kept out. During the third night a marvellous peace came over him suddenly and he was permanently freed from possession by the evil spirit thereafter.

21

Why does he see the guide's photograph emanating light and charging him with spiritual power? A photo, after all, is a light-phenomenon

charged with the electromagnetic ray connection of the person pho-
tographed. When the guide tries to help him, his auric mental energy
immediately expresses itself through the picture and affects the seeker's
mind as its percipient. However, at a certain stage of development, when
that energy of the Overself which the Indians call Kundalini is being
awakened so as to enable him to do what is then put into his hands to do,
the photo carries something more than mere thought; its mental radia-
tions are actually transmuted into light-radiations and so it may at times
appear to be suffused with light. And needless to say the most sensitive
points in such a picture are the eyes; the help given will therefore affect
these points most.

22

The more developed a man is, in intelligence character and spiritual
consciousness, the larger is the auric field around him.

23

There are times when one may share the Life-Force's ecstasy in feeling
and even see it at work in light. It is an inner experience but linked to the
outer world.

24

The unpleasant feeling he sometimes gets either momentarily or suddenly on meeting certain persons may be merely the echo of his own
dislike or prejudice, or it may be a psychic reaction and authentic warning,
or it may even be a souvenir from an earlier incarnation.

25

During the early stages of his Quest, the neophyte will have to take
some protective measures against the mental auras, the emotional influences, and the psychic magnetisms of other people whose character or
conduct may have an obstructive effect upon his Quest or a disturbing
effect upon his mind. The total avoidance of such people, or at least a
reduction in the number of contacts with them, is one such measure; a
special vigilance, when he is with them, over his thoughts and feelings, so
as to discriminate those which come from them and those which are really
his own, is another measure.

26

The thoughts one gets in the vicinity of certain persons may well be the
psychic reaction to their auras, the intuitive indication of their characters.
But it may also be this mixed with one's own opinion, or even mere
opinion only.

27

To sit in a public vehicle or popular café and be stared at by others is
discomforting to the sensitive person. He knows by his own experience

that the glance carries with it mental characteristics, projects the other's thought and feeling of the moment.

28

He must be careful not to accept other people's moods, not to assimilate their thoughts, but to detect such intruders and reject them.

29

It is interesting to note that the Bavarian mystic Theresa Neumann told investigators that she lived not only on the eucharist wafer, which she took once a day, but mainly on light. It is interesting because light is the original substance of matter.

30

The folkloric belief that a string of garlic stretched across the threshold of a door keeps off evil influences is not entirely without a ground. Garlic is found in Europe and in Asia in the same position and for the same purpose. Outside the house, flowers of sulphur (powder) dusted inside the shoes is also used in occult circles here.

31

I mentioned the flowers of sulphur used in occult circles as a protective influence against undesirable influences; there is another preventive used there and that is a couple of tablespoonfuls of vinegar mixed into the bathwater. Incidentally, such a mixture in about the same proportions may be used to clean wooden floors or their linoleum coverings. On the subject of floor coverings, note that woolen carpets are best cleaned by hand with a hard brush and not by vacuum cleaners, which are harmful to them, or by the non-electric roller type of carpet cleaning apparatus.

32

He who is sensitive to the auras of other persons becomes quickly affected by contacts with them. He must take care that, whether through empathy or sympathy, he does not desert himself in order to be with others.

33

The psychically sensitive man will note in many cases that as another person comes closer to him he feels increasing awareness of the alien aura until finally it fully interpenetrates his own.

34

The auric vibrations which accompany a letter often indicate the state of mind of the writer. Holding it in one's hand or touching the forehead with it makes the reception of these vibrations more acute. But, of course, meditation definitely directed towards the letter will widen and deepen the result.

35

It is better not to shake hands with everybody, for then one picks up their conditions, briefly of course. There is an auric deposit on one's own hand from the other person's aura. Ordinarily, this is an unpleasant sensation, for few people have reached a sufficient measure of fineness or purity to provide an uplifting rather than a depressing effect.

36

He may suffer from his own bodily infirmities and other people's malice or enjoy his bodily delights or other people's.

37

The aspirant whose sensitivity creates a psychic reaction of discomfort in the presence of certain persons may overcome this negative situation by learning the art of building a mental wall around himself the moment he becomes aware of what is happening—that is, as soon as he experiences the impact of this undesirable atmosphere. It must be done swiftly and with an attitude of calm deliberation and emotional detachment.

38

As he progresses on the path he must be careful of his personal contacts. He becomes increasingly sensitive to other persons' auras and thoughts. He should, for instance, refrain from associating with anyone who is a failure, as not only will this affect his own attitude, but he will tend to pick up something of the other's bad karma and defective mental tendencies.

39

An intuitive sensitivity to both negative and positive phases manifests itself naturally to him at one stage on the path. Certain drawbacks cannot be helped because the same sensitivity which makes him aware of the finer things also makes him aware of their opposites. To correct this condition a twofold process is needed. First he must strengthen the idea of the spiritual *centre* within himself as providing a kind of gravitational spot upon which his consciousness should revolve. Second, the moment the negative awareness arises he must be able to switch his attention instantaneously to an altogether different subject. The second part does not mean that he is totally to ignore the negative awareness but that he is to recognize it for what it is. He must understand whence it emanates, comprehend its character and place, and be guarded as to what action, if any, is to be taken; but when he has done this, as in a flash, he must switch attention elsewhere.

40

There is a light which, produced by higher beings and seen by ordinary ones, can make them turn dizzy, or lose consciousness, or even go mad.

41

A sensitive person will prefer not to be touched. He feels the touch of others conveys their aura. There are more hygienic ways of greeting a person than shaking hands with him, a close proximity of flesh which is as psychically undesirable as it is physically disagreeable.

42

In all encounters or confrontations with others, he must take care not to get involved, either needlessly or more than is necessary, in that telepathic swirl which sets up from the impact of two consciousnesses meeting.

43

How often have I seen this radiation of bluish white light appear round the head of some person, flicker for a few seconds, and vanish. Whenever this happened that person was marked out for this quest, for I knew also, as by an instinct, that a glimpse had been, or would be, received.

44

These centres, as well as the aura itself, are affected by health conditions, low or high vitality, mental and emotional conditions, and self-control or the lack of it. By special exercises, physical postures, breath regulation, willpower, and stimulation, the centres can be affected.

45

Madame Helena Rubinstein: "I hate being touched."

Nicole, Duchess of Bedford: "I dislike being touched intensely."

Such sensitivity is a very real thing. For the mingling of invisible auras is expressed by the visible physical bodies' unwanted contact.

46

Some persons are irritated by the mere presence or atmosphere of certain other persons even though no word has been spoken. This may happen especially when he feels that he understands that the other person's mental attitude is hostile to him.

47

The occult basis of the power of eyes to emit rays that carry something invisible yet real of the personality is the existence of an aura. In India this is why a taboo is applied to pariah outcastes and in Japan why the roof of the tallest building in Tokyo, the Marcinouchi Building, is closed to visitors, for they would be able to look down on the Emperor's Palace.

48

If he is entitled to avoid obnoxious people socially, he is still more entitled to avoid dangerous people spiritually.

49

If he is feeling and thinking what the other person is, then he is failing to pay attention to what he himself is, to his Overself. He cannot afford to remain on a merely psychic level.

50

When in a difficult position with other persons, especially hostile ones, practise *Hara*.

51

Hara is a Japanese term which equals the soul and centre of energy, which is situated below the navel and in the centre of the human body.

52

One man's eyes may evade other people's glances through shiftiness but another man's through shyness. Thus the value of appearances as a guide to what lies beneath them is limited.

53

When he first encounters this unlooked-for phenomenon, he will be shocked and withdraw into aloofness like a tortoise into its shell and perhaps take refuge in a hard-held cynicism. But although it forges an armour around a sensitive man and provides him with a protection, it offers no adequate solution.

54

The enforced association of living in apartment buildings with many families huddled together, this close community of persons who may be, and behave, far below one in spiritual caste, thought, and manner, is unwelcome to a sensitive temperament.

55

He does not *consciously* put himself in someone's place. He cannot help finding himself in it—such is his developed sensitivity.

56

Before each world war the sensitive suffered from foreboding of coming sinister calamity, like that which hovered in the atmosphere when a Greek theatre audience watched the unfoldment of a tragic play.

Telepathy, mental influences

57

It is a strange fact to which science as well as philosophy, experience as well as intuition, can testify, that thought from one mind can be brought into another mind, that the feeling of one man may affect the feeling of another without the use of written message or spoken word. If there were no common mind among all men, this could never happen, could never have been possible. If they were not all rooted in a universal consciousness, however secret and hidden it be, such silent transmission between their individual consciousnesses could never have been possible.

58

The sensitive person cannot help receiving impressions about the mood or character or feeling of another person with whom he is in contact. But this is quite apart from, and not necessarily accompanied by, knowledge of the particular object or person being thought of in connection with such a mood. Usually the sensitive will not know towards what or whom it is directed; that is, such knowledge will not form part of his impression.

59

He finds that he is receiving influences from others all the time. It is necessary to protect himself against them or, in a few cases where uplift comes, open himself to them.

60

He will be astonished to find out how many feelings and thoughts which appear to be genuinely his own really emanate from other persons with whom he may be in contact at the time.

61

Unspoken thoughts may cross space and enter another mind, which may become aware of them and, at times, of even their source.

62

There is something mysterious about the way a thought intended to benefit the consciousness of someone else living far off reappears in that person's mind, although he does not know that it is not of his own origination.

63

It is a fact that a practised passive receptive mind can be sensitive over long distances.

64

If one kind of mentality is sensitive to waves of feeling or thought, another is concentrated enough to emit them.

65

At times you may know what is in someone else's mind, but your knowledge is neither certain nor complete. For in the end your ego is alone and isolated.

66

There are differences of course, one being that the creator feels the experience more strongly, sees the point more clearly, and presents it more articulately than the receiver.

67

He becomes aware of receiving communications, though not on the usual verbal level.

68

It is like hearing an echo from a long way off.

69

Telepathy is science's established fact, not somebody's fanciful theory.

70

The sensitive person may or may not know when thoughts pass through him from someone else. Among other things, it depends upon what he has to do with his time.

Clairvoyance

71

The faculty of clairvoyance is really an extension of the imagination. If the ordinary man's use of the latter is nonclairvoyant, fanciful, or even misleading, that is because he has not divested it from the ego's wishes, habits, and rule.

72

If time is as mysterious, as flexible, and as variable as analysis shows, a hint of justification appears for the belief that predictions may sometimes be made in advance of the actual events, that under certain conditions the inevitable may be foreseen and the trend of things calculated—in short, that the future may on occasions be anticipated.

73

The clairvoyant instinct which guides the carrier pigeon to its distant loft is possessed by no man.

74

Clairvoyance is true imagination—a rare thing.

75

The untrained aspirant may easily mistake the products of exuberant fancy for those of authentic clairvoyance.

76

If it is regrettable that few men can foresee events, it is nevertheless useful in that it forces the others to develop their reasoning abilities and judicial capacities.

77

To make accurate forecasts of future events, to learn in advance what is going to happen tomorrow, is to be ready for all possibilities.

78

Everyone may be wise after the event but few are sensitive enough to receive ahead of time intimation of the event.

79

If the clairvoyant vision is not produced by other causes, then it is usually produced by the subconscious mind automatically taking a familiar form, thus creating an intelligible means of communication with the conscious mind.

80

Clues to what is coming, indications of probable happenings, and pictures from karmic programming may at times show themselves in various ways.

81

A continental friend visited a celebrated clairvoyant who described to him a scene from the times of Jesus and a setting within ancient Rome. The description was extraordinarily detailed and vivid. The seer concluded it with the statement that "this was one of your previous incarnations." My friend was amused because the description could have been taken from a book which he had read a week earlier, or from a film based on the book which he had seen some years earlier but which the reading had brought back to his memory again. The title of book and film was *Ben Hur*. The clairvoyant was a firm believer in reincarnation. It is easy to see that he correctly picked up these thought-forms from his sitter's mind, but incorrectly if unconsciously added his own opinion to the picture.

82

Strange things may happen to the consciousness in that half-world when one is unsure whether it be the state of sleep or waking. Images may be seen that have a clairvoyant quality about them or truths may be perceived that have an intuitive one.

83

It is interesting to note that most of the very very early scriptures were passed down through generation after generation by word of mouth and not in writing—not only scriptures, but also mythological histories and chants. This shows that those earlier races, or rather peoples, had a prodigious capacity to keep hold of statements and not to forget them. Why is it that has mostly disappeared among us today? The reason is the same one that explains why the primitive peoples were closer to nature, were much more psychic, more aware of the psychical planes. And that reason is that the logical intellect has since then been developed and has replaced, to a certain extent, the instincts, clairvoyance, and so on.

84

There is clairvoyance. To see things this way is not the best or most accurate. The better way is to know intuitively by that something, that voice within you, which can tell you the truth about things and people.

85

Clairvoyance and Telepathy

Clairvoyance is that abnormal awareness which enables one to know a fact or perceive a scene which ordinarily could not be known or perceived at all. Such a state may or may not be accompanied by reverie. It may operate in time, as when past or future are read. It may operate in space, as when scenes or persons in some remote city or land are seen. Its mildest form is the sensing of someone's presence; its fullest form is vivid vision.

The scientific rationale of both clairvoyance and telepathy will now be exposed and from this it will be seen how superstitious are many occult theories on the one hand and how materialistic are many sceptical theories on the other hand. What happens in the case of clairvoyance is that the act of concentration, whether voluntary or involuntary, induces an activity in the subliminal mind which in turn presents the result of this activity as an impression of the scene or person concentrated on. This subconscious impression is then made to appear to the waking consciousness as a mental image. In the practical technique, attentive concentration is usually followed by the shutting down of waking consciousness, thus inducing a dreamlike state. It is in such a state, resembling half-trance, that most occult powers, visions, and so on usually become active.

If it be asked how it is possible to become aware of distant scenes and far-off persons, unuttered thoughts and the projection of personal atmospheres, the answer is that quite obviously there must exist some connecting medium between both seer and seen, sender and receiver. And mentalism asserts that this medium is and can be none other than the same mind whose universal existence makes us all percipients of the world-show and recipients of the divine World-Idea.

These strange phenomena are possible because one man's mind is connected with another and all form part of a unitary whole. None exists in isolation. There is an inclusive mind which subsists beneath them all, a thread-Mind which runs through all minds. When we work out the implications of these cases we find that they suggest a larger mind whose limits we cannot trace. Each individual mind is like a bubble on the surface of a lake. The water in the lake brings all the separate minds into connection with one another. There is not only an individual subconsciousness but also a collective and comprehensive subliminal mind, a cosmic consciousness.

The deeper layers of the mind in which one man abides are indissolubly the same as the deeper layers of the mind in which his neighbour abides. Thus the link among all the finite egos of mankind cannot from its very nature be cut. This ultimate unity of the unconscious renders possible a reasonable explanation of those mysterious happenings called telepathy, occultism, prevision, and clairvoyance. Whoever can succeed in withdrawing his attention from the surface consciousness—however involuntarily or momentarily—to that substratum which underlies it, will naturally find in himself the possibility of closer touch with other finite minds irrespective of the distance between their bodies.

All genuine occult happenings find their basis in the fact that Mind is the single and supreme principle of the world and that all things are primarily mental things. All those strange happenings like clairvoyance, second-sight, premonitions, and telepathy testify also that the existence of this mind is free from space-time limitations. When we understand that Mind is itself a reality apart from the fleshly brain, we can also understand why telepathy between two persons is perfectly possible. When we perceive that time and space are not absolutes but forms of mental experience, we can also perceive why reading the past, foretelling the future, and seeing something far distant from the body are likewise possible.

Evaluating intuitions and "messages"

86
It is only after the mystic has felt human desires and known human joys, come up against intellectual limitations, suffered worldly disappointments, that he can evaluate. If he has not had sufficient experience of common life, he may not adequately assess the values indicated by mystical intuitions nor properly understand the meaning of his mystical experiences themselves. Thus, what he gets out of both depends to some extent on what he brings to them. If he brings too little or too lopsided a contribution, then his higher self will gradually lead him to seek development along the lines of deficiency. And to compel him to make the diversion when he fails to respond to the inner leading, it will throw the terrible gloom of the dark night over him for a time.(P)

87
He must learn to recognize the infrequent voice of real inspiration when he hears it, no less than the many inferior voices that make pretension to its quality.

88
Be passive only to the Overself but positive to people.

89
The student trained along philosophical lines approaches the interpretations of his inner experiences with restraint laid heavily upon his ego by the feeling of his own limitations, his own weaknesses. If therefore he errs at all in such interpretation, it will be in the direction of an unflattering one.

90

It is hard for a foreigner entering a strange country for the first time to get true and correct impressions of it. They will necessarily be surface ones and may therefore be misleading ones. In the same way, without this previous instruction and training, it is hard for a mystic to get true and correct reception of the revelatory experience. This is because his mind will unconsciously reflect its personal limitations into the reception, so that what he gets is not the experience itself, but the experience in conjunction with those limitations, and therefore under them. He does not get direct reception at all.

91

The philosophic student must watch himself vigilantly and examine his experiences critically, determined to stretch mental honesty to the farthest point. He must, in fact, safeguard himself against his auto-suggestions. He must test every claim and challenge every internal voice and vision.

92

He must eliminate all those intellectual ideas which stand between him and the Real, all those emotional states which cloud it. Otherwise his mystical deliverances will merely reproduce those ideas and states interwoven inextricably with real inspirations.

93

If he were philosophically trained, he might know when to stop reception of the message and thus refrain from adding his own dubious opinions to its certain truths.

94

In discussing the nature of a revelation we need to remember that, however little or however much, it must be coloured by the man's own past history, traditions, and surroundings, his present conceptions, beliefs, and imaginations. Only when every possible effort has been made by a man to free himself from all these influences can they be reduced to a minimum, and that is the task of philosophy. But that requires that he should really be free outwardly as well as inwardly and therefore not a member of any group, coterie, institution, religion, or organization dealing with the subject upon which he has had a revelation. The more he fails to combat these influences, the more likely is it that some portion, whether it be small or very large, of his revelation is merely an arbitrary creation of his own.

95

Not to all mystics are the special revelations about the World-Mind's operations and processes made. The recipients are only a fraction in number, but it would be an error to believe that they are more saintly or more ego-free than other mystics. It is simply that, having occult tendencies, these have been made use of, since such revelations are not made on the highest possible level where such tendencies could not find fulfilment. Generally, but not always, the persons who are chosen and are used to communicate the revelations have still to complete their spiritual development. The exceptions are those who have undergone the philosophic training.

96

It is safer to take any of these approaches in a cautious and conservative way. The mind will then remain steady, better able to perceive truth.

97

It requires only a little philosophical training to be able to distinguish what part of these revelations is merely parochial and what part is really universal, what is the tinsel of human opinion and what is pure gold of divine truth, what is the work of irresponsible imagination and what is the activity of Overself. One can see where the contribution of established religion or mystical sects ends and where that of original seership begins.

98

The best practical advice to beginners, and even to many who think they are proficients, is a warning. However solemn the message seems to be, however inspired the accompanying state of mind apparently is, do not automatically and unquestioningly believe that the Lord is speaking to them. If they object that surely at such a time as sacred prayer or uplifting meditation the Lord would not let them be deceived by evil forces, the answer is that the question is wrongly put. It is *they*, and not necessarily the evil forces, who deceive themselves.

99

Because the guidance comes to him from such a medley of sources, he is in danger of being seriously wrong and of making grave mistakes. For the glamour and strength of the higher source may unconsciously be bestowed upon the lower ones.

100

They form a mind-picture of the experience or enlightenment that they expect to get as a consequence of their practice, or of their discipleship, but in the end the expectation either proves illusory or imagination fabricates the fulfilment for them.

101

The message or revelation, the clairvoyant picture or clairaudient voice, presents itself as if it were newly originated from outside the personality when in fact it was all along present in the subconscious.

102

The Baroness von Krudener was a mystic who at one time greatly influenced Czar Alexander I. She gave him the idea of the Holy Alliance of Russia, Prussia, and Austria. She undertook fantastic missions. Not long before her death, however, she confessed: "Very often I have taken for the voice of God what was nothing but the fruit of my own pride and imagination."

103

The messages are certainly not produced by the conscious mind but they may still be produced by the subconscious mind. To call in, for the purpose of explanation, some outside and unearthly force, some unseen spirit, can only be justified after the subconscious' power and operation have been first called in and adequately heard.

104

Do not mistake imaginations or speculations for knowledge of truth: too often they show up personal attachments and wishes, expectations and inclinations.

105

Why attribute to a high source what is of merely natural origin? Why offer everything that comes into the mind as a divine revelation?

106

Too many clergymen, laymen, and leaders have spoken for God, as if they knew God's mind and did God's will. In most cases it is safe to say that they either understand very imperfectly the divine nature or interpreted very fallibly the divine communication.

107

Doctor Frank Buchman, founder of the Oxford Group, illustrates one defect of mysticism. Before the war he endorsed and even praised Hitler. Yet, for at least twenty years before this endorsement, he was practising meditation every morning without fail. He was getting, he claimed, guidance from God. Was it God's guidance that induced him to praise Hitler?

108

A millionaire Englishman who made his fortune selling rails, locomotives, and metals lost it later because he decided his financial investments by the method of sticking a pin at random into his copy of the Bible and accepting the text therein indicated as a reliable guide for the purpose.

109

Joanna Southcott was honest enough to tell the doctor who attended her during the few weeks before her death that she considered her inspiration and prophecies as delusion. Indeed she was scrupulously honest, for then she called her leading disciples to her bedside and confessed her doubts and despairs to them. "Feeling as I do now, that my dissolution is drawing nigh, it all appears delusion," she told them, "but when the communications were made to me *I did not in the least doubt.*"

110

When dealing with the origin of inner experiences, visions, and so forth, do not ascribe it to expectancy alone—link it with imagination also.

111

Too often in the history of mysticism impulses from the ego have been mistaken for spontaneous intuitions from the higher individuality.

112

The same God who showed Spanish Saint Teresa the necessary holiness of poverty showed several American cult-leaders the necessary holiness of riches! Is it not more sensible to assume that one or the other was not in communication with God at all?

113

It is insufficient understanding of the mental processes behind an intuition, a message, or a revelation which causes would-be mystics and even quite a number of practising mystics to accept without question these inward impressions as being of divine origin when they are nothing of the sort. When this ignorance is allied to insufficient emotional control and insufficient knowledge of the history of mysticism, both past and current, both Occidental and Oriental, then a fanatic is bred and truth is lost or missed; then danger besets him and all those who put themselves under his influence.

114

Let us not mistake the folly of man for the wisdom of God, nor the impulse of man for the will of God. Let us not accept the perversion of truth for the purity of truth.

115

But alas, too often the grisly truth is that it is not the genuine intuition at all but rather the intellect trying to be intuition. In his eagerness to get a result he, unconsciously of course, tells a lie to himself.

116

The experiences which may be read about in books and which are so confusing are not all on the same level. The chief cause of this confusion lies in the failure to separate the intellectual from the truly spiritual in the descriptions. Under the former heading come most of the occurrences. They are mostly projections of the seer's ego and reveal what he is most familiar with, what he believes in, what he expects, and so on. Few seers have a scientific outlook and most mix together the essential with the incidental quite indiscriminately.

117

If he receives flattering messages from his mysterious source, whether it claims to be a master or a god, a good spirit or his soul, he may be sure that he is being led astray by his own ego and that the source is not what it claims to be.

118

We need not wonder that the experience fattens his ego and swells his head, that he comes to regard the revelation as entirely exclusive to himself, and that finally he announces himself as a new Messiah born among men as their sole saviour.

119

"I believe that I am acting on the order of the Almighty Creator," announced Hitler one day to the Germans. The ignorance of his credulous people of the correct method of testing the infallibility of mystical announcements made them his blood-bathed victims.

120

The most pompous declarations of mystical knowledge are often nothing more than empty asseverations of personal opinion.

121

Often the first impression should be accepted because it is the correct one. But sensual attraction or aversion may provide a false one.

122

Snap decisions, actions done impulsively, and judgements rendered on first impressions may seem at the time to have intuition as their source but it is not necessarily so. They may be based on outward appearances alone and thus lack its depth, or may be emotional alone and suffer from the ego's bias or defects.

123

He cannot afford to put himself at the mercy of every subconscious impulse, even if it takes the name of God.

124

It is easy for the impatient student to mistake the ego's voice for the Overself's.

125

The capacity for intuition is born from a long experience in bygone lives but the psychological reality of it was always present—because the Overself was.

126

All communications of a psychical or intuitive, visioned or heard character must be tested warily and judged critically by their results in experience. Otherwise the false, the fraudulent, the unfactual, the misleading may be accepted as the true and real. This of course is a rule mainly for beginners.

127

The standard classics of mystical experience should be referred to occasionally so as to check the vagaries through which his own inner experience is likely to pass.

128

He must test these experiences not only by their internal evidences but also by their external results. Do they make him humbler or prouder? Do they improve the balance of his faculties or disturb it?(P)

129

Make it a definite rule in every single instance to check your intuitions by the light of reason.(P)

130

He should take scrupulous care to discriminate between the ego-prompted emotions and the intuitive, impersonal feelings. Since this will be a none-too-easy task he will have to walk carefully here. Where he knows that he cannot trust himself he should refuse to be carried away by his promptings, no matter how vehement they may be. But where the depth, the calmness, and the certitude of his inner experience combine to give him conviction of higher guidance, he may make the experiment and surrender to it. In this way and with such care, he will not give himself too easily or too quickly to inner messages. On the other hand, he will not overplay the sceptic thereby and lose the benefit of an authentic whisper from on high.

131

Irony is a good servant of inspiration if it cuts away the debris of false belief which chokes the passage of profound thoughts.

132

Clearer thinking about his experience and more careful description of it is needed if he is to keep out of confusion or error.

133

We cultivate intuition not so much by strengthening it little by little as by removing the obstacles to it.

134

The highly personal man is too full of himself to leave any room for the soul, with its utter impersonality, to enter his field of awareness.

135

He must be on his guard against mixing doctrine brought up from the lower state with the experience of the higher state. It is not only the sceptic and outsider who must test the mystic's claim to divine revelation, but also the mystic himself.

136

To admit the human origin, whether in whole or in part, of a so-called divine revelation is an act which only those who have mortgaged their reason to mere sentimentality need fear.

137

As a result of such impersonal self-examination, the content of some mystical experience or psychical vision may have to be disavowed: but the result will be that his future experiences or visions are likely to be truer ones.

138

The subjective feeling of certainty is no certificate of its truth.

139

A further way in which we can test the value of their theory is by its effect upon the character and behaviour, its results in the ethical attitudes and personal actions.

140

His humility will be a natural protection against the ego's self-flattering exaggerations or the intellect's arrogant assumptions.

141

It is less easy for an aspirant himself than for an experienced observer to detect the influences which impregnate his inner experiences.

142

Cause and effect is plain enough a relationship in this physical world but becomes disturbed and unreliable when research penetrates a different level of being. If it moves on, it finds itself in a new order of knowledge where a new faculty—intuition—must become active through concentration and contemplation and—dare it be said?—worship.

143

The intuition which fails when checked, tested, and verified by every other possible source must be treated with caution.

144

I have indeed said that intuition should be cultivated as a help to successful accomplishment of meditation exercises, but I have never said that it should be cultivated at the expense of reasoned thinking, common sense, and practicality. When the healthy balance has been upset, pseudo-intuitions have an easy triumph.

145

If his mind is too passive it becomes open to all sorts of suggestions, but if it is too positive it misses clues, hints, intuitions. It misses inspirations and messages from within, or guidance from without. Therefore a fine, even, and delicate balance between these two extremes is needful.

146

The first awareness of this feeling is so impalpable, so delicate, that it is easy to miss: attention turns away into some thought or activity without even knowing its loss.

147

Intuitions move in on us in one of two ways: either so soft and gentle at first as almost to be missed or with such aggressive forcefulness as to allow no other way.

148

This intuitive feeling is a clue. It must be yielded to; the delicate emotion must be allowed to move him to a higher view.

149

A profound assurance will slowly come to settle itself within the innermost depths of his being. It will endorse or negate read or heard statements.

150

It is not easy for the beginner to know how valid is the intuition he feels or the guidance he gets. Where any doubt exists it is better to wait before accepting the one or obeying the other.

151

Recall the feeling with which the earlier experiences of alleged intuition were born.

152

Intuition is always to be trusted but we must first be sure that it is intuition and not its imitation, or its admixture.

153

It is easy to take one's opinion as something more than it is. But no one who really gets an intuition, a revelation, or an awareness from the Overself can mistake it as something less than it is. For it is unique in presentation and experience.

154

He may test the authenticity of his inner experiences in various ways but one of them is to remember that if they begin with doubt and end with certainty, or begin with fear and end with joy, they represent a movement from the ego to the Overself. But if this order is reversed, they represent nothing more than a movement within the ego and are therefore to be distrusted.

155

In *The Hidden Teaching Beyond Yoga* the student was cautioned to check his intuitions by reason, lest they are really pseudo-intuitions. This is a necessary counsel to all except the very few whose intuition is thoroughly tested by results and whose experience is abundant enough to detect the false at once and reject it without further ado. Once so established, the intuition needs no checking, only unreserved acceptance.

156

The untrained blindly accept their message; the informed and disciplined mystics scrupulously examine it.

157

How much of the glimpse, experience, or message is truly inspired by a higher source, and how much is merely added, imagined, or misconceived by his own little ego-mind, is a question that the beginning quester should have the humility to ask himself. What is authentic will easily survive such careful discriminating judgement.

158

He must not be content to accept the communication entirely as presented but should sift it and seek the origins of its various parts. But he must sift it critically and seek these origins open-mindedly.

159

His inner experiences should be checked by those of the great sages and philosophic seers.

160

When it first comes, and for many occasions afterward, the intuition is subtle to the point of being barely felt, delicate to the point of being scarcely experienced.

161

As such possibilities of error and deception exist along the aspirant's path, it is needful for him to lay down a safe rule for his self-protection. And that is to regard all his revelations as being projections of his subconscious ego, with all the ego's limitations and defects, until they prove themselves in time to be otherwise.

15

ILLUMINATIONS

Properties of imagination

In the mystical aspirant's life, his imaginative faculty, when properly used, keeps the Guide or Master constantly and vividly before his attention to inspire, to correct, and to lead him. But improperly used, it leads him astray into fantasies and falsities.

2

If he continues to gaze at the mental images which he thus sees in his vision, rapt and absorbed as he is, he may eventually mesmerize himself into a firm belief in their external reality. But whether they be Gods and saints or lights and colours, these strange visions which pass before his eyes are partly creations of the mind itself. Many so-called clairvoyant and occult phenomena are really mental projections, but it is perfectly possible for them to be so vivid as to appear as if they were outside their seer. The experiences of them have been largely, if unconsciously, created within the tortuous recesses of the narrator's own cranium. He visualizes mental images with such intensity and exuberance that the imagined forms and events appear to him as external objects. This kind of thing has now come even within the sweep of scientific investigation. A group of psychologists, professors attached to American universities, have discovered that the faculty of perceiving mental images so vividly that they appear to be outside objects is not uncommon among children, and they have bestowed the term "eidetic imagery" on this power. There is little difference between such imagining and that of those grown-up children who unconsciously create their own visions. In both cases the visions are the result of the percipient's own mental construction and have no independent existence.

3

The mind can make its own experiences, from the lowest to the highest, by imagination or by intellection, by faith or by expectancy. They may seem real enough to the experiencer but yet be mere aberrations, illustrating only this power of the mind, rather than its capacity to find truth. Worshippers of cults, devotees of gurus, do not usually know this.

4

Let us not be misunderstood. We are not decrying either the worth or the utility of imagination properly used. We are decrying its degeneration into wild fancy, its caricature by foolish hallucination, its misuse and abuse. On the Quest, as in other fields, it is a valuable faculty which can help the aspirant actualize his ideal in everyday living. By its use in intensive meditation it enables him to put into pictorial form what he wants to become. This literally *creates* his ideal.

5

Just as the dream-mind of sleep creates pseudo-personalities with utter ease, so the reverie-mind of meditation creates images and messages with the same ease.

6

Visions may be nothing more than rambling imaginations yet are mistaken for revelations.

7

The intensity of a man's thinking will help to determine how long or how short the thought-form thus created will survive and its influence endure; for all thought-forms must die in the end.

8

Too often the picture he builds up in his mind is painted with baseless assumptions, exaggerated expectations, and ungrounded suppositions. It does not coincide with the reality which life itself provides. A blind faith is not necessarily a correct one.

9

The world into which he thinks he has penetrated exists inside his own head alone. It is a private one. It is a fantasy, not a reality.

10

In short, a man must become aware of his relationship to the Spirit before he will drop his relationship with spiritualism.

11

When these pictures in the mind pose as psychical realities, they may easily lead him astray from the true path.

12

Its apparent clairvoyance or psychic faculty or strong detailed memory is largely due to possession of picture-vision.

13

Although he feels that the communication originates from outside himself, from a spiritual leader or disembodied being, it is part of his own inner life nevertheless. The thoughts are of his own making even though projected into space and associated with someone else. Their seeming outwardness is no proof of their actual outwardness. He has unconsciously deceived himself, and yet not altogether done so.

Spiritual reality, mental imagery

14

The problem of extraordinary psychic phenomena which sometimes arise in the course of meditation is puzzling but not insoluble. Visions may be seen, voices heard, revelations automatically written down, or conversations carried on with another entity. We propose to deal here with authentic phenomena and not with cases of insanity, epilepsy, hysteria, and neuroticism, which unfortunately get mixed up with mystical aspiration and, unjustly but not unreasonably, bring censure down on mysticism itself.

15

The reality of the soul is one thing, the image under which many mystics experience it is another. Any effort to identify the one with the other under all conditions is a misconceived and misguided effort.

16

Where the psychical manifests itself and mixes with the aspirant's mystical experience, this may happen because he has some psychical sensitivity or a strong emotional nature or a vivid imaginative faculty. If the ego inserts itself, as it often does, the result will be a confused one. In such a case, the aspirant has to separate the psychical element from the mystical one, which is higher. He has to force himself by rigorous analysis to become aware of what has really happened.

17

A strange happening which cannot be explained at present is not necessarily a miracle. There might be a supernormal explanation.

18

There is a danger in the case of those who practise meditation and seek psychic "experiences," without a sufficiently strong character, of developing a double personality, one which mixes together in ill-assorted union the most exalted moments felt in meditation with the lowest ones felt in the animal nature. In spite of the loftiness of one part of the nature, the other may become weak and faulty.

19

Instead of truth being sharply revealed by such religio-psychic states, it is pleasantly fogged and speciously avoided.

20

A psychic experience which is also emotionally absorbing in a self-centered way is one to beware of. If it throws him off-balance, it is useless and unimportant to his quest.

21

It is true they may believe they feel peace of mind, but an inner peace which is grounded on the false creations of fantasy will not stand the tests of life. They may go about their business in this delusion for some time, but sooner or later something will happen to expose it for what it is.

22

Most occult meditations and exercises are done within, by, and for the ego! Their special danger is self-deception since it is an ego no longer openly materialistic but masquerading as highly spiritual!

23

A neurotic experience often masquerades as a noumenal one!

24

Every psychic vision is really seen outside his being.

25

Those who lose their heads and become hysterical over their own mystical experiences have probably had only psychical ones.

26

The experience may be gratifying but it may also be of little value; it is cozy but not cosmic!

27

When we comprehend the mentalist character of the whole of our world-experience, it is easy to comprehend that a mystic's intuition may symbolize itself in a perceived form, his thought may express itself in a heard voice, his supersensual experience may translate itself into a sensory one, and his higher self may project itself in a revered master's face.

28

Those to whom the higher power has to reveal itself through visions seen clairvoyantly, or sounds heard clairaudiently, or teachings impressed mentally are helped in this inferior way only because they lack the capacity to receive in a superior way. And this remains just as true if the vision is of their most respected Spiritual Leader, the sound none other than the mystic Sanskrit syllable OM, and the teaching fully descriptive of the seven planes of progressive being. If they had possessed the capacity to receive by pure insight without any reference to the method by which we receive through the agency of five bodily senses and the intellect, they would not have needed such occult experiences, which are in a sense semi-materialistic. Only when these agents are stilled, and the image-making faculty silenced, and the time or place lost, is pure Spirit known. Not only must the body and its activities, the intellect and its movements be forgotten, but even their representation in an occult or psychical manner must be absent. It is then only that there can be true identity with the Overself. All other experiences are mere projections going *out* from it, and hence involved in references to the ego.

29

If the voices which he hears are audible in the same way that one hears the voices of people through the ears, it is merely psychic and undesirable. If, however, it is a very strong mental impression and also very clear, then it is the mystic phenomenon known as the "Interior Word" which is on a truly spiritual plane and therefore is desirable.(P)

30

H.P.B.'s *Voice of the Silence* tells of seven mystical sounds which are heard by the aspirant. The first is like the nightingale's voice, whereas the sixth is like a thunder-cloud. This passage has been much misunderstood both by novices and by unphilosophical mystics, whilst in India and Tibet whole systems of yoga have been built up on their supposed psychic existence. The sounds are not actually heard. The reference to them is merely metaphorical. It speaks rather of the silent intuitive feeling of the Overself's existence which becomes progressively stronger with time, until finally, in H.P.B.'s own eloquent words, "The seventh swallows all the other sounds. They die, and then are heard no more." This represents the stage where the voice of the ego is completely unified with the voice of the Overself, where occasional realization is converted into a constant one.(P)

31

Some see lightning flash across the eyes, others feel a glowing point within the heart. These are not the Overself but the human and psychic *reactions* to the experience of it.

32

There are certain principal phenomena—especially visions that are seen, rapturous ecstasies that are felt, revelations that are impressed on the mind, and communications that are uttered within by an interior voice— which may appear at various stages (or may not).

33

It would be a gross error to believe that *all* visions are to be regarded with caution, let alone suspicion. There is one which is a complete exception to this rule. This is the vision of Light.

34

The Infinite and Absolute Power which transcends time could never reveal itself by any seen vision or heard sound. Sects like the Rahasoami which offer both as a divine experience are still pandering to the psychic thirst and occult hunger of half-developed minds unable to understand the relativity and inferiority of such inner experiences.

35

The faith which is already in the heart, the image which pre-exists in the mind, these are drawn upon and used by the man's soul to give him the experience of and message from itself.

36

The Overself can never be seen or heard, touched or tasted. Therefore no visions of a pictorial kind, no voices of a psychic kind, no musical sounds of a "mystical and cosmic" kind, no outer form or manifestation of any kind which comes to you through the senses can be the real authentic experience of it.

37

Most of the visions and many of the voices experienced by them are within a strange sphere, compounded partly of thought-forms created by their own imagination and partly of denizens in a spirit underworld.

38

The pure growth of the inner life is not compatible with the dubious activity of dramatic occult-psychical forces, even though these assertedly emanate from God—firstly because the assertion is a false one, secondly because the resultant experiences keep the man within the realm of form, illusion, and even more especially, egoism.

39

All visions in the end are visions which occur in mind. Do not think that vision of anything is the goal. The one thing you must find is reality of being, that which you are.

40

We must be sharp enough to observe that even when it is occupied with any mental image of God or the Soul, the consciousness is still objective, still directed to something apart from and other than itself.

41

God will appear to us in Spirit alone, never in Space. To see him is to see the playing and posturing of our own mind.(P)

42

A mystic experience may come with a seen vision of the spiritual Guide or a felt—not heard—voice communicating a message, teachings, or guidance, or it may come with none of these things as intellectual insight into the Real.

43

The God with whom he communicates is indeed an aspect of his own consciousness, a higher state of his own being.

44

The fact that God is formless suffices to show that He cannot be seen as an external or internal form. Whoever declares that God has taken shape before him, whether in tangible flesh or untouchable vision, thereby declares his own ignorance.

45

What they think to be the solemn voice of God is really the voice of their

own higher self commingled with, or influenced by, the expectations of
their conscious and subconscious mind.

46

He inevitably thinks of God through his own experience and so through
his own mental images. But the God of reality is utterly beyond him and
utterly unpicturable. It is the Unknown God.

47

Many a mystical experience of "God" is really an exalted emotion shaped
by the power of suggestions received from outside or from within.

48

Only in relation to our human nature can we make these attributions to
the Divine. Only in their human reactions do mystics have their various
mystical experiences of the Divine.

49

The danger of mistaking his mere opinion for God's voice is a real one.
It can be averted only if he will allow himself to be guided by the wider
experience of Masters and disciplined by the rejection of egoistic influences.

50

The Infinite Reality could only be known by an infinite mind. If any
finite human intelligence—however mystical it may be—consciously
claims such knowledge, it unconsciously proclaims at the same time that
its knowledge is ultimately only an opinion.

51

The danger of taking every idea that comes into his head as a communication from Jesus or Buddha, as so many take it even today, is a real one.

52

He imagines himself to have attained union with God or to be on the
path to it, and the irony is that it is this very imagination which prevents
him from attaining it.

53

Whether divinity appears to man as the world outside him or as an
inward experience, it is still an appearance.

54

The differing human imaginations about God and the various human
ideas about God's response to human attitudes in no way affect or alter the
actual situation.

55

Psychic phenomena, whether of a sensory or mental kind, which insidiously flatter the ego should be ignored, or discounted as illusory. The
most absurd effect is the Messiah complex.

Conditioning factors

56

The importance of the mental attitude with which the meditator enters this supreme experience is immense. For it is truly creative. Thought maketh the man. It is here that the meditator's interference may alter the results that should legitimately be expected from this enlargement of consciousness. Such interference may take the shape, for example, of insisting on attaching his intellectual preconceptions and emotional complexes to the Overself in anticipation of what he thinks it is or ought to be. He will usually emerge from this experience with a view of the significance coloured by his previous habitual thought and distinctive life. If, for instance, he enters it out of ascetic escapism, as often happens, out of a quest of refuge from a world with whose trials or temptations, existence or values he cannot cope, he will return with a strengthened denunciation of the world's worthlessness. This faulty interpretation of his mystical experience is due not only to the immaturity of his intellectual ideas but also to the bias of his emotional temperament.

57

When a man receives or communicates a mystic experience, a divine revelation, he naturally receives it through, or communicates it along with, his preconceived opinions and traditionally absorbed views, his emotional prejudices and intellectual bias, his particular situation in time and place and his conscious or unconscious self-interest. It is limited by them, while his pronouncements are conditioned by them. A further element which intrudes into his interpretation is that of hidden desires and unconscious wishes. Rawson with his cult of an immortal bodily life represents this type of intrusion.

58

Although these visions of a spiritual guide maybe are the outcome of the man's own previous desires and thoughts, there is no reason why he should not profit by their limited usefulness. It is only when they keep him permanently caught, as in a trap, that they hinder his further advance and render him a disservice.

59

Ideas picked up by association or inherent in the mentality or lurking in the character may become as operative during the illumination as before it. They will then seem to be an integral part of it.

60

His own imaginings enter into his highest mystical experience and give a spurious validity to the intellectual, emotional, and traditional tendencies which birth and environment have implanted in him.

61

Mystics see in vision the leader they believe in. "According to talmudic tradition, the prophet Elijah never died, and many saintly persons in the period of the Talmud and thereafter, down to recent times, have been reputedly visited and taught by him. Such a privilege is called *gillui Elijah*—Elijah's self-revelation."

The Kabbalah has admitted that the *gillui Elijah* does not necessarily imply a visual manifestation: "To some Elijah reveals himself through the soul, by way of the intellect, to some by the way of wisdom, and to some—face to face."—*Tikkunei Zohar Hadash*. The Maharal of Prague, creator of the famous *golem* (robot), wrote (*Nezah Israel*, chapter XXVIII): "There is no difference whether Elijah's presence be seen or not seen, for often Elijah tells one various things without the recipient's awareness of the source of his information."— H.L. Gordon, *The Maggid of Caro*

62

His ego, with its preferences and repulsions, will stamp its character upon his interpretation unless in the moment of revelation he can abandon it utterly.

63

The emotions swiftly insert themselves into the experience and give it a personal bias. The thoughts wrap themselves around it and, following confirmed habit, give it a familiar shape.

64

It is a well-known fact in Muhammedan religious history that visions of the Prophet have often been granted to Islamic Holy Men, and are indeed much prized by them. But the question comes up: Why did not Jesus or Buddha appear to them instead of Muhammed?

65

Even Ramakrishna once admitted that the enlightenment attained by the most highly spiritual person is slightly coloured by his own ordinary human mind! It is obvious that differences of education or intellect, upbringing or tradition, will be responsible for some of the differences of teaching among mystics.

66

The ego not only inserts itself into the experience at the very time that it is happening but also after it is over when remembering or communicating it.

67

Why did Swedenborg, for instance, see an inner world which was but a continuation of, and entirely coloured by, the religious tradition into which he was born? Why was it so completely Christian and Western? Why were the Buddhistic characteristics of the Eastern half of the planet's traditions utterly absent?

68

He who finds in the revelation precisely what he expected to find may have unconsciously contributed towards its making.

69

He is being affected by suggestion all the time. If he could catch it at the point of entry, he might be able to protect himself. But this presupposes the ability to recognize the influences for what they are, or to detect their real source.

70

Imagination, desire, emotion, or expectancy get involved with the real glimpse because the man has not purged his character enough, nor developed his intelligence sufficiently, to arrive at pure perception.

71

The illumination is one thing, its emotional additions another. A beginner confuses the two. When the emotional excitement wears off and only the *ideas* left by illumination remain, he feels disappointed, frustrated, unhappy.

72

Even in moments of highest exaltation he has to receive the inspiration with the limited consciousness and imperfect character which he possesses at the time it comes.

73

A separation must be made between the mental-emotional fact of the experience and the message, revelation, or expression which it contains. Such an analysis will not hurt a true experience and a true message but only tend to confirm them.

74

When any mystic assigns a supreme and unique place to the Person with whom his native religion is identified, and assigns an inferior and commoner one to the other prophets, his mystical revelation is faulty and imperfect.

75

Suggestion from outside as well as from inside himself supplies much of the interpretation of his message. To that extent it may distort the message.

76

What the ego contributes to his illumination is an unwitting contribution. Nevertheless, it is present; thus and to that degree it stops him from being fully and finally illumined.

77

Mystical experiences do happen and only the purblind materialist, who will not trouble to investigate, dares deny their occurrence. But when each mystic tells of seeing only that God or that Saviour or that Guide whom he already worships or honours, the thoughtful scientific enquirer naturally and rightly becomes suspicious. The Christian sees Saint Teresa or Jesus or pictures of the orthodox heaven which were taught him in youth and childhood. The Hindu sees the Rama or Shiva with whom he is already familiar. The situation in mystical circles is today, and always has been, an anarchical one. What else can be expected where men are free to mistake private opinion for divine guidance, human ambition for sacred mandate? But even in loftier levels, where vision is authentic and intuition is a fact, the intellectual unity in such circles is a precarious one. How can we imagine a common denominator of outlook between such diversified mystics as Plotinus and Swedenborg? What unity of belief can there be between Eckhart, the German prophet, and Joseph Smith, the Mormon seer? This raises a question which has to be settled and which the advanced mystic must face if he is going to be honest with himself and others.

Philosophy's answer will not be palatable to most mystics, but the inconsistency of such experiences cannot otherwise be explained. It declares that the actuality of a mystical revelation may be accepted without by any means accepting all its content. It explains that if the heart yearns intensely for the Overself but, whether through environmental suggestion or historical tradition, associates this in belief with a particular mental image, there will be an unconscious projection of the image into mystical experiences, should they eventually occur. The Overself uses the man's own imaginative faculty as a medium of its communication to him. It helps him by couching its message in an idiom which is familiar to, and easily understandable by, him. Thus he first puts a picture of God or a Saint in his mind and then these experiences follow after intense concentration upon it. But it is really his own mind which works all these wonders and which gives the impression of an external power, whether of God or of man, acting upon him. His interpretation has been unconsciously laid over the delight and grandeur of the inner experience itself and presented to the world as if it were an inherent and integral part of that experience.

Paul's previous familiarity with the name and notions of Jesus account for his identification with Christ of the vision which appeared to him on the road to Damascus. Had he been unaware of Jesus' existence, had he known only of Krishna's existence, for example, he would have attributed this mystic experience not to the first but to the second source. This does not in the least derogate from the genuine character of Paul's vision nor the truly spiritual authenticity of his conversion. His experience would have been equally exalted, equally divine whatever attribution he gave it, because it was a veritable visitation, sudden and unexpected, by the Overself.

Thus what is already familiar to the mystic, such as images out of his own past or out of the conventional traditions or religious dogmas in which he has previously been instructed, adds itself to the initial inspiration. But it often adds itself so largely as to assume an importance beyond its right. He himself is unfortunately in no position to distinguish the original from what has been added to it, for the frontier between them has been obliterated by the force, heat, and immediacy of his experience. The mystic who has striven is entitled to his reward and gets it through such experiences, but so long as he is unable to separate what is essential in them—the sublime tranquillity and serene immateriality that abide in their inmost being—from what is accidental—the presupposed mental figures and pictures he sees, the inward message he hears, and the intuitive thoughts that arise—so long will he be blind to the fact that the latter is veridical only for himself, being hatched in his own mind, and not for others.

78

He enters this Light with the equipment of experience, knowledge, mentality, and character which accompany the intuition leading him into it. The condition of such equipment cannot help but affect what he sees or learns.

79

Even the vocabulary with which he explains the mystical experience to himself or transmits it to others is manufactured for him by the religious tradition of his land. It limits and even shapes his understanding, so that he does not receive the knowledge yielded by this experience as it is in itself.

80

The visions represent no new knowledge but only a development of his inherited beliefs or subconscious influences.

81

The revelation will be conditioned by his own mentality, his racial tradition, his point of view, his area of experience, and his grade of development. These constitute the channel in which it has to manifest and through which it has to pass to others. They may interfere to the point of rendering it inaccurate.

82

The kind of spiritual experience a man gets depends upon the degree of development attained by his character, intelligence, and aspiration.

83

The character of these visions is often traceable to previously held ideas, to strongly held beliefs, or to hoarded suggestions. Ideas which he previously knew contribute towards and may even determine the ideas which are supposed to be revealed ones. Thus his interior revelation or clairvoyance is usually conditioned by his personal history and temperament.

84

It is a noteworthy historical fact that out of the list of known stigmatists, only two of those were men—Francis of Assisi and Padre Pio. All the others were women. It is equally noteworthy that this strange phenomenon has never appeared among the mystics and monks of the Eastern Greek Orthodox Church—and they have been many.

85

Generally the most powerful of these formative influences are the suggestions which he receives and accepts from his environment. Parents, family, country, and race have acted upon him since his infancy, always openly and often subtly. They have imposed their own traditional ideas, to which he has unconsciously fallen victim unless he is one of the few who have had sufficient independence to think for themselves.

86

In the end all suggestion is auto-suggestion. An idea which has been introduced into the mind by an outside agent becomes our own only after *we* have accepted it.

87

The group he belongs to, the organization of which he is a member, the very language he uses—all this conditions his illumination.

88

The materials stored in his memory will help to shape the finished revelation, just as the literary models to which he is accustomed or with which he has had contact will influence the form of his composition.

89

His personal characteristics, personal history, and personal habits constitute the glasses through which he looks at Truth. If they are coloured or biased, too inadequate or too one-sided, then this will affect his vision of the truth.

90

Suggestion pours in from his origins and devotions, his background and dedications, his experience and relationships, from all the past generations and past reincarnations which have made his ego what it is.

91

He is a slave to the beliefs put into his head in childhood and adolescence, by society and education, and simply echoes them back for the rest of his lifetime, even when he enters the light of a mystical experience.

92

His ideas of God and his intuitions of the Soul do not come from himself alone nor from his mystical experience alone. They have come also from his parents, his educators, his spiritual pastors, from intercourse with the society in which he has lived, and from reading the books he has owned or borrowed.

93

Just as a dream so often dramatizes the simplest mental or physical stimulus, so the mind of a psychic dramatizes some of its own ordinary content and projects that upon an event, an object, or a person.

94

The true being is one thing, a human being's experience of it is another, while the individual reaction to it is a third thing. So when two people report their communion with, and communication from, God, remember not to expect identical statements. There will be differences and colourings, agreements and, to some extent, contradictions. There are no two individualities absolutely alike, no two personal histories which duplicate one another. So—"the observer enters into the observed object," as they say of the most difficult stage in formulating the theory of atomic physics. Each prophet gives you his way of receiving and articulating truth: it cannot be otherwise. Silence alone can then hold the answer to Pilate's question: "What is truth?" But, because few people are sensitive enough to comprehend such an answer telepathically or to "deny" themselves sufficiently to let its grace enter their hearts, most prophets will continue to speak.

95

If visions and voices, forms and messages, often enter the mystic's field of consciousness at a certain stage of his experience, they are like the similes and metaphors which poets and writers use in order to express the feelings aroused by something or other. They ought not to be confused with the deeper psychological experience to which they are related, any more than we ought to confuse a writer's allusion in the expression "the man was a Napoleon in daring" with thinking that the man in any way became a real Napoleon instead of a figurative one. The educational and theological ideas familiar to a mystic are similar figurative projections when they reappear in his visions, although he is usually too confused or too unscientific or too carried away to separate them from their psychological basis. Nevertheless it may still be the divine Overself which supplies the original inspiration for them, and the thrill of uplift or peace which he experiences does then come from such a basis. The mystic is too close to his experience, too enthralled with its wonder, to notice how far he is himself contributing a genuine and how far a dubious or even a fictitious element to it, or to comprehend that it is the act of meditation itself, and not the object meditated on, that really produces results. The inspiration may be indubitable, but it is a common mistake to superimpose upon such a feeling the intellectual image which memory constructs or the theoretical interpretation which natural bias or human expectation provides. The nugget of inspirational gold is hidden within a fantasy created by his own desires and emotions, by his strong wishful thinking. It is a more refined version of the old story of making God partly but not wholly in man's image.

Thus these experiences do not really originate from an outside source. It is his own mental pictures that are brought up out of the subconscious and reflected into his conscious mind, even when he believes that they are visions of something external. The message he hears may only be the echo of his own voice, a subtle psychic self-deception. The content of many clairvoyant visions and portentous prophecies, as of many dreams, is determined by what has previously been read, thought, or experienced. Hence they are only projections of mental images already familiar to him. These ideas may simmer in the mind's depths for a long time but eventually they float to the surface. The mental phenomena obtained differ according to the notions previously entertained and are consequently coloured accordingly. This is inevitable because his mystical study or practice is usually and unconsciously carried on under the sway of such educational preconceptions and experiential bias as he brings to it. The historical variations in mystical phenomena are too wide, and the visions themselves are too similar to the expectations of the mystic to be acceptable as valid, even when their actual occurrence is undeniable, as it often is. We see wish-fulfilment at work here, whether it be the consequence of unconscious wishes or conscious ones. These experiences form too frail a foundation to hold up a true conception of the world or of God.

96

The mystic must beware of the effusions of his all-too-vivid imagination. The confusion wrought by those earnest but inexperienced aspirants who associate their wrong intellectual beliefs, their narrow emotional pre-possessions, and their foolish hopes with the Overself's inspiration is immense. They enthuse about what is inconsequential and neglect what is important. So long as they insist on taking the imaginations they revel in so uncritically as a basis for the understanding of life, so long will that understanding itself remain shallow and inadequate. So long as they are less interested in the pure experience of the Overself and more in the fanciful drapery which the mental complexes unconsciously wrap around it, so long will their knowledge of divine matters be halting and uncertain. An unexamined and uncriticized mysticism, which carries a heavy cargo of wishful thinking, is not good enough.

97

In the content of his message there is both an impersonal element and a personal one. The first is derived from his higher self, which is often mistaken for God. The second is derived from his own characteristic mentality, whose contribution is seldom recognized or admitted. The essential idea comes from a higher source but the words expressing it do not.

98

He imagines that his intuitive message is pure undefiled and authentic, whereas he has brought into it what he has learned read and heard—in short his own beliefs and opinions. But he has done this so unconsciously, his ego has interposed itself so cunningly, that it is nearly impossible for him to discover not only how far this process has gone but even that it has happened at all.

99

The initial impetus and dynamic force of all these mystical phenomena come from the Overself, whereas the forms taken in consciousness by them are the ego's own manufacture. When the ego receives the impact from the Overself, it visualizes a face or figure, an event or scene, according to its habitual trend of thinking and experiential familiarity. In this natural but limited way it gives expression to the Formless in the world of forms. The wisdom of this process is that the ego naturally supplies a form with which it is familiar and, therefore, which is comprehensible to it. This explains why, for example, a mystical message is always couched in the same language as that spoken by its recipient. But it also explains why the very intellectual and experiential limitations of the ego are so often and so unfortunately mistaken for divine revelations!

100

Few find the pure truth: most find what they desire, expect, or prefer, which is merely the mental creation of their own ego. Of course it will probably be mixed with some part of the pure truth, or they would be led astray indeed, but both parts are so hopelessly intertwined that separation is hard or impossible.

101

The mystic's own personality and his previous way of thinking and believing will lead him unconsciously into interpretations of, and deductions from, his inner experience conformable with what he is. The truth of his revelation or experience is not absolute, but relative to his own particular human personality.

102

A part of the illumination does not rise from within. It is implanted from without. It is not a contribution from divine wisdom, but a suggestion from human thought. It is really an activation, by the soul's newly found power, of ideas put into the mind previously by others. For example, many Indian yogis actually hear the word "aum" sounding through the mind in their deep and prolonged meditation. A few, belonging to a particular sect, hear the word "Radhasoami" in the same condition. Why is it that no Western mystic, uninitiated into Eastern Yoga, has ever recorded hearing either of these words? This phenomenon is really due in one group of cases to hypnotic suggestion by a guru, and in the other group to unconscious suggestion by a tradition. All that does not however negate its actuality and genuineness, nor detract from its value in first, strengthening the aspirant's religious faith, second, promoting his mystical endeavours, and third—which is the most important of all—providing him with a diving board whence to plunge into the vast silence of the Void, where no words can be formulated and no sounds can be heard, because it is too deep for them or anything else. These, being the most advanced form of psychic phenomena, occur in the last stage of meditation and just before contemplation proper begins.(P)

103

What he takes to be a completely mystical experience is really mixed up with quite ordinary non-mystic all-too-human feelings.

104

When it is said that the mystic's own mental construction is responsible for the visions he sees, whether these be of a living guru distant in space or a dead one distant in time or a scriptural God, it is not meant that such construction is a voluntary activity. On the contrary, it is both involuntary and subconscious. This is the psychological explanation of such phenomena, but what is the metaphysical one? This is that the mystic, not having evolved to an understanding of the formless, timeless, matterless character of true being, nor to the capacity to concentrate on it, is given a spaced-timed-shaped image on which to concentrate. What gives him this image? It is his own Overself.

105

The divine adapts itself to the seeker's understanding in the same moment that it blesses him by its presence. The latter acts as a catalyst. It causes him unconsciously to formulate ideas and create pictures which, being of his own making, are easily comprehensible.

106

The form under which the experience came to him was partially or wholly a contributed one—that is, he unconsciously built it out of familiar elements. In this way it had meaning for him, was acceptable to him, and was instantly recognizable by him. But if the mold was partially or wholly undivine, the inspiring force, truth, and reality which flowed into it was not.

107

The words and images, the phrases and symbols, come from his own mentality or experience, but their inspiration comes from that part of himself which is not in time.

108

It is not altogether his own fault that he grafts his passionately held opinions upon the stem of his mystical experience, for the process is quite unconscious.

109

The interference with an illumination occurs when it is being transmitted through the everyday normal consciousness of the mystic.

110

A brilliant young astronomer at a famous English university said to me recently that what seemed to be needed was an agreed standard of criticism for religious truth, as he called it, a criterion of validity, as he explained. But if a synod of competent saints or mystics were to meet privately, they would still not agree. For at the core of every authentic mystical experience the mystics are united, but at its surface, where the power of suggestion and the limitations of ego come into play, they are not.

111

His own thoughts come back to him in his new revelation. His limited personal views return on themselves, energized by the exhilarated feeling which results from his fresh contact with the Impersonal. Nevertheless his mystical experience is a real one.

112

His *feeling* of inspired revelation is correct but his *inference* of its purity is not. His own uncontrolled imagination forms a substantial part of it.

113

The genuinely inspirational part of his message is what helps him and others, what ought to be respected and honoured even by those who cannot share the belief, illusion, or dogma in which he entwines it.

114

The experience reveals the Overself as it really is but their ego's vanity or preconceived ideas about it try to tell them something else. If they are intent on finding truth, there will be the wonder of new discovery; but if they are intent on finding confirmation of those ideas, there will one day be a hard inner struggle.

115

It is highly significant that nowhere in the history of the Eastern Orthodox Church has any saint appeared bearing the blood-flowing marks of the
stigmata. It may well be asked why this should be so when the Western or
Latin Church has produced a number of saints whose lives were notable
for this phenomenon. The only answer that a scientific but spiritually
sympathetic psychology could accept is that the Greek mystics were not
attracted towards the figure of the suffering Christ and therefore did not
meditate upon it, whereas the Latin mystics, like Padre Pio, for instance,
have always been attracted to this figure and given themselves up to frequent meditation upon it. A further point worth noting is that few Hindu
mystics have had any vision of Jesus—Ramakrishna, Sunda Singh, and a
couple of obscure holy men are the only ones I have ever heard of in this
connection. All this points to the tremendous power of *suggestion*.

116

The ultimate unity of spiritual teachings, which some profess to see,
applies rather to spiritual experience. As soon as the mystic attempts to
understand, interpret, or communicate his experience, differences set in.
This is partly because the intellect gets to work, partly because he unconsciously obeys the bias given him by the nature of his past experience,
study, education, and environment, and partly because he may not have
undergone the philosophic discipline to its fullest extent.

117

How much man owes his spiritual revelations to tradition and environment, how little to the pure and primal waters of actual inspiration, only
the philosophic investigator really knows.

118

It is his own mind, using its imaginative power, which creates the vision
he sees. But it is not a false vision since it assumes the form which appeals
most to him, and because its purpose is to enable him to believe, accept,
the divine presence as a real fact. That presence is what matters most in all
such experiences and is their chief inspirer.

119

How else explain why Francis of Assisi saw a vision of Jesus nailed to
the cross whereas William Blake saw a vision of the Devil? We know that
Francis poured out devotion, thought, and prayer to Jesus whereas Blake
admitted, "For many years I longed to see Satan."

120

Why is it that to Saint Gregory in the third century and to Pope Pius XII
in the twentieth the Virgin Mary appeared, surrounded by a bright light?
Why did not Sri Krishna appear?

121

In its passage from Mind to mind the revelation gets somehow mixed up, adulterated, and despoiled.

122

Because he cannot accommodate the whole of the Real in all its purity but must needs pass some of it through his own ego, his resultant experience or understanding of it becomes partly involved in illusions.

123

Why did Sri Ramakrishna see God as the Mother, Kali, during his numerous mystical experiences? The answer must be traced back to his boyhood history. He was then a young priest serving in a temple dedicated to Kali. He performed his ceremonies with intense faith and devotion. The power of involuntary and subconscious auto-suggestion explains the rest.

124

Subliminal suggestion enters into the message, submerged memories influence it. The pure gold of divine truth lies at its core but these inferior metals turn it into an alloy.

125

It is the fate of all human speech and writing to reveal something of the instrument through which they manifest. They may reveal his mental greatness and moral integrity but they may also reveal his littleness and bias.

126

He has received a real message from the Overself but he has subconsciously manufactured the form it has taken and consciously clothed it in familiar words.

127

Inspiration is still a living reality in the prophet's heart even though his ego limits or interferes with its messages.

128

He carries his ego into the experience itself; the two get mixed together. It is not his fault, for he is ignorant, does not clearly understand what is happening to him, while the egoistic instinct has hitherto been the driving power behind his life.

129

It was Lu Hsiang-shan, the twelfth-century mentalist, who remarked—whether simply or sarcastically is of no point here—"If the superior minds and virtuous worthies of a thousand epochs of antiquity were to be brought together at the same table, there would of a certainty be no complete agreement on Truth."

130

The ego thrusts itself into his revelation, blatantly if he is ignorant of its wiles, subtly if he is not.

131

The idea with which he approaches God, the soul, or the Overself is a human creation, whether it be his own or more generally derived from traditional religious belief. It reflects his personality and the quality of his mind. When divine inspiration comes, he unwittingly attaches this idea to it.

The true Word of revelation

132

The true Word of revelation is an eternal one. The varieties of human hearing do not affect it. Can we recover it in all its immaculate purity of sound?

133

Personal factors help to mold the revelation not only from the conscious surfaces but also from subconscious depths beyond them. The ego-complex insidiously penetrates it; the emotional nature immediately permeates it. The question arises whether these limitations can be transcended, whether a genuinely universal and impersonal condition can be attained in the seer himself, so that the resultant revelation shall be a "pure" one. The answer is that it certainly can, but that it is a rare and exceptional attainment.

134

When we understand that it is not possible for any man to free himself totally from personal standpoints, we understand that all mystical communications and religious revelations are afflicted with relativity and are consequently imperfect—all, that is to say, except those where the recipient has sought and sought successfully to transcend his humanity. Such an effort is embodied in the philosophic discipline. Such recipients were men like Gautama and Jesus.

135

Before he permits others to saddle him with the pretense of having achieved omniscience or to receive his pronouncements under the belief that he is incapable of making mistakes, the mystic needs to ask himself, "What is the source of my revelation?" How far it may be trusted as being infallible depends on his discovery of the correct answer to this question, on his penetration through the relative elements in it to the absolute one, on his separation of the durable essence from the ephemeral covering.

136

By a "pure" interpretation of the experience, we mean one wherein not the slightest intrusion of personal complexes, limitation, or temperament has happened, one where the mind has not been held captive by the educational or environmental thought-forms implanted in it by others.

137

He will receive the truth in all its purity only when he himself has attained utter purity, only when he can go beyond his own limited views, only when he can set aside every kind of personal emotion, only when he can forget completely what others have suggested to him, only when he can liberate himself from the conditioning he has undergone by society and tradition, only when, in short, he can sacrifice his whole psyche to the truth.

138

An absolute and irrefutable truth can exist only for a mind freed from the predicament of relativity into which human beings, finite and conditioned as they are, are plunged. Each man, therefore, states his own personal version of truth. Only the sage, deep in the meditation of *nirvikalpa samadhi*, temporarily deprived of personality, gets absorbed for the time in the Absolute. But when he returns to ordinary consciousness and tries to state what he knows, it is through the ego that his communication is made.

139

A mystical revelation can be considered as trustworthy if the revelator has not only purged his mind and heart by philosophic discipline but also developed them by philosophic cultivation. It is the absence of this precautionary preparation which accounts for the conflicts among the recorded revelations of history.

140

While the mentality retains the colouring of any personal bias it will colour truth, for which it is a medium, accordingly. But when it attains colourlessness and becomes a transparent jewel, it will transmit truth in its purity.

141

It is true that even in the prose of a philosophically trained sage his intellectual development, emotional disposition, and individual character will influence the choice of words and the style of language in which he expresses his revelations or knowledge. But the value of his self-criticizing discipline will also show itself in that they will not be permitted to influence the revelation or the knowledge itself. The personality of the inspired writer or speaker cannot be eliminated from the phraseology he employs, but the purity of his receptivity to the true Idea requires and is dependent on such elimination. The philosophic discipline secures it.

142

Some of the more advanced tenets of this teaching do not belong to the world of ordinary things and familiar relations. The attempt to communicate them in language derived from that world is necessarily a difficult one.

143

If the Overself meets with no obstructions in his mind, its manifestation will be perfect. But in the ratio that it does meet with them, its manifestation will be imperfect. The mind must not only be made sensitive enough to be guided by the Overself, it must also be made pure enough to interpret such guidance correctly and egolessly.

144

To get at the essential and authentic elements in a mystical revelation, all those which arise from the personal ego, the sense perceptions, and the imaginative faculty must be either discounted or wholly eliminated.

145

Authentically inspired revelations, least mixed with the human ego's opinions, are never as befuddled, turbid, and mystery-mongering as the pseudo-revelations.

146

Only in the attainment of the pure atmosphere of this mystical summit does he also attain freedom from the risk of deception and illusion, for where there is no imagery and no words there is no root whence deception and illusion could possibly arise. All the foolishness and falsity which have done so much harm to individual seekers and brought so much discredit on their search itself have their source in psychic experiences that appeal to egotism and pride.

147

Although the response of the Overself ordinarily conforms to the faith and mentality of the worshipper, to one who has undergone the discipline and finished the preparation which philosophy imposes, it comes in all its own original purity.

148

Nature sends her messages to man through his body and mind. But his denseness obscures them altogether, or receives confused versions of them. This is one reason why he needs interpreters and prophets. So long as he remains unaware of what she is saying to him, so long must others with better hearing appear in his history.

149

Eloquent communications reach him through the silence.

150

It may be distressing to those who have full faith in the revelations of seers and ardent devotion for them to learn that these revelations may not always be what their receivers believe them to be, that they may not be sacred at all, but only human, or partly sacred and partly human. They may be even deceptive, mistaken, or imaginary. Those who know nothing of the controversies which agitate mystical circles may regret this statement but it would be easy to document it fully. But such remarks do not apply to *philosophic* insight, its personalities and tenets. Its entire approach and method are sufficiently protected against aberrations to avoid them. For philosophy insists on asking—and finding the answer to—the question: "What is it that seers attain during their highest meditation? Is it their own imagination, their own idea, or is it truth and reality?"

151

Only a poet could portray these experiences as they deserve; to write of them with outer photographic exactness only is to half-lose them.

152

If the mystic has perfectly undergone the philosophic discipline, his messages will contain universal truths; if he has not undergone any discipline at all, they will contain private fancies; if some discipline, then the result will be a mixed one and he will not be able to distinguish between them.

153

Although the truth—as being—cannot be passed by the illuminate who has it to the unenlightened ones who do not have it, that does not deter him from making the effort. What he is able to give them is either an intellectual formulation or an emotional presentation but in both cases it is something made in his own image because passed through his own personality. So his followers receive not the inspiration which lit up the universe for him, but the imagination which he is forced to substitute in its place.

154

A true inspiration communicating a true revelation must still find a perfectly ego-free mind through which to operate, if there is to be publication to others in any way through spoken or written words.

155

To the degree that he can free himself from the personal ground that he stands on, to that degree can he transmit the message pure and undefiled.

156

The truest mystical doctrines are the commonest, yet they have come as personal revelations. The mystics who embraced them did so out of the loneliness of their innermost being, not out of the suggestion or influence of other men.

157

He to whom the disciple turns for advice and inspiration is but a fellow-worshipper with him—and, perhaps, a humble messenger, too.

158

The Overself is not poor. It has all the servants it needs to act through, or the voices to speak through, or the pens to write through. But it can do so only in harmony with the karmic laws, with the state of humans' present evolution, and with their needs or deserts.

159

We hear the echo of the divine in these revelations, but we do not hear its original voice. That is not possible, except in the silence of all ideas.

160

It would be more correct to say, and more relevant to affirm, that although no mystical experience may be communicated by telling about it, such communication may eventually be achieved over a period of years through a long process, of which the telling is the first item.

Index

Entries are listed by chapter number followed by "para" number. For example, 11.147 means chapter 11, para 147, and 5.109, 111 means chapter 5, paras 109 and 111. Chapter listings are separated by a semicolon. Please note also that, for the reader's convenience, the first number in the right-hand running heads throughout the text indicates chapter number.

The 28 Categories from the Notebooks

This outline of categories in *The Notebooks* is the most recent one Paul Brunton developed for sorting, ordering, and filing his written work. The listings he put after each title were not meant to be all-inclusive. They merely suggest something of the range of topics included in each category.